MW01119884

*Trauma Fiction*

# Trauma Fiction

Anne Whitehead

Edinburgh University Press

© Anne Whitehead, 2004

Edinburgh University Press Ltd
22 George Square, Edinburgh

Typeset in Baskerville
by Hewer Text Ltd, Edinburgh, and
printed and bound in Great Britain by
The Cromwell Press Ltd, Trowbridge, Wilts

A CIP record for this book is available from the British Library

ISBN 0 7486 1857 0 (hardback)

# Contents

# Acknowledgements

A version of Chapter 1 appeared in *Critique*, published by Heldref Publications. Chapter 2 first appeared in *Discourse*, published by Wayne State University Press. The book was written during a period of research leave jointly funded by a University of Newcastle upon Tyne Internal Research Fellowship and an AHRB Research Leave Award. I would like to thank Moyra Forrest for her work on the index and the School of English at Newcastle University for covering the indexing costs. I am grateful to Jackie Jones, my editor at Edinburgh University Press, for her encouragement, support and judicious comments. I am also grateful to Cathy Caruth and Sue Vice who, as readers for Edinburgh University Press, offered valuable feedback in the early stages of writing, and provided particularly helpful suggestions for the introductions and conclusion. My thinking has been stimulated by conversations with various friends and colleagues, most notably John Beck, Kate Chedgzoy, Marita le vaul-Grimwood, Jonathan Long, Michael Rossington and Victoria Stewart. I would especially like to thank Linda Anderson for her encouragement of this project and for reading through and commenting on a draft version of the book. The symposium 'Trauma: Narratives/Theory/ Politics', held at the University of Salford in May 2003, provided me with food for thought in relation to Chapter 1, and I would like to thank Erica Burman, Richard Crownshaw and Jane Kilby for their rigorous and detailed readings of my paper. Carl Good and Anne Cubilie gave valuable suggestions for revising Chapter 2. I would finally like to thank Mark Gillingwater, for cheering me up along the way.

# Part I

# *Theme*

# Introduction to Part I

The term 'trauma fiction' represents a paradox or contradiction: if trauma comprises an event or experience which overwhelms the individual and resists language or representation, how then can it be narrativised in fiction? This monograph seeks to suggest that there are various ways of thinking through the relation between trauma and fiction. The rise of trauma theory has provided novelists with new ways of conceptualising trauma and has shifted attention away from the question of what is remembered of the past to how and why it is remembered. This raises, in turn, the related issues of politics, ethics and aesthetics. The desire among various cultural groups to represent or make visible specific historical instances of trauma has given rise to numerous important works of contemporary fiction. We can think, for example, of Toni Morrison's attempts to gain political recognition for the suffering of African Americans during and after slavery in novels such as *Beloved* (1987) and *Jazz* (1992). It is also clear that fiction itself has been marked or changed by its encounter with trauma. Novelists have frequently found that the impact of trauma can only adequately be represented by mimicking its forms and symptoms, so that temporality and chronology collapse, and narratives are characterised by repetition and indirection. Trauma fiction overlaps with and borrows from both postmodern and postcolonial fiction in its self-conscious deployment of stylistic devices as modes of reflection or critique. My aim in what follows is to consider trauma fiction first by addressing the impact of trauma theory on the ways in which trauma is conceptualised and understood and how this has in turn been reflected in contemporary fiction. In the second half of the volume, I will explore the literary techniques by which novelists have sought to represent trauma, or to narrate the unnarratable, and I will outline the (necessarily provisional) range of literary devices which characterise the emerging genre of trauma fiction.

The term 'trauma fiction' also signals the recent journey of the concept of trauma from medical and scientific discourse to the field of literary studies. The origin of contemporary trauma studies can usefully be dated to 1980, when post-traumatic stress disorder (PTSD) was first included in the diagnostic canon of the medical and psychiatric professions. The formal recognition of PTSD was the result of sustained political campaigning by Vietnam veterans, who organised agitation groups against the continuation of the war. These groups rapidly spread throughout America and served a dual purpose: to raise public awareness about the effects of the war and to offer support and counselling to returning soldiers. The veterans also commissioned research into the impact of wartime experiences on combatants. This resulted in a five-volume study on the psychological legacies of Vietnam, which clearly delineated the syndrome of PTSD and demonstrated its direct relationship to combat exposure. In formally recognising this condition as a new diagnostic category, the American Psychiatric Association acknowledged for the first time that a psychiatric disorder could be wholly environmentally determined and that a traumatic event occurring in adulthood could have lasting psychological consequences.

Trauma theory emerged in the United States in the early 1990s and sought to elaborate on the cultural and ethical implications of trauma. The first three chapters of this volume explore the work of trauma theorists Cathy Caruth, Shoshana Felman and Geoffrey Hartman. Each of these theorists emerged out of Yale University, where they worked alongside or were taught by Paul de Man, and each took a surprising journey from literary criticism to trauma studies. My choice of theorists reveals a specific affinity of literary criticism with trauma theory and suggests that trauma theory is inherently linked to the literary in ways that it has not always recognised. In reading literary texts alongside trauma theory, this volume does not simply attempt to 'apply' a psychological or psychoanalytic theory to the text. More profoundly, I seek to remark on a resonance between theory and literature in which each speaks to and addresses the other. The literary readings in each of the chapters add something, or speak something, that the theory cannot say. Rather than simply illustrating the theory, the readings are an extension of the theory's own silences. Theory and literature both speak to and

4

displace one another throughout the volume, signalling to the reader the complex and supplementary relation between the two discourses.

Cathy Caruth's edited volume *Trauma: Explorations in Memory* appeared as a landmark publication in 1995. Caruth combined essays and interviews by literary theorists, film-makers, sociologists and psychiatrists in order to emphasise the trans-disciplinary nature of trauma theory. Introducing the volume, Caruth summarised the definition of trauma which emerged from the diagnostic category of PTSD:

> The pathology consists [. . .] solely in the *structure of its experience* or reception: the event is not assimilated or experienced fully at the time, but only belatedly, in its repeated *possession* of the one who experiences it. To be traumatized is precisely to be possessed by an image or event. (1995: 4–5)

Caruth's interest lies in the collapse of understanding which is situated at the heart of trauma. Trauma emerges as that which, at the very moment of its reception, registers as a non-experience, causing conventional epistemologies to falter.

Caruth's conceptualisation of trauma profoundly problematises the relation between experience and event. Trauma carries the force of a literality which renders it resistant to narrative structures and linear temporalities. Insufficiently grasped at the time of its occurrence, trauma does not lie in the possession of the individual, to be recounted at will, but rather acts as a haunting or possessive influence which not only insistently and intrusively returns but is, moreover, experienced for the first time only in its belated repetition. Unsettling temporal structures and disturbing relations between the individual and the world, trauma represents for Caruth a profound crisis of history:

> If PTSD must be understood as a pathological symptom, then it is not so much a symptom of the unconscious, as it is a symptom of history. The traumatized, we might say, carry an impossible history within them, or they become themselves the symptom of a history that they cannot entirely possess. (1995: 5)

Caruth's articulation of a crisis of historical experience resonates powerfully with the broken narratives and disrupted lives which have emerged out of the debris of recent traumatic events. Focusing on the structure of trauma, Caruth knowingly risks the accusation of losing the specifics of an event in a generalisable condition, but far from seeking to minimise or downplay suffering, her work represents an important attempt to think through the hiatuses and dislocations which necessarily inhabit trauma.

Caruth's emphasis on trauma's disruption of time or history draws on Freud's concept of *Nachträglichkeit*, which has been translated as 'deferred action' or 'afterwardsness'.[1] *Nachträglichkeit* describes a complex and ambiguous temporal trajectory and has proved to be a useful model for those (like Caruth) who seek to rethink the relation between memory and trauma and to construct models of historical temporality which depart from the strictly linear. For Freud, the concept refers to the ways in which certain experiences, impressions and memory traces are revised at a later date in order to correspond with fresh experiences or with the attainment of a new stage of development. Freud's conception involves a radical rethinking of the causality and temporality of memory. The traumatic incident is not fully acknowledged at the time that it occurs and only becomes an *event* at some later point of intense emotional crisis. Caruth's understanding of trauma reworks 'deferred action' as belatedness and models itself on Freud's conception of the non-linear temporal relation to the past.

In Chapter 1, I explore the implications of Caruth's conceptualisation of trauma for narrative fiction. Her work suggests that if trauma is at all susceptible to narrative formulation, then it requires a literary form which departs from conventional linear sequence. The irruption of one time into another is figured by Caruth as a form of possession or haunting. The ghost represents an appropriate embodiment of the disjunction of temporality, the surfacing of the past in the present. In contemporary fiction, there has been an abundance of novels which explore haunted histories. The traces of unresolved past events, or the ghosts of those who died too suddenly and violently to be properly mourned, possess those who are seeking to get on with the task of living. Toni Morrison's *Beloved* is the most influential of these novels. Sethe is haunted by the ghost of her murdered daughter, Beloved, who returns to claim the mother-love that she was so brutally denied. Beloved also represents the unresolved trauma of slavery, which haunts each of the characters in the novel and cannot be laid to rest. In Michèle Roberts's *Daughters of the House* (1993) and Anne Michaels's *Fugitive Pieces* (1997), the ghosts of Jews murdered in the Holocaust have not been properly buried and so return to haunt the succeeding generation(s).

Pat Barker's Booker-prize winning *Regeneration* trilogy (1991–95) explores the history of the First World War as a site of haunting and demonstrates that 'regeneration' is not possible until the past has been worked through. In Chapter 1, I focus on Barker's *Another World* (1998), the sequel to the *Regeneration* trilogy, which reveals that the Great War shows no sign, at the turn of the millennium, of being laid to rest. First

World War veteran Geordie is troubled in his nightmares by the ghost of his brother, Harry, and the unresolved effects of his death. The ending of the novel appears to suggest that after Geordie's death, the past can be resolved and forgotten. However, my reading indicates that the consolations of the ending provide a vehicle through which Barker comments on and critiques our need for a past which is easily packaged and resolved. I argue that the novel offers a version of history as revenant, in which the effects of the war are far from over. In contemporary fiction, then, the ghost story is reconfigured to explore the nature of trauma as psychological possession. The ghosts embody or incarnate the traumas of recent history and represent a form of collective or cultural haunting. The novels raise the important question of whether the ghosts of the past can be exorcised. Psychoanalysis claims that it can work through the past and make the ghosts go away. However, many of the novels implicitly critique this notion. As John Brannigan points out, haunting in contemporary fiction often represents the figurative return of elements of the past which have been silenced or culturally excluded, and the attempt to exorcise these ghosts can represent 'merely an attempt to prolong the repression of voices of protest or difference' (2003: 21).

If trauma emerges in Caruth's writing as a 'crisis of truth' (1995: 6), then this crisis extends beyond the individual to affect the ways in which historical experience can be accessed at a cultural level. The effects of the inherent latency of trauma can be discerned in the broken or fragmented quality of testimonial narratives which demand new structures of reading or reception. The 1980s witnessed the emergence of the genre of Holocaust video testimony, which originated in New Haven and was rapidly absorbed into the Yale University library archives. In *Testimony: Crises of Witnessing in Literature, Psychoanalysis and History* (1992), Shoshana Felman and Dori Laub elaborate a contemporary crisis of historical witnessing which necessitates a profoundly ethical response. In the face of narratives burdened by the incoherences of trauma, Felman and Laub insist on the possibility of nevertheless transmitting truth in the new space opened up by testimony. Speaking beyond understanding, testimony requires a highly collaborative relationship between speaker and listener. The listener bears a dual responsibility: to receive the testimony but also to avoid appropriating the story as his or her own. A fragile balance is engendered between the necessity to witness sympathetically that which testimonial writing cannot fully represent and a simultaneous respect for the otherness of the experience, which resists rendering it too familiar or indulging in too easy an understanding or identification.

The ethical questions raised by testimony are inherently literary. Geoffrey Hartman observes that trauma theorists are trying to find 'a way of *receiving* the story, of listening to it, of drawing it into an interpretative conversation' (1995: 541). In literary studies, interpretation is too often construed as a binary process which takes place between the active subject (the reader) and the passive object (the text). Trauma theory readjusts the relationship between reader and text, so that reading is restored as an ethical practice. Hartman argues that the text addresses the reader as a 'responsive, vulnerable, even unpredictable being' (1995: 549). This new mode of reading and listening opens out, in turn, into public- and mental-health issues. Trauma studies work against medical reductionism by exhorting practitioners to attend to a voice which is not fully known or knowable, and to bear witness. The experts are not given the last word; rather, their role is to return to the patient his or her own story.

Anne Michaels's *Fugitive Pieces* offers the reader a model of the witnessing process. As Nicola King has pointed out, the novel is structured around different layers or levels of witnessing: Athos listens to or receives Jakob's testimony; this enables Jakob to write his memoirs which are found and read by Ben, who in turn shares them with the reader. W. G. Sebald's narratives share a similar construction. In *Austerlitz* (2001), the narrator receives Austerlitz's testimony from him over a number of years. In recording or writing down the story, he both returns it to Austerlitz and simultaneously passes it on to the reader. Both of these novels foreground the role of language and storytelling. They create a community of witnesses which implicitly includes the reader, so that the very act of reading comprises a mode of bearing witness. At the same time, the novelists position the narrator as a mediator of others' stories and so find a way of expressing an experience which is not directly their own. The risk of appropriation is ever present in these narratives, however; in *Austerlitz*, for example, Sebald's distinctive omission of paragraphs and quotation marks from the novel potentially obscures the distinction between Austerlitz and the narrator.

The problem or predicament which testimony raises is how to avoid sympathy turning into over-identification. Dominick LaCapra has attempted to establish a boundary between the two by distinguishing empathy from identification. Empathy combines a rapport or bond with the other person with an affirmation of otherness and it emphasises the importance of 'cognition and critical analysis' (2001: 213). Identification fails to recognise such limits and the receiver of testimony succumbs to a secondary trauma. LaCapra's model provides an important caution against appropriating the experience of another. In Chapter 2, I explore the transmissibility of trauma through reading Binjamin Wilkomirski's *Fragments: Memories of a Childhood, 1939–1948* (1996). Wilkomirski's memoir represented a crisis point in Holocaust studies, because after publication it was revealed to be a fake. 'Wilkomirski' was a pseudonym; the author of *Fragments* was in actuality a Swiss musical-instrument maker named Bruno Doessekker.[2] Wilkomirski had not deliberately set out to produce a forgery; he apparently believed the experiences he described to be his own. His internalisation of Holocaust memoirs and testimonies points to the transmissibility of trauma and the hazards of over-identification. In assuming the identity of the survivor, Wilkomirski goes beyond the bounds imposed by LaCapra, who rightly insists that the experience of transmitted trauma should necessarily differ from the trauma experienced by the survivor. However, this distinction risks simplifying the issues that are at stake in Wilkomirski's narrative. Although he was not a Holocaust survivor, he did suffer trauma in the early loss of his parents and his subsequent adoption. The 'case' of Wilkomirski raises the fraught and complex question of how to think through the relation between different types and levels of trauma.

My reading of *Fragments* seeks to demonstrate that Wilkomirski closely replicates the literary techniques associated with the genre of testimony. He creates a narrative which is full of gaps, to be filled in by the reader using his or her own knowledge of the Holocaust, and he makes liberal use of synecdoche and continuous present tense. Wilkomirski's replication of the conventions of testimony enables him to produce a highly convincing account of trauma which implicitly positions the reader as an empathetic listener or witness. *Fragments* notably departs from the testimonial mode, however, in the narrator's adoption of the child's perspective. I argue that Wilkomirski is influenced in his use of this technique by Jerzy Kosinski's *The Painted Bird* (1965). Although Kosinski published *The Painted Bird* as fiction, he – like Wilkomirski – displayed a notable tendency to internalise his own fictions as part of his process of self-invention. My reading of *Fragments* also explores the immediate context in which Wilkomirki's 'memoir' was published, namely the crisis of memory which took place in Switzerland in the mid-1990s regarding the nation's involvement in the Holocaust. I suggest that the original impact of Wilkomirski's text derives, at least in part, from its offering its Swiss readers a defamiliarised view of themselves, through the eyes of a refugee child.

Reflecting on the notion of transmissibility, Hartman questions how traumatic knowledge 'can [. . .] extend into personal and cultural memory' (1995: 552). His response draws on the poetry of William Wordsworth to emphasise the importance of place. Hartman was evacuated from Germany to England on one of the last children's transports and he associates his love of Wordsworth with his childhood perception of the English countryside as a refuge from the wartime traumas occurring in Europe. Nevertheless, his childhood experience of displacement left its own irrevocable legacy. In *The Longest Shadow*, Hartman unequivocally states: 'An organic relation to place is what I lacked and would never recover' (1996: 19). Hartman's writing on trauma questions whether the figure of the pastoral can survive the Holocaust. He discerns in Wordsworth's writing a conjunction of memory and place, so that the scenes that he describes take on an almost visionary quality. However, Hartman questions whether Wordsworth represented the end of a viable pastoral tradition. He cannot equate the concentration camps with Wordsworthian memory places; burdened with the non-experience of trauma, the camps act as sites of stasis and form non-places in the minds of survivors. Although memory is strongly attached to place, the effect of trauma, it seems, has been to destroy the symbolic function of place.

In Chapter 3, I argue that Anne Michaels's *Fugitive Pieces* explores the role of landscape after the Holocaust and suggests that it can help to absorb the shock of trauma. Michaels breaks down the landscape into its constituent components: wood, water and rock. Throughout the novel, nature records its own memory traces: tree rings document in wood the history that they have witnessed; the sea preserves and washes clean the bones of the drowned Jews of Corfu; and rock conceals in its strata the fossilised remains of the past. Michaels's treatment of landscape combines a Romantic pantheism with the Jewish mystical tradition of kabbalism, in which nature has its own agency. The fugitive pieces of memory are scattered across the landscape and it is the task of the kabbalist to laboriously gather them together. Both Athos and Jakob devote their lives to collecting the shattered remnants of the past, rescuing and redeeming the stories of the conquered and the dispossessed. In containing within itself the fugitive pieces of memory, the landscape provides for Michaels an important and potentially redemptive counterforce to the catastrophe of the Holocaust. Sebald's fiction likewise suggests that there is an underlying pattern or design in nature, which would restore meaning if only it could be properly discerned. I question whether such a trajectory is appropriate in post-Holocaust fiction, and I echo Hartman's concerns as to whether the notion of the landscape as cathartic can be reinstated in this context.

The important work on collective memory carried out by Maurice Halbwachs, Pierre Nora and James Young highlights the fact that memory is not indigenous to a place but relies on human activity and will. In *Fugitive Pieces*, Michaels demonstrates that in the aftermath of the Holocaust we need to improvise new rites of grief and mourning. This commemorative work begins with a collective investment of memory in the landscapes of atrocity and mass murder in order to create 'sites of memory'. In *Another World*, Barker represents the First World War cemeteries in France as alternative 'sites of memory', where the dead can be commemorated and the memory of the past transmitted to the next generation. In her preoccupation with the relation between memory and forgetting, Barker questions how long the memory of the dead should be preserved. In their novels, both Barker and Michaels interrogate what it means to 'remember' the First and Second World Wars as the last remaining survivors are dying and the events are passing out of living memory.

The contemporary fascination with sites of memory, evidenced in the current proliferation of public memorials, raises the important question of the politics of place. Problems inevitably arise when a single site is invested with different commemorative significances by contending interest groups. Michaels's 'fugitive pieces' evoke the Jews of the diaspora who are scattered across the globe. I suggest that one of the questions that her novel raises but does not explicitly address is whether the gathering together of these scattered elements implies that the promise of redemption is synonymous with the founding of Israel. Caryl Phillips's *The Nature of Blood* (1997) serves as a timely reminder of the dangers that are inherent in building contemporary identities around symbolically invested spatial and geographical sites. For Phillips, the identification with place inevitably leads to tribalism and the erection of fences, borders and barriers. He emphasises the value of a diasporic or rootless identity which does not identify itself with any one particular cultural or geographical location, although I suggest that this strategy, in turn, potentially raises its own political problem of an evasion of history, especially when it arises in connection with Israel.

# Chapter 1

## *The past as revenant: trauma and haunting in Pat Barker's* Another World

In *Trauma: Explorations in Memory*, Cathy Caruth formulates the structure of trauma as a disruption of history or temporality. The traumatic event is not experienced or assimilated fully at the time that it occurs, but only belatedly in its insistent and intrusive return, and hence is not available in the usual way to memory and interpretation. Caruth's description emerges out of Freud's famous account of trauma in 'Moses and Monotheism' (1939), in which the event returns after a period of latency or delay:

> It may happen that a man who has experienced some frightful accident – a railway collision, for instance – leaves the scene of the event apparently uninjured. In the course of the next few weeks, however, he develops a number of severe psychical and motor symptoms which can only be traced to his shock, the concussion or whatever else it was. He now has a 'traumatic neurosis'. (Freud, 1990, XIII: 309)

The victim gets away from the scene of the accident 'apparently uninjured'. The event is not experienced as it occurs, but is fully evident only in connection with another place and in another time.

For Caruth, trauma is not a symptom of the unconscious but of history. The experience of trauma has not yet been assimilated by the individual and so cannot be possessed in the forms of memory or narrative. On the contrary, trauma assumes a haunting quality, continuing to possess the subject with its insistent repetitions and returns. In 'Beyond the Pleasure Principle' (1920), Freud observes of the shell-shocked soldiers who suffer battle nightmares: 'The impression they give is of being pursued by a malignant fate or possessed by some "daemonic" power' (Freud, 1991, XI: 292). In its disturbed and disrupted temporality, trauma is inextricable for Freud from the ghostly or spectral, and it testifies to the profoundly unresolved nature of the past. For Caruth, likewise, trauma represents a mode of haunting: 'To be traumatized is precisely to be possessed by an image or event' (1995: 4–5).

Caruth's insistence on the inherent belatedness of experience and understanding challenges the notion of a straightforward textual referentiality. If history is characterised by its continually delayed or deferred entrance into experience, as Caruth suggests, then there is a need to profoundly rethink the modes of our engagement with the past. History is no longer available as a completed knowledge, but must be reconceived as that which perpetually escapes or eludes our understanding. Such a notion of history implicitly repositions the relation between language and the world, so that the text shifts from a reflective mode – based on a position of self-awareness and self-understanding – to a performative act, in which the text becomes imbricated in our attempts to perceive and understand the world around us. For Caruth, literary fiction plays a crucial role in providing the reader with a narrative which is not straightforwardly referential, but which nevertheless offers a powerful mode of access to history and memory.

> How can we think of a referential – or historical, or material – dimension of texts that is not simply opposed to their fictional powers? How might the very fictional power of texts be, not a hindrance to, but a means of gaining access to their referential force? (Caruth and Esch, 1996: 2)

For Caruth, referential truth or experience is no longer opposed to fiction but is inextricable from it, providing the reader with radically new problems of interpretation and understanding.

LaCapra has sounded a note of caution in relation to Caruth's work. He seeks to circumscribe or limit the concept of trauma by distinguishing between absence and loss. For LaCapra, absence represents a transhistorical or foundational loss, a structural trauma that is not related to a particular event and to which we are all subject. Loss, on the contrary, represents a specific historical trauma to which not everyone is subject. Loss can be narrated and is capable of transformation or reconfiguration in the future. LaCapra argues that theorists such as Caruth and Felman risk conflating structural and historical trauma, thereby situating historical losses on a trans-historical level. Such conflation, LaCapra argues, results in a melan-

cholic paralysis and potentially obfuscates or generalises the significance of particular historical losses. Trauma theory can seem to imply
that everyone is a victim, that all history is trauma and that we share a
pathological 'wound culture'. LaCapra urges us to remain mindful of
the distinction between structural and historical trauma, for their
conflation 'tends to take place so rapidly that it escapes notice and
seems natural or necessary' (2001: 48). LaCapra's argument has
repercussions for the consideration of trauma fiction. Literary fiction
relies on and encourages empathic identification. While LaCapra
allows that empathy is important in attempting to understand traumatic events and victims, he cautions against identifying with the
victim to the point of making oneself a surrogate victim. He alerts us
to the issue of what we (seek to) gain from reading trauma narratives,
and he questions what is at stake for both writers and readers in
taking on the pain of other people's stories.

Caruth's notion of belatedness also raises the question of the
duration and extent of the period of delay in trauma. Theories of
trans-generational trauma suggest that affect can leak across generations; that a traumatic event which is experienced by one individual
can be passed on so that its effects are replayed in another individual
one or more generations later. Nicolas Abraham and Maria Torok's
work on trans-generational haunting suggests that symptoms are
transmitted from one generation to the next when a shameful
and therefore unspeakable experience is barred from consciousness
or kept secret. The trauma is communicated without ever having
been spoken, and resides within the next generation as a silent
presence or 'phantom'.

> Should the child have parents 'with secrets' [. . .] he will receive from
> them a gap in the unconscious, an unknown, unrecognized knowledge.
> [. . .] The buried speech of the parent becomes a dead gap, without a
> burial place, in the child. This unknown phantom comes back from the
> unconscious to haunt and leads to phobias, madness and obsessions. Its
> effects can persist through several generations and determine the fate of
> an entire family line. (Rashkin, 1988: 39)

The phantom is a variant of the return of the repressed, for what
returns to haunt is the trauma of another. In describing trans-
generational trauma, Abraham and Torok notably evoke the metaphor of a building: the psyche of the next generation becomes a
'crypt', a container that houses the seemingly unthinkable and
unrepresentable residue of the past. LaCapra endorses in his work
the importance of Abraham and Torok's writing on the intergenera-

tional transmission of trauma. For him, the concept is suggestive for analysing the often ill-defined feelings of guilt that inform our emotional investments in the past and that can lead to an unwitting over-identification on the part of both readers and writers of trauma narratives.

## The ghosts of the First World War

Pat Barker's Booker-prize winning *Regeneration* trilogy (1991–5) represents one of the most influential contemporary literary recuperations of the First World War. In the trilogy, Barker reconfigures history as a trauma that needs to be acknowledged and worked through.[1] She draws on and revises the literary genre of the ghost story, so that the spectres that haunt the soldiers represent a form of psychological possession. Each of the soldiers in the trilogy is haunted by his own particular ghost(s). Siegfried Sassoon sees corpses on the streets of London and the dead men of his company visit his room. The ghosts embody his guilt at not fighting in the war and his grief for the men he has lost. In *The Ghost Road* (1995), Geoffrey Wansbeck is visited by the ghost of a German prisoner whom he murdered; the spectre embodies his unresolved guilt over the act of killing. In treating his patients, W. H. R. Rivers finds himself unable to dismiss the reality of their ghosts and at the end of the trilogy, it seems that he, like his patients, is marching on the 'ghost road'. Barker suggests that history after the First World War is continually and unredeemably haunted by the memory of loss.

In this chapter, I aim to offer a reading of Barker's *Another World* (1998) as a narrative of traumatic haunting. This novel followed the *Regeneration* trilogy and continued its First World War theme. It was inspired by Barker's interviews with veterans and her visit to the war cemeteries in France. The novel is set in the present day and Barker explicitly addresses the question of what meaning or significance the First World War holds for us today. She explores what it means to 'remember' the First World War when it is passing out of living memory, as the last surviving veterans are dying. *Another World* concerns the trauma of fratricide across three generations: the Victorian murder of the toddler, James Fanshawe, by his elder brother and sister; Geordie's murder of his elder brother, Harry, in the First World War; and Gareth and Miranda's attempts to murder their brother, Jasper, in the present day. Barker writes a history in which the present is overshadowed and haunted by the unresolved effects of the past. Trauma is transmitted across the generations and the novel questions whether there can be an end to this process. This chapter looks, in turn, at how the legacy of the war affects the first generation, the third generation and the fourth generation. The second generation is notably absent from Barker's narrative. This signals a reticence in Barker's writing relating to the Second World War, and to the Holocaust in particular. In interviews, Barker has expressed discomfort with the issues of entitlement raised by the Holocaust, pointing to the difficulties of representing the Holocaust for those who are not survivors or who are not Jewish. The First World War arguably represents in her work the trauma of all twentieth-century conflicts. On this level, her writing on the First World War risks generalisation; the First World War subsumes other, later conflicts, and displaces the specificity of historical trauma in a generalised narrative of haunting.

The epigraph to the novel is taken from Joseph Brodsky: 'Remember: the past won't fit into memory without something left over; it must have a future' (Barker, 1998: unnumbered). The quotation speaks of the overwhelming nature of the traumatic past, which cannot be contained by memory but always and necessarily leaks into the future. Even more explicitly than in the *Regeneration* trilogy, Barker calls into question the processes of 'regeneration' and recovery in the face of the overwhelming social traumas of the twentieth century. Time no longer flows smoothly and seamlessly back into the past, as the tourists in the 'time wagon' at Jorvik Viking Centre in York are able to do (231). Instead, Barker explores the achronology of trauma: 'Suppose [time's] not an ever rolling stream, but something altogether more viscous and unpredictable, like blood. Suppose it coagulates around terrible events, clots over them, stops the flow' (270–1). Such a history seems to defy recovery and even remembrance itself. Although the ending of the novel offers a tentative promise that there is wisdom in forgetting and that the past can finally be laid to rest, the conclusion rests uneasily alongside what has gone before. Barker arguably presents the novel's ending as the comfort or 'discharge of feeling' (276) that Nick seeks in the wake of Geordie's funeral, and that the reader correspondingly desires at the close of the novel, but that is nonetheless deceptive and does not hold out the promise of resurrection or recovery.

## The first generation

The central character in *Another World* is Geordie Lucas, a First World War veteran who is still haunted by his wartime experiences. Barker's main focus in her portrait of Geordie is on the effects of trauma on memory, and she draws closely on Freud's 'Beyond the Pleasure Principle'. Freud observes that the shell-shocked soldiers return in their battle nightmares to the scene of trauma, only to awaken in a state of terror. The nightmares represent a re-entry into the experience. Freud notes of the soldier: 'He is obliged to *repeat* the repressed material as a contemporary experience instead of, as the physician would prefer to see, *remembering* it as something belonging to the past' (Freud, 1991, XI: 288). Geordie likewise escapes the past during the day, only to find that his sleep is haunted by the 'upside-down time of the trenches' (148). Sleepwalking, he re-enacts the war and his nights are spent in working parties and on patrol. Barker explicitly states that Geordie re-experiences the war as if it were happening in the present: 'it's not like he's remembering it, it's like he's actually seeing it' (69). Like Freud's soldiers, Geordie awakens from his nightmares in a state of terror: 'He wakes up and it's still happening' (69). He cannot escape from the past, but seems doomed to an endless and interminable replay of events. Barker's portrait of Geordie does not simply draw on Freud, however; she also extends his discussion of shell-shock. Freud's soldiers suffered their symptoms during or in the immediate aftermath of the war; Geordie suffers his nightmares over eighty years later. If Freud gestures towards a past that haunts the present and resists assimilation, Barker emphasises the lasting and seemingly irresolvable nature of this possession.

The novel charts Geordie's final illness and ends with his funeral. Although the doctors diagnose that Geordie is dying of cancer, he is convinced that he is dying from another cause. His body bears the traces of two wounds: the scar on his stomach from his recent cancer operation and the old wound in his side that he brought back from France and that marks the site of a bayonet attack. Like the nightmares that receded after the war only to return eighty years later, the bayonet wound has not bothered Geordie since the war but is now 'playing up' again (63). In contrast to the operation scar, which is healing well, Geordie complains that the bayonet wound bleeds and hurts. Geordie's obsessive focus on his war injury powerfully symbolises and externalises the resurfacing of his painful wartime memories: 'The bleeding bayonet wound's the physical equivalent of the eruption of memory that makes his nights dreadful' (227).[2] The traumatic wound does not heal over the course of time and is not susceptible to recovery or regeneration.

As he is dying, Geordie confesses to his grandson, Nick, that he killed his own brother, Harry, in No Man's Land. It is only after Geordie's death, however, that Nick hears his recorded account of the event. At the core of Geordie's testimony lies an essential incomprehensibility. Although he remembers reaching his injured brother in No Man's Land and the sight of his screaming face lit momentarily by a flare, he cannot recall the extent of Harry's injury and so does not know whether his killing was an act of mercy or an act of murder. He is haunted not by the memory of what he has done, but by a shocking and paradoxical failure of memory which produces in him a deep and painful uncertainty regarding both the truth of the past and the significance of his own action. He takes with him to the grave a suspicion that the war gave him an opportunity to act on a 'child's hatred' (264) of his brother that would otherwise have existed only in fantasy. Barker implicitly comments here on a war that utilised children as soldiers and killers, enlisting boys of eighteen or nineteen and sometimes younger. In his nightmares, Geordie calls out the name of Harry and it is his brother's death, rather than his own wartime experiences, that haunts him. His nightmares are of Harry's face which, like the Cheshire cat, gradually disappears so that only the mouth remains: 'Night after night he feels himself falling towards that mouth' (146). Unlike the grinning cat, however, Harry's mouth lets out a terrible scream that echoes unceasingly through Geordie's dreams: 'A scream begins and never ends' (241). The image of the open mouth recurs throughout *Regeneration* (1991), where it symbolises the soldiers' protest against the war which is effectively silenced by the intervention of the medical authorities. Harry's open mouth represents for Geordie a protest against his own death, a protest that Geordie can silence in waking life but not in sleep.

Geordie's last words, whispered to his grandson Nick, are: 'I am in hell' (246). The inescapable present tense powerfully articulates Geordie's trauma and forcefully denies the prospect or consolation of eternal rest. His words echo Siegfried Sassoon's famous declaration in his poem 'Memorial Tablet': 'I died in hell – / (They called it Passchendaele)' (1983: 137). Sassoon's speaker is a dead soldier who can consign the war to the past tense. Geordie's words disturb Nick because, having survived, he continues to experience the war in an ongoing traumatic present. Geordie's words also recall Wilfred

Owen's poem 'Strange Meeting', in which the speaker enters hell to find himself face to face with the soldier whom he killed. His former enemy greets him and suggests that they put aside their differences and rest together. Owen's poem provides a powerful contrast to Geordie's terror of meeting in death the brother he killed who will now recognise him as an enemy. The sleep with which Owen's poem concludes eludes Geordie before his death and his prospects of eternal rest appear remote. Through intertextuality, Barker clearly signals her own mediated points of access to the First World War, in the medical literature relating to the condition of shell-shock (Freud) and in the writing of the First World War poets (Owen and Sassoon). These sources emerge more explicitly in the *Regeneration* trilogy, in Barker's depiction of Rivers's medical practice and in her portrayal of the wartime experiences of Sassoon, Owen and (to a lesser extent) Robert Graves.

The novel closes with Geordie's funeral, and Barker questions whether the ghosts of the First World War can be laid to rest after his death. Nick derives comfort at the funeral from the nature of the cemetery itself which offers consolation in decay. The moss-covered stones and half-obscured names suggest the wisdom of forgetting and offer the promise that life will renew itself in the wake of Geordie's death. It seems that life can return to its normal course now that the ghosts of the past have been exorcised: 'Life's sorting out, settling down, arranging itself into new patterns' (275). However, the text raises notes of caution. Nick's response derives from his own desire for reassurance. He prefers not to confront the more disturbing aspects of reality and his desire to forget represents a defensive reaction. In offering an ending which is cathartic for the reader as well as for Nick, Barker implicitly comments on our need for a past that is neatly packaged and easily resolved. The novel suggests a more troubling version of history and, even in the final pages, the trauma of the war continues to cast its shadow.

At the funeral, Gareth finds Geordie's shaving mirror in Nick's bathroom and it is clear that this object forms part of Nick's inheritance from his grandfather. The steel mirror accompanied Geordie throughout the war and he subsequently used it every morning for shaving. Throughout the novel, the descriptions of the mirror emphasise its capacity to distort that which is reflected. As a child, Nick gazed into the mirror only to find that his reflection was 'blurry, swollen, distorted by the irregularities in the metal' (57). In *The Fantastic* (1975), Tzvetan Todorov indicates that eyeglasses and mirrors, as distorters of vision, can reveal a world beyond the ordinary: 'To see through eyeglasses brings the discovery of *another world* and distorts normal vision. The derangement is similar to that provoked by the mirror' (122; emphasis mine). Geordie's attachment to the mirror resides in its subversions and distortions, which reveal to him the other world of the war and the trenches. The mirror likewise reveals to Nick an aspect of himself that he does not recognise. After shadowing Geordie in one of his waking dreams, he finds that his grandfather does not recognise him, and the mirror similarly refuses him recognition: 'it doesn't reflect his face' (164). Immediately after Geordie's death, Nick looks into the mirror again only to find himself estranged from the reflection once more: 'the face that stares back at him is nothing like his own' (257). Barker significantly withholds from us what it is that Nick does see. If the face is his own but defamiliarised, the mirror reveals the extent of his own dissociation and denial. If the face is Geordie's or Harry's, the mirror reflects the power of his grandfather's trauma over Nick. The mirror may, however, reflect nothing more sinister than Nick's own cumulative stress and exhaustion. In the subtle movement of the mirror from Geordie's bathroom to Nick's, Barker symbolises the transmission of Geordie's trauma to the next generation, so that his terrible secret continues to haunt and disturb the family line.

## The third generation

The main narrative focus in *Another World* is Geordie's grandson, Nick, and it is his perspective that is foregrounded throughout the novel. Through Nick, Barker explores the meaning and significance of the First World War for the present generation. Nick has found it impossible throughout his childhood to communicate with Geordie about the war. His main point of access to the First World War is his visit with Geordie to the war cemeteries in France. He is most affected by his grandfather's experiences at Thiepval, and for Geordie himself the war cemetery acts as a vehicle for the transmission of the past, where he can 'graft his memories' onto Nick (74). Nick finds himself repelled by Lutyens's memorial to the dead at Thiepval which invokes, but simultaneously refuses, the consolations of Christianity. It resembles a cathedral that refuses to soar, but remains resolutely earthbound. Nick's response to the memorial closely echoes Geoff Dyer's description of Thiepval in *The Missing of the Somme* (1994):

Its predominant relation is to the earth – not, as is the case with a
cathedral, to the sky. A cathedral reaches up, defies gravity effortlessly, its
effect is entirely vertiginous. And unlike a cathedral which is so graceful
(full of grace) that, after a point it disappears, becomes ethereal, the
Thiepval memorial, after a point, simply refuses to go any higher. It is
stubborn, stoical. Like the deadlocked armies of the war, it stands its
ground. (126–7)

With the wound in his side, Geordie represents for Nick a latter-day
Christ and Thiepval is his 'Golgotha' (73), the site of his suffering.[3]
However, Geordie, unlike Christ, does not attain the promised
resurrection or salvation: 'this place represented not the triumph
*over* death, but the triumph *of* death' (74). Geordie's 'Golgotha' is
'the place of a skull' (73), associated only with death and mortality.
Throughout the novel, the skull symbolises the vulnerability of the
human body to harm, from Geordie's skull rising to the surface as he
dies to Jasper's skull revealed on the X-ray screen. The message of the
war that Nick derives from his visit to Thiepval is: '*You can get away with
it*' (85). He consciously refers to the politicians and war profiteers
who led a generation of young men to their deaths. However, his
failure to pronounce the word 'murder' also suggests an unconscious
knowledge of Geordie's fratricide. Trying to talk about his visit to
France on his return, Nick admits that 'he hasn't succeeded in telling
himself about Thiepval yet' (85). In order to 'tell himself', Nick would
have to recognise the murder that Geordie committed, allowing his
knowledge of the past to surface within himself. Geordie's secret lies
buried within Nick, and Barker suggests that the aspects of the past
that are transmitted to the next generation are precisely those that
remain unspoken and unacknowledged. When Geordie does give an
account of Harry's death, it is significantly recorded for a public
archive rather than passed on as a familial narrative. Through
Geordie's fratricide, Barker gestures towards a broader question
concerning the stories of war veterans. She raises the issue of whether
the act of killing can form part of a war narrative that is passed on as
family history. How many war stories, like Geordie's, circle around a
'central silence' (158), a legacy that cannot be passed on or acknowledged? Geordie's fears about his brother's death highlight the
profoundly troubling nature of wartime violence. Is the act of killing
in war a necessary act or is it an act of murder? The novel suggests that
the fact of killing troubles the memory of the First World War, and
Barker signals the difficulty of reconciling wartime and familial
narratives.

The war cemeteries in France offer Nick an alternative to his consoling vision of the decaying churchyard. He is struck by the 'ageless graves' and the 'devotion that kept the graves young' (278). In their defiance of time and change, the war cemeteries mirror Geordie's traumatic memories. Like the words on the memorial stones, Geordie's memories are 'carved in granite' (86) and will not alter or change. Barker's image suggests that Geordie himself becomes a form of memorial to the dead, keeping their memory alive within himself.[4] At the close of the novel, Nick suggests that the past can be resolved by allowing the war cemeteries to decay, so that the names of the dead are 'half-erased' and the headstones are covered by the 'obliterating grass' (278). However, there are dangers in such an approach, for it threatens oblivion and forgetting. Nick's desire to move on is poised between renewal or regeneration and an impulse to cover over or bury the past. Nick's is, furthermore, an impossible vision, for grass cannot obliterate the traces of the past. In the so-called Iron Harvest, each year's ploughing in the Somme brings to the surface tons of wartime ammunition. The effects of the war are far from over, even though the last surviving veterans are being laid to rest. Nick remains resistant to Geordie's lesson that the past cannot always be resolved. His desire to 'erase' or 'obliterate' the past protects him from confronting the ways in which Geordie's wartime legacy troublingly and painfully plays itself out in the present.

## The fourth generation

Nick's failure to acknowledge Geordie's fratricide is paralleled by his refusal to confront the danger posed by his elder two children to the life of his toddler, Jasper. The threat of fratricide is not laid to rest with Geordie's death but returns to haunt the younger generation. The novel dramatises Nick's increasing sense of powerlessness in the family, for he can neither help his wife nor protect his children. As an impotent father, Nick represents an icon of contemporary vulnerable masculinity. In *Another World*, Barker explores the loss of masculinity as one of the legacies of the First World War, and Nick's actions call into question whether this lost masculinity can be recuperated or reinstalled.[5] Nick's family is fractured by divorce and the children – Miranda, Gareth and Jasper – are all from different relationships.[6] Jealousy and violence mark the relations between them. Barker significantly writes the contemporary narrative of fratricide as a ghost story, suggesting the power of the past over the present. Nick's family work together to strip the paintwork at his new house, Lob's Hill. In the course of this activity, they uncover a painting of the Fanshawes, the original owners of the property. The painting is a cruel satire of the idealised Victorian family but it also bears an uncanny resemblance to Nick's own family, mirroring the violence and sexual tensions that underpin their relationships. At the heart of the composition stands James Fanshawe, one hand resting on the knee of each of his parents. The painting reveals the hatred that circulates around the family 'with the golden-haired toddler at its dark centre' (40). The picture was whitewashed in order to conceal the crime of fratricide at which it hints. Nick discovers in a book of local murders that the two elder Fanshawe siblings, Muriel and Robert, were charged with the murder of their younger brother, James. Although they were subsequently found innocent, local rumour suggested that their father had paid for their acquittal and that they were indeed guilty. The painting reveals the threat of fratricide that haunts Nick's family. Nick characteristically suppresses his own knowledge, covering the picture over once more. However, his conviction that the picture revealed itself of its own volition suggests its inexorable surfacing to consciousness: 'it would have been impossible to keep it hidden any longer, rather as a mass of rotting vegetation, long submerged, will rise suddenly to the surface of a pond' (43). The uncovering of the painting and the subsequent revelation of the Fanshawe murder parallel the gradual surfacing to Nick's consciousness of Geordie's fratricide.

Barker's narrative of the fourth generation self-consciously draws on the literary ghost story. On Miranda's arrival at Lob's Hill, Nick points out to her the lintel of the house which is inscribed with the words: 'FANSHAWE / 1898' (13). Miranda immediately recalls the lintel carved with the name of Earnshaw in Emily Brontë's *Wuthering Heights*, and the association suggests to her that the house is haunted. Miranda's thoughts act as an important narrative indicator, so that even in the opening pages of the novel an atmosphere of brooding menace is associated with Lob's Hill. *Another World* also draws inspiration from Henry James's *The Turn of the Screw*. In James's novella, the governess describes her arrival at Bly House where she is to care for her two charges, Miles and Flora. The governess quickly becomes aware of the presence of ghosts, whom she identifies as Quint, the gardener at Bly before he died, and Miss Jessel, her predecessor as governess who had a sexual relationship with Quint. The governess spends much of her time trying to work out whether the children are aware of the ghosts and what their attitude is towards them. At every point in the story, the ghosts can be read equally in either of two senses. If the governess alone sees the ghosts, they can be read as symptomatic of her own neurosis, and in particular her repressed sexual feelings for her employer. If the children are in communication with the ghosts, however, this suggests that they were corrupted and that the ghosts are now returning to claim them. The question of the reality of the ghosts becomes inextricable in James's story from the question of the nature of childhood. The governess's obsession with what the children 'know' about the ghosts conceals her fear that they have been tainted with sexual knowledge through their constant association with Quint and Miss Jessel. James's ambiguous narrative leaves the nature of the ghosts unresolved and it also leaves open-ended the question of childhood. The children remain uncertainly suspended between knowing and not knowing, between innocence and corruption.

The spectral figure of a young woman appears throughout *Another World*. In Barker's descriptions, she is finely poised between the real and the imagined. She closely resembles Miranda, but she could equally represent the ghost of Muriel Fanshawe. Barker's merging of the two suggests that Miranda is possessed by the ghost of Muriel and clearly positions the attempts on Jasper's life by his elder siblings as actions that repeat or replay a past trauma. The young woman appears first to Nick as he is driving home on a dark and rainy night and is dismissed by him as a '[h]ypnogogic hallucination' (89). Miranda sees her next looking in through the window at Lob's Hill, as if she were searching for something or someone. Her actions recall the governess's description of the ghost of Quint, whom she sees peering through the window at Bly searching for the children, and suggest that Muriel is seeking to claim the life of Jasper. The apparition through the window also echoes the ghost of Cathy in *Wuthering Heights*, hinting that Miranda may be imagining a ghost that she is already half expecting to see. Miranda rushes outside and peers through the window herself, repeating the young woman's actions in a manner that suggests she is possessed by the ghost of Muriel. This impression is reinforced when Jasper fails to recognise her and 'screams and screams and screams' (177).

When Gareth tries to kill Jasper by throwing stones at him from a clifftop, the young woman appears once more. The ghost of Muriel is appropriately present as her act of fratricide is replayed. However, Gareth believes the figure to be Miranda, suggesting that Miranda is either possessed by Muriel or that her resentment towards Jasper is repressed and she has entered a fugue state, acting without her own knowledge and control. The final appearance of the young woman is when Miranda sleepwalks into Jasper's nursery and places her hands over his face, as if to suffocate him. It is unclear whether Miranda, possessed by the ghost of Muriel, seeks to murder her brother in a traumatic re-enactment of the past or whether she acts on her own suppressed and denied desires. Her actions recall the governess's suffocation of Miles at the close of *The Turn of the Screw*, an act which is also ambivalently poised between supernatural possession and the governess's own repressed desires.[7] The narrative of the Fanshawes powerfully suggests that Gareth and Miranda are possessed by the ghosts of the past. They are caught in a traumatic repetition-compulsion, in which they are no longer in control of the plot of their own lives but enact other people's stories. Through the device of the ghost story, Barker explores the nature of contemporary childhood. Miranda and Gareth act out of their own agency but also under the influence of the past. They are ambivalently suspended between knowing and not knowing, between innocence and cruelty.[8] Barker's intertextual references to *The Turn of the Screw* reinforce this ambivalent view of childhood, for James's novella circles around the question of what the children 'know', and whether they are innocent or corrupted.

In *Another World*, the young woman is both real and imagined and Barker deliberately does not resolve this ambiguity. The novel accords with Tzvetan Todorov's definition of the fantastic, which emerges when a person is confronted by a phenomenon that cannot readily be explained by the laws of his familiar world. The person who experiences such an event has two choices: either he must conclude that he is suffering from an illusion or fantasy, in which case the laws of the world remain intact, or he must decide that the event has indeed taken place, in which case this reality is controlled by unknown laws. The fantastic is located in the period of hesitation before either of the two choices is taken. Todorov notes: 'The fantastic occupies the duration of this uncertainty. Once we choose one answer or the other, we leave the fantastic for a neighbouring genre' (25). The fantastic is a device used to considerable effect in narratives of trauma. It is most notably deployed in the novels of Toni Morrison. In *Beloved*, Beloved is both an abused black girl who has escaped from the house where a white man was holding her prisoner and Sethe's murdered daughter returned from the grave. In *Jazz*,

Wild is both a wild woman who lives in the woods and the spectre of Beloved not yet laid to rest. The hesitation between real and imagined reflects the contradictory nature of the traumatic event, which has happened and therefore has a form of historical reality, but which has not yet been fully assimilated and so is not susceptible to conventional modes of reference or reality. In *Another World*, the spectral girl embodies the unspoken secret of fratricide (Geordie's and the Fanshawes'), which has a form of historical reality – Harry's death is documented on tape in Helen's archive, and the Fanshawe murder is recorded in the book of local murders – but which remains unacknowledged within the family narrative.

Nick resists understanding the threat of violence posed by his own children, just as he suppresses his knowledge of Geordie's fratricide. The novel charts his increasing but reluctant acknowledgement of the murderous impulses that haunt his family. At the opening of the novel, Nick allows his worries about Miranda's safety to surface in an image of the boys who abducted and murdered James Bulger: 'three figures smudged on a video surveillance screen, an older boy taking a toddler by the hand while his companion strides ahead, eager for the atrocity to come' (3). This vision significantly surfaces again when Nick searches for the children on a family outing, in a state of panic for Jasper's safety. He thinks he has found them when he sees 'two taller figures holding a small boy by the hand' (117), but this turns out to be a couple with their child. Nick's mistake reveals his barely submerged anxiety that the two older children represent a threat to Jasper, a fear that he will not admit even to himself: 'Nick's mind skitters away from the real source of his fears' (116). When Nick encounters the history of the Fanshawe murders, he likewise locks the book in the boot of his car, concealing the past from his family but also from himself. When Miranda enters Jasper's nursery, Nick prevents her from killing Jasper, ensuring that the past (Geordie's and the Fanshawes') does not play itself out in the present. However, this act does not restore his control of the family or reinstate his masculinity, for he intervenes in order to evade his knowledge of Miranda's intentions: 'He has to stop whatever's going to happen next. Or rather he has to shield himself from ever knowing what it is' (219). Throughout the novel, Nick deliberately refuses to know or to recognise the violence that exists within his own family. He wishes to know less, to ignore the events that occur around him. This is a hazardous approach that twice almost results in Jasper's death. At the close of the novel, Nick justifies concealing the Fanshawe murder from his family, observing: 'It's easy to let oneself be dazzled by false analogies – the past never threatens anything as simple, or as avoidable, as repetition' (278). The evidence of the novel works against Nick's statement, however, for the past seems all too liable to repetition and return. Nick's reassurances that the past does not repeat and is capable of resolution ring false, and Barker's ending implicitly offers a critique of the reader's (and Nick's) desire for comforting, neatly packaged conclusions.

## Haunted histories

As in the *Regeneration* trilogy, Barker draws on the discourse of trauma in *Another World*, in order to reconfigure history as a site of haunting and to suggest the pervasive influence of the unresolved effects of the past. LaCapra reminds us of the risks entailed in such an approach to trauma. In particular, Barker's writing risks losing sight of the historical specificity of trauma. I have indicated that she tends to use the First World War as an icon or cipher for twentieth-century warfare, which runs the risk of over-generalisation. In *Another World*, the narrative of the First World War is combined with an exploration of child murderers, so that the trauma of Geordie's war experience is displaced onto the narrative of the Fanshawe murder. It becomes difficult to determine exactly what the trauma is in the novel or where it resides. Is the central trauma Geordie's murder of Harry, or the Fanshawe murder, or even the Bulger murder that surfaces in the course of the narrative? Furthermore, Barker's emphasis on the effects of Geordie's trauma on subsequent generations risks appropriating or belatedly acting out the experience of the trauma victim. The loss of specificity in a generalised narrative of haunting potentially undermines the possibility for transformative social and political engagement. In its exploration of child murder, Barker's narrative raises further problems in its implicit positioning of the child as a source of trauma, which reinforces a cultural ideology of the child as origin. In addition, Barker does not address the question of child sexuality alongside the issue of child violence. This is particularly noticable given that she draws on the Bulger case which raised important questions about the place of children's sexuality, and given that she refers intertextually to James's *The Turn of the Screw* which precisely questions the extent to which children are sexually aware.

The form of Barker's novel suggests the disruption of referentiality that lies at the heart of Caruth's definition of trauma. The Fanshawe murder relates closely to Geordie's war trauma, for both narratives represent a legacy of fratricide that plays itself out in the present. The painting on the wall acts as a distorted mirror that reflects both Geordie's past and the relations between Nick's family in the present. The Fanshawe narrative both acknowledges and displaces Geordie's secret, pointing to the complex intersections between knowing and not knowing that extend throughout the novel. If Geordie's secret cannot be articulated or passed on in the context of the family narrative, then the Fanshawe murder offers an alternative discursive site for confronting and working through trauma. Barker's narrative demonstrates that the past is no longer straightforwardly available as a completed knowledge, and the indirectness of trauma in the novel signals a new form of referentiality that does refer, although not in a traditional semantic sense.

*Another World* powerfully dramatises the notion of trans-generational haunting. In the *Regeneration* trilogy, the ghosts represented the soldiers' dead companions, or those whom they killed, and Barker emphasised the unprecedented loss of the war. In *Another World*, the ghosts haunt subsequent generations. Family secrets that are unspoken or unresolved are communicated to the next generation and lie buried within them. Abraham and Torok's architectural image of the 'crypt' resonates in Barker's novel in the motif of the haunted house. Lob's Hill acts as a container which holds the unthinkable and unrepresentable residue of the past. The house also represents, on another level, the 'crypt' within Nick's psyche: the painting surfacing beneath the paintwork is analogous to Geordie's fratricide rising to the surface of Nick's consciousness. The haunted house is a common literary device in novels that explore the theme of trans-generational haunting. In *Beloved*, the trauma of slavery is initially contained within 124 Bluestone Road before it is embodied in the person of Beloved, and Baby Suggs points out that every house in the neighbourhood has its own ghost(s). In Michèle Roberts's *Daughters of the House*, the old Normandy house in which Thérèse and Léonie grow up is haunted by voices that whisper, chant and mourn. At the end of the novel, it is revealed that these are the ghosts of Jews who were arrested by the Germans and locked in one of the rooms on the night before they were shot. These haunted houses both externalise or symbolise psychic processes, drawing on Abraham and Torok's metaphor of the 'crypt', and suggest a connection between trauma and place, so that something of the trauma remains or inheres at the site of its occurrence. Trans-generational haunting offers a powerful figure for writers who wish to explore the impact of traumatic events on those who were born after. Although LaCapra has rightly raised concerns regarding the dangers of appropriating the experiences of trauma victims, and has drawn a distinction between the survivor-witness and subsequent generations, nevertheless traumatic events clearly do have a significant effect on those born later. The notions of belatedness and trans-generational haunting have been utilised by a range of contemporary novelists as a powerful and effective means of exploring, and representing, the lasting and ongoing effects of traumatic events.

# Chapter 2

## Telling tales: trauma and testimony in Binjamin Wilkomirski's Fragments

In the context of Holocaust literature, there has been much recent discussion regarding the boundaries between fact and fiction.[1] It has been recognised that Holocaust fiction is often based on extensive historical research and documentation, while Holocaust testimony is subject to the inaccuracies and distortions of memory. Thomas Keneally, author of *Schindler's List* (1982), argued that his novel, based on interviews with survivors and extensive archival research, comprised a hybrid form, suspended between fact and fiction which he termed 'non-fiction fiction'.[2] Art Spiegelman's *Maus* comic books, based on historical research and interviews with his father, took thirteen years to complete. Spiegelman protested when the *New York Times* classified *Maus* under 'Fiction' in their bestseller list; in response to his letter, the *Times* changed the classification of *Maus* from 'Fiction' to 'Fact'. Of Holocaust testimony, Primo Levi, in *The Drowned and the Saved* (1988), insisted that '[h]uman memory is a marvellous but fallacious instrument' (11), liable to deterioration and decay, especially in the wake of such a catastrophic experience as the Holocaust. Elie Wiesel, in his memoir *All Rivers Run to the Sea* (1995), revised and commented on a passage in *Night* (1960) in which he described the horrific train journey to Auschwitz. Wiesel revealed that his description in *Night* mingled fact and fantasy, and distorted the truth of the event, and he observed of the process of testimony: 'No witness is capable of recounting everything from start to finish anyway. God alone knows the whole story' (1995: 17).[3] If testimonies inevitably contain errors and omissions, writers and scholars nevertheless agree that they remain fundamentally accurate.

Levi defended the consonance of his memories with the historical record, arguing that his own published writings are 'unaffected by the drifting I have described' (1988: 21). Other Holocaust survivors have likewise defended the accuracy of their testimonies, despite the unreliability of memory. The critic Lawrence Langer observed that the essence and substance of Holocaust testimonies takes priority over inconsistencies or contradictions in their detail (1991: xv).

The recent controversy surrounding Binjamin Wilkomirski's *Fragments: Memories of a Childhood, 1939–1948* (1996) represented a crisis point in this discussion. *Fragments* narrated the story of its author's childhood experiences, which included escaping from the persecution of the Jews in Riga, surviving imprisonment in concentration camps in Poland, and being smuggled from a Polish orphanage to Switzerland immediately after the war. On publication, the text was widely hailed as a literary masterpiece and received numerous prestigious awards, including the American National Jewish Book Award for autobiography and memoirs, the *Jewish Quarterly* prize for non-fiction, and the Prix Mémoire de la Shoah from the Fondation Judaisme Français. However, extensive research by Elena Lappin (1999), Philip Grourevitch (1999) and Stefan Maechler (2001) has convincingly demonstrated that Wilkomirski invented the history in *Fragments*. Wilkomirski was born in Switzerland in 1941, under the name of Bruno Grosjean. He was brought up by his mother until he was two years old, when she was forced by the Swiss authorities to give him up for adoption because he was illegitimate. He was officially adopted by the Doessekers in 1945, when he was four years old. In the wake of the revelations concerning Wilkomirski, the publishers withdrew *Fragments* from print in autumn 1999.[4] Many critics turned against the work, arguing that it no longer had any literary value. However, influential scholars stood against the tide of opinion and defended the text. Susan Suleiman described *Fragments* as 'a work of literary art, powerful in its effect' (2000: 553), Lawrence Langer regarded the book to be 'a very compelling work of literature' (quoted in Eskin, 2002: 107) and Deborah Lipstadt agreed, arguing: 'If [Wilkomirski] had told the same story in terrible prose, it wouldn't have been mesmerizing' (quoted in Eskin, 2002: 108).

*Fragments* collapsed the boundary between fact and fiction in an unprecedented manner and critics were at a loss as to how to categorise the text. Although it was published as a memoir, this description was clearly no longer appropriate because memoir, by definition, describes experiences that the author has lived through.

Wilkomirski self-consciously presents *Fragments* as a memoir, observing in the 'Afterword' that he was persuaded to forget the past by
those around him and that it took many years before he was able to
write about his memories. He claims that he is one of the 'children
without identity' (154), who survived the Holocaust because they
were provided with false documentation but who consequently
lacked any clear information about their own origins. In deliberately
framing his text as a memoir, Wilkomirski breaks what Lejeune has
termed the 'autobiographical pact', whereby a text can be classed as
autobiography if the author and the narrator-protagonist coincide.
Sue Vice has suggested that *Fragments* can be straightforwardly
recategorised as fiction, arguing that 'the work of textual analysis
can begin on what remains a striking and unusual *novel*' (2000: 164).
However, as Suleiman points out, Wilkomirski's text obscures the
difference between fact and fiction by insisting on its own accuracy
and truthfulness. The unique character of *Fragments* emerges from
the fact that this obfuscation does not seem to be deliberate; to all
appearances, Wilkomirski genuinely believes himself to have experienced the past that he describes. Based on Wilkomirski's own
insistence and apparent belief that his text is factual, Suleiman
observes that 'we must call *Fragments* not a novel but a false – or
better a deluded – memoir' (2000: 552).

This chapter explores, in the first instance, the literary context
which enabled *Fragments* to be read as an authentic and convincing
Holocaust memoir. In recent years, Holocaust testimony has
emerged as a distinct genre, which is governed by its own rules
and conventions. By writing within these conventions, Wilkomirski
was able to produce a powerful and moving narrative of trauma which
seemed to collapse under the burden of its own unbearable recollections. I will argue that Wilkomirski was also influenced, in writing
*Fragments*, by Jerzy Kosinski's *The Painted Bird* (1965), and in particular
by Kosinski's view of memory, which does not accord to fact but
reflects an inner or subjective truth. I will discuss the relation between
*Fragments* and *The Painted Bird*, and argue that Wilkomirski's adoption
of the child's perspective owes much to Kosinski and marks a striking
departure in the text from the testimonial genre. One of the key
questions for critics, in relation to *Fragments*, is whether the text
deserves to fall into oblivion and, if not, how it can be constructively
read or interpreted. The chapter concludes by seeking to reorient
current discussions of *Fragments* away from the notion of individual
memory and towards ideas of cultural or collective memory. I will

argue that one way of rehabilitating Wilkomirski's text is to regard it as reflecting and helping to shape a singular moment of crisis in Swiss cultural memory of the Holocaust. *Fragments* emerged in the highly charged cultural atmosphere of a society split along generational, racial and political fault lines. In the mid-1990s, the Swiss were bitterly divided between those who defended the traditional image of Switzerland as a neutral and independent power, and those who regarded Switzerland to have been complicit with National Socialism. I will discuss the publication of *Fragments* as a key watershed in the Swiss cultural debate about the Holocaust and as a text which is itself, in turn, shaped by the emerging discourses of the guilt and culpability of Switzerland, both during the war and in the immediate postwar years.

## The genre of testimony

It has long been recognised, in thinking about fakes and forgeries, that producing a fake is only possible in relation to a form with a clearly established genre. The fake relies on a skilful mimicry, which is indiscernible or imperceptible to the untrained eye, of the conventions associated with a particular form. In the 1980s and 1990s, Holocaust testimony emerged as a distinct genre and its rules and conventions were defined by key trauma theorists, such as Lawrence Langer, Shoshana Felman and Dori Laub. In highly influential studies on testimony, these theorists established the formal expectations of the genre, to the extent that Robert Hanks, in a review of *Fragments*, felt justified in noting: 'a peculiar set of conventions has come to cluster around depictions of the Holocaust [. . .] the effect has been to turn the literature of genocide into a genre, with rules almost as constricting as those binding the Agatha Christie-style detective story' (1996: 31). Once the conventions of a genre have been defined, they are open, as Amy Hungerford observes, to the possibility that they may be 'met fraudulently' (2001: 69). It was arguably not until the mid-1990s, that the genre of Holocaust testimony was sufficiently developed or distinct for a text such as *Fragments* to emerge, or for this genre to be of sufficient cultural prestige and value (in terms of literary prizes and awards) that it would have been desirable to fake.

Lawrence Langer's *Holocaust Testimonies: The Ruins of Memory* (1991) has been highly influential in the fields of Holocaust studies and trauma theory. Langer's dissociation-related theory of testimony is primarily concerned to demonstrate the ways in which the Holocaust unsettles and disrupts traditional moral and historical accounts. He argues that the experiences of the Holocaust isolated the individual from conventional moral frameworks based on agency and choice. Survival in the ghettos or camps depended on an alternative code of behaviour, in which victims were confronted with what Langer terms 'choiceless choice' (1991: 83). The extremity of the concentration camps produced a rupture in the lives and selves of Holocaust victims which, for Langer, is not susceptible to recovery or repair: 'What we are really speaking of [. . .] is a festering wound, a blighted convalescence' (1991: 92). The testimonies strive towards a new form of representation, which seeks to articulate the unprecedented reality of the camps. In collapsing chronology and refusing the coherence of closure, survivors seek to reflect their own experiences of rupture. Langer discerns in the testimonies a conflict between concentrationary modes of behaviour and conventional moral values which reflects the perpetual struggle, in which survivors are caught, between the extreme and the everyday.

In *Testimony: Crises of Witnessing in Literature, Psychoanalysis and History* (1992), Shoshana Felman and Dori Laub describe testimony as fragmented and broken in form, 'composed of bits and pieces of a memory that has been overwhelmed by occurrences that have not settled into understanding or remembrance' (5). Testimony represents a joint process or event, which can only take place in the presence of an empathetic listener. Laub, in particular, bases his notion of testimony on the conventions of psychoanalytic practice. By definition, the traumatic event takes place outside of the structures of normal reality; the work of testimony accordingly begins with a 'joint acceptance' of the 'Holocaust reality' between survivor and listener (69). Both parties enter into a contract or understanding relating to the testimonial process, which Laub defines as follows:

> Implicitly, the listener says to the testifier: 'For this limited time, throughout the duration of the testimony, I'll be with you all the way, as much as I can. I want to go wherever you go, and I'll hold and protect you along this journey. Then, at the end of the journey, I shall leave you.' (70)

On the part of the listener, there is a necessary emotional investment in the testimony. The trauma returns in disjointed fragments and the role of the listener is to 'move quietly and decisively in bringing things together' (71), making sense out of the broken fragments that emerge. Such a commitment is not without hazards for the listener, who risks experiencing a modified version of the survivor's trauma:

'the listener to trauma comes to be a participant and a co-owner of the traumatic event: through his very listening, he comes to partially experience trauma in himself' (57). Other trauma theorists have responded with caution to Laub's understanding of the role of the listener. Geoffrey Hartman is wary of what he considers to be Laub's 'positive view' (1996: 165, n. 10) of secondary trauma. Kali Tal is critical of what she regards to be an appropriative gesture on Laub's part, which makes no distinction between the primary trauma suffered by the victim or survivor and the secondary trauma suffered by the testimonial audience (1996: 56–7). LaCapra warns that over-identification with the victim of trauma can lead to 'surrogate vict-image' (2001: 211). In an attempt to impose a limit on our response to traumatic events, he distinguishes empathy – in which an affective response to trauma is combined with cognition, argument and critical judgement – from identification, in which a sense of critical and emotional distance has been lost.

Langer distinguishes in the testimonies between story and plot.[5] If the story is the chronological narrative, beginning with 'I was born' and ending with 'I was liberated', the plot of the testimony 'meanders, coils back on itself, contains rocks and rapids, and requires strenuous effort to follow its intricate turns' (1991: 174), revealing that the witness is seized by instead of selecting incidents. In *Fragments*, the past emerges in bits and pieces and the plot strays in time, resisting chronology and closure: 'My earliest memories are a rubble field of isolated images and events. [. . .] Mostly a chaotic jumble, with very little chronological fit; shards that keep surfacing against the orderly grain of grown-up life and escaping the laws of logic' (4). The immediacy of the past, overwhelming and flooding the present, is powerfully represented in Wilkomirski's distinctive use of tenses. Andrea Reiter observes of the sections into which the German text of *Fragments* is divided that each characteristically opens with a short passage in the imperfect, followed by an extended description of the camps in the present tense and concluding with a brief reflective passage in the imperfect. The present-tense narration is further characterised by the use of 'short and excited main clauses' (Reiter, 2000: 239). This method of narration emphasises the traumatic nature of the memories described, which are not so much remembered as re-experienced or relived. The transition into the present tense is typically marked by an associative image or link which causes the past to surface. The most notable use of this technique is the smell of bread, which transports the narrator from the Swiss orphanage to the day in the camp when he met his mother and received from her a piece of bread. As the smell of the bread 'envelope[s]' the narrator, it evokes 'pictures' in him which take him back into the past (46).

The narrator's memories of the camp reflect Langer's notion of 'choiceless choice', so that at key moments of self-preservation such as the betrayal of the new boy in the barracks (60–7) or the death of Jankl (74–6), the child experiences a splitting or rupture of the self, evident in symptoms such as deafness or dissociation, which reveals the extremity of the situation and highlights his lack of agency or choice. Although the narrator clearly recognises the threat to his own life caused by the new boy in the barracks, who has not yet learnt the 'rules of the game' (60) and consequently 'could be the end of us all' (62), he nevertheless cannot remember his death without conventional morality asserting itself: 'I'm guilty, I'm a murderer. If it hadn't been for me, it wouldn't have happened' (66). The narrator cannot reconcile the codes of survival which he learnt from Jankl in the camp, with the morals of Swiss society and the two value systems conflict throughout the narrative.

Laub's representation of testimony as a joint project can be linked to the process of reading, which necessarily entails a relationship between reader and author. *Fragments* opens with an implicit pact or contract, in which Wilkomirski vouches that the text is based on accurate and truthful childhood memories: 'I'm not a poet or a writer. I can only try to use words to draw as exactly as possible what happened, what I saw; exactly the way my child's memory has held on to it' (4–5). In return, the reader accepts as genuine the 'Holocaust reality' which is represented and enters into a commitment to accompany the author for the duration of the narrative unfolding. *Fragments* continually shifts in time between the narrator's early childhood in Poland and his first years in Switzerland. Wilkomirski relies on the use of synecdoche, which is particularly prevalent in the descriptions of the concentration camps in the frequent use of the detail from a uniform to represent a camp guard. He is extremely vague in the details of the text and we are given few clear dates or places. Even the child's name and the identification of his mother and father are not definite. The more traumatic the event described, the more fragmented the narrative becomes, so that Wilkomirski's descriptions of the gas vans and mass burial are barely decipherable (90–7). In order to make sense of the highly impressionistic narrative, the reader must draw on his own knowledge of the Holocaust. Reader-response critic, Wolfgang Iser, sees the reader as someone who is, above all, concerned with coherence and sense-making. Faced with a fragmentary narrative, the reader will search for connections between the pieces and actively provide the unwritten part of the text. Blake Eskin observes that *Fragments* operates in precisely this way: 'The episodic, non-linear narrative [. . .] requir[es] us to connect dots to create [Wilkomirski's] biography' (2002: 16). Laub indicates the depth of emotional investment required in fitting together the broken pieces of a narrative of trauma. The letters that were sent to Wilkomirski from readers, before the text was revealed to be a false memoir, bear witness to the extent of their identification and the depth of betrayal that they felt on learning the truth.[6] In replicating the conventions of testimony, Wilkomirski produces a convincing account of extreme trauma and positions his readers as empathetic listeners so that they necessarily respond to the text with an intense emotional and subjective involvement. The initial responses to *Fragments* highlight the risk that over-identification can lead to the loss of critical reflection and distance.

It appears that Wilkomirski did not consciously deceive his readers but wrote what he believed to be an authentic memoir. Suleiman has argued that the process of reading Holocaust testimonies provided Bruno Doesseker/Grosjean with the identity of Binjamin Wilkomirski and convinced him of his identity as a survivor: 'His powerful memoir is based not on his experiences but on his fantasies and on the memories of others; before writing his book, Wilkomirski/Doesseker/Grosjean had read thousands of testimonies and historical works in his obsessive pursuit of a Holocaust identity' (2000: 549). Hungerford correctly points out, however, that Wilkomirski did not read trauma theory and other memoirs 'in order to learn the conventions of the Holocaust memoir, his extensive personal archive of such books becoming [. . .] a "laboratory" for creating his fraud' (2001: 68). The case of Wilkomirski is fascinating, because it gestures towards the unforeseeable effects of the Holocaust as story, and demonstrates the ways in which the Holocaust is implicated in uncontrollable and as yet unknown ways in individual fantasy. Felman explores the unpredictable effects of the Holocaust in her story of screening a video testimony to her class of students at Yale (Felman and Laub, 1992: 1–56). The students experienced a crisis as a result of the screening and Felman suggests that testimony not only refers to a private life but can act, beyond this, to *'penetrate us like an actual life'* (2). Although LaCapra accuses Felman of blatant '[s]elf-dramatization' (1998: 113n.) and insists that there is clearly a difference between primary and secondary trauma, it nevertheless seems that traumatic experience can transmit itself, through sympathetic iden- tification, in profoundly unpredictable ways. Wilkomirski clearly exceeds this boundary between the trauma that the survivor has experienced and transmitted trauma. In his case, trauma does not penetrate *like* a life; the penetrating effect of the Holocaust replaces his own life and he assumes the identity of the survivor.

## Through the eyes of a child

*Fragments* most notably departs from the techniques of testimony and enters the realm of Holocaust fiction in Wilkomirski's use of the child's narrative viewpoint. At the opening of the text, the narrator clearly states that he can only represent his childhood experiences by returning to the child's perspective: 'If I'm going to write about it, I have to give up on the ordering logic of grown-ups; it would only distort what happened' (4). Wilkomirski's narrative technique has a number of effects on the reader. Most obviously, it increases identi- fication with the protagonist, because the reader is naturally inclined to feel more sympathy for the experiences of a young child. Readers encountering the overwhelming details of the Holocaust can often feel disoriented and at a loss, and the child's perspective mirrors their own response. The view through a child's eyes estranges the familiar facts of the Holocaust, providing an unfamiliar perspective on the events because a child is liable to notice details and is not always able to interpret what is going on around him. In the terms of reader- response criticism, the limited insight of the child creates a hiatus in the text, which relies on the knowledge or imagination of the reader to fill in the gap and to make sense of the narrative. Reiter observes of the child's viewpoint that it 'moves the facts – so well known that they are easily disregarded – into a brightly illuminated field of attention' (2000: 239). The adoption of the child's perspective acts as a powerful literary device in *Fragments*, which both increases the reader's in- volvement and presents the facts of the Holocaust in a new and innovative light.

The child's perspective is used to particular effect in the episode in *Fragments* in which the narrator encounters a pile of women's corpses in the camp, shortly after meeting his mother. Looking at the dead women, the child remembers the story of origins which was told to him by one of the older children in the barracks, 'that little children grow in women's bellies before they're born' (85). This leads him to wonder about his own origins in relation to his mother's body: 'everyone keeps saying I'm so small, that must mean that I grew in a belly too' (85). As he ponders, the stomach of one of the corpses begins to move and the child remembers that babies move when they are ready to be born. In the place of the human child, however, a rat emerges from the stomach and darts away. The narrator mistakenly assimilates this new fact into his emerging theory of human origins: 'I saw it, I saw it! The dead women are giving birth to rats!' (86). He leaps to the conclusion that the rats which plague the children in the camp are the offspring of the camp women who have died. Returning to the question of his own origins, the boy suffers a profound crisis of identity in which he is no longer able to discern whether he is human or animal: 'I'm a child – but am I a human child or a rat child, or can you be both at once?' (87). The passage relies on the reader being able to perceive, where the child cannot, that the rat has been feeding on the dead woman's body. The confusion of the child reflects the brutalisation of the Holocaust and calls into question the extent to which Nazi propaganda was internalised by its victims, to become an element of their self-perception and identity. Reiter observes of the episode: 'What Wilkomirski narrates here in this sensational fashion accords well – irrespective of its autobiographical authenticity – with the experience of alienation attested by many survivors' (2000: 238). The reader's superior knowledge increases identification with the narrator because he cannot understand or interpret what is happening around him and, in the absence of parents to teach or guide him, he relies on the gossip of the older children in the barracks to provide him with an interpretative framework.

In narrating the experiences of a young boy in Poland from the limited viewpoint of the child, Wilkomirski's *Fragments* closely echoes Jerzy Kosinski's *The Painted Bird*. Langer was one of the few critics to recognise that *Fragments* was fiction from the outset, precisely because of its remarkable similarities to *The Painted Bird*.[7] In each text, a young child is left alone in a world dominated by brutality and cruelty and the child temporarily loses the faculty of speech in his struggle to survive. Although the boy in *The Painted Bird* does not enter the concentration camps, both children are subjected to the terror of Nazi-occupied Poland and both miraculously survive a series of savage and violent attacks. Wilkomirski first encountered *The Painted Bird* in the 1960s, and described it as 'the most touching and most shocking thing I had ever read' (quoted in Maechler, 2001: 59). In particular,

Wilkomirski was struck by Kosinski's method of narration through the child, which he subsequently adopted in his own work. Wilkomirski recognised the powerful effect of the boy's misunderstandings, observing of the child's viewpoint that it is '[v]ery matter-of-fact, just as he saw it, whether he understood it or not' (quoted in Maechler, 2001: 59).

The controversy which surrounds *Fragments* bears a remarkable similarity to the reception of Kosinski's novel. Initially greeted with favourable reviews, *The Painted Bird* was published as fiction but was predominantly read as a historical testimony to Kosinski's wartime experiences. Kosinski encouraged such readings and claimed that his own childhood experiences were, if anything, worse than those suffered by his child protagonist. When it was subsequently discovered that Kosinski had spent the war in hiding with his parents, he was widely attacked.[8] In an 'Afterword' to the German edition of *The Painted Bird*, Kosinski sought to explain the relation between his life and the text, discussing his ideas on the literary treatment of memory. Rejecting the strict binary of fact and fiction as too neat, Kosinski coined the term 'autofiction' to describe his writing. He regards the act of writing *The Painted Bird* as a therapeutic project, 'the result of the slow unfreezing of a mind long gripped by fear' (quoted in Maechler, 2001: 243). For Kosinski, memory is inherently a process of editing, so that the writer 'creates his own personal pattern out of his memories'; he shapes experience into stories or fictions which can, in turn, be accommodated by the individual (quoted in Maechler, 2001: 242). Kosinski is less concerned with factual autobiography – 'an examination, or a revisitation of childhood' – than with a 'vision', in which objective reality acquires a secondary importance (quoted in Maechler, 2001: 243). The child's journey in *The Painted Bird* is 'metaphorical' and it 'could actually have taken place in the mind' (quoted in Maechler, 2001: 243). The story corresponds to an internal landscape and is strongly allied to the genre of the fairy tale: '*The Painted Bird* can be considered as fairy tales *experienced* by the child, rather than *told* to him' (quoted in Maechler, 2001: 243). Kosinski provides an unconventional and distinctive literary model, in which autobiography and fantasy merge and the truth of memory is highly subjective: 'One cannot say that memory is either literal or exact; if memories have a truth, it is more an emotional than an actual one' (quoted in Maechler, 2001: 242).

Wilkomirski owned a German edition of *The Painted Bird* and was undoubtedly familiar with Kosinski's ideas. Kosinski's views initially seem far removed from *Fragments*. Wilkomirski has repeatedly asserted that his memories correspond to fact and he is concerned to emphasise the accuracy of his childhood recollections, which are 'planted, first and foremost, in exact snapshots' (4). However, *Fragments* often reads like a fairy tale in which the child acts as the protagonist, improbably surviving unscathed all of the dangers which threaten him, including being thrown violently to the ground. In *The Uses of Enchantment* (1976), Bruno Bettelheim observes that the fairy tale invariably signals its own beginning through a sequence of recognisable devices:

> 'Once upon a time', 'In a certain country', 'A thousand years ago or longer', 'At a time when animals still talked', 'Once in an old castle in the midst of a large and dense forest' – such beginnings suggest that what follows does not pertain to the here and now that we know. This deliberate vagueness in the beginnings of fairy tales symbolizes that we are leaving the concrete world of ordinary reality. (62)

Wilkomirski ushers the reader into the world of his early childhood in terms which evoke such fairy-tale beginnings: 'it seemed a long way away and a long time ago. It was in the farmhouse, away somewhere in amongst the Polish forests' (19). The boy is the youngest of six brothers and they live with the farmer's wife, an archetypal wicked stepmother who is 'severe, rough, full of punishments' (27). In a contemporary rewriting of the Grimm brothers' 'Hansel and Gretel', the child takes on the identity of a resourceful little Hansel. Separated from his brothers, he is imprisoned in concentration camps where his tasks are precisely those of Hansel, namely to outwit the adults and to save himself from the ovens. Through the eyes of the boy, the Holocaust persecutes and kills children and the ovens in the camps are made for children, just as the witch's oven was designed to cook Hansel and Gretel. Even after the war in Switzerland it seems that he is not safe; when his adopted mother shows him the cellar, with its fruit racks and coal furnace, she momentarily metamorphoses in the boy's response into the figure of the witch.

> So – my suspicions were right. I've fallen into a trap. The oven door is smaller than usual, but it's big enough for children [. . .] Wooden bunks for children, oven doors for children, it's all too much [. . .] My thoughts were falling over each other. I was right. They're trying to trick me. That's why they want me to forget what I know. The camp's still here. Everything's still here. (125)

The boy in *Fragments* relies on Hansel's strategy to save himself. Just as Hansel lay trails of stones and bread to find his way back home, so the child, in his new home in Switzerland, lays a trail of memories to trace his way back into the past: 'I wanted to get back, somehow. I thought the only way I'd find my way back would be if I remembered every place, every street, every house, and every barracks' (67). The narrator finds the technique reliable, so that the first time he returns to Kraków after the war he is able to retrace the route from the station to the Miodowa synagogue 'like a sleepwalker' (113). In broader terms, however, it seems that Wilkomirski does not learn the lesson of Hansel's over-reliance on this method. Like Hansel, Wilkomirski learns to his cost that such traces are apt to disappear and to prove untrustworthy and unreliable as signposts or markers.

In identifying Kosinski as a literary influence on Wilkomirski, I am not seeking to argue that *Fragments* deliberately or consciously echoed *The Painted Bird*, or that Wilkomirski set out to provoke a similar controversy. The parallel between the two writers is potentially more interesting than this. Kosinski famously internalised or lived out the fictions that he invented for himself, so that the stories became a part of his life. Daniel Schwarz observes of Kosinski: 'Not only did [he] create imaginary worlds in his novels, but his novels played a crucial role in creating his character and personality' (1999: 176). There is arguably a self-conscious theatricality or opportunism to Kosinski's self-inventions, which seems absent from Wilkomirski's pained insistences that his text is a true representation of his child-hood. *Fragments* was written after Wilkomirski had received psycho-analytic treatment, which he obliquely refers to in the text as a 'long journey' (10).[9] Psychoanalysis is famously less concerned with auto-biographical actuality than with the patient's 'vision' of childhood, which reflects a subjective or emotional rather than an objective truth. The convergence of Wilkomirski's and Kosinski's texts speaks of the uncomfortable and insecure boundary between text and life so that we cannot entirely separate one from the other. The text can absorb life in complex, indirect and unpredictable forms, while life can absorb the text in equally unknowable and unsettling ways. In Wilkomirski's case, the relation of psychoanalysis to the fictions of the self is just as complex and troubling. Psychoanalysis works at the interstices of fantasy and reality in the realm of the 'as if'. In writing *Fragments* and in assuming the identity of the survivor, Wilkomirski has arguably taken the 'as if' beyond the confines of the psycho-analytic encounter and has internalised or acted out as his own experience the productions of fantasy and identification.

## Switzerland is not a beautiful country

*Fragments* cannot properly be read as fiction because of Wilkomirski's own insistence and apparent belief that his text is factual. Neither can *Fragments* be read as testimony, in spite of its close mimicry of the form, because it does not describe Wilkomirski's own experiences but comprises, in Suleiman's terms, a 'false' or 'deluded' memoir (2000: 552). The genre of testimony is based on individual memory and critical discussion of *Fragments* has accordingly focused on the unreliability of personal recollection and its susceptibility to distortion and external influence. In what follows, I suggest that *Fragments* can be reinvigorated as a text if it is placed in the theoretical context of cultural or collective memory. Maurice Halbwachs argued in *On Collective Memory* (1992) that both individual and collective remembering are concerned to represent the past in the light of the needs of the present, and that both modes of remembrance therefore employ mechanisms of selection and reconstruction in ordering their narratives. However, Nancy Wood has pointed out a crucial distinction which Halbwachs has drawn, between individual and collective acts of remembrance:

> What differentiates these two modes of memory is that while the emanation of individual memory is primarily subject to the laws of the unconscious, public memory – whatever its unconscious vicissitudes – testifies to a will or desire on the part of some social group or disposition of power to select and organize representations of the past so that these will be embraced by individuals as their own. (2000: 2)

Collective memory is imbricated in political structures and produces narratives which are used to support group interests and mobilise loyalties. However, these narratives are also, to some degree, integrated at the level of individual memory, so that socially organised representations of the past influence and inform personal remembrance and the constructions of autobiographical memory are inevitably implicated in wider social frameworks of meaning.

*Fragments* was first published in Switzerland in 1995. This date marked a period of crisis in Swiss collective memory, which was highly fractured and divided. Caroline Wiedmer has argued that, at this time, Switzerland was suffering a 'crisis of national self-assessment' regarding its wartime past (2001: 467). In the mid-1990s there developed in Switzerland, largely as a result of external pressures, a critical discussion concerning the Swiss involvement in the crimes of the National-Socialist regime. The Swiss banks were initially at the centre of the controversy. International Jewish organisations, headed by the World Jewish Congress, accused the Swiss of co-operating with the Nazis. During the war, gold reserves were sold to Switzerland which had been acquired by force from the banks of occupied countries or confiscated from the victims of Nazism. After the war, Swiss banks were accused of the insensitive or cynical handling of claims by Holocaust survivors in relation to dormant accounts. In 1995, the Swiss Federation of Jewish Communities, the World Jewish Congress and the Israeli government urged Swiss banks to look again for Holocaust-era assets. In response, the Swiss government established two international committees of experts: the Volcker Commission, which investigated unclaimed accounts in Swiss banks, and the Bergier Commission, which looked into Switzerland's business dealings and Swiss refugee politics during the Second World War. Under the pressure of external accusations and charges, the traditional image of Switzerland as a neutral or independent nation became increasingly impossible to sustain.

Two statements, in particular, stand out among the heated debates which circulated around the so-called Nazi Gold Affair. On 7 May 1995, the fiftieth anniversary of D-Day, President Kaspar Villiger became the first to officially apologise for the Swiss refugee policy during the war, and particularly the Federal Council's role in introducing the J-stamped passport, which marked Switzerland's recognition of the racial categories established by the Nuremberg Laws.[10] Villiger observed: 'To me, it is beyond doubt that we incurred guilt with our policies regarding the persecuted Jews. We can only bow in silence before those who on our account suffered, were imprisoned, or even died' (quoted in Wiedmer, 2001: 467–8). In 1998, the former president Jean-Pascale Delamuraz, interviewed by the French-language Swiss newspaper *24 Heures*, argued that the Nazi Gold Affair was based less on historical truth than on an American intention to destabilise Switzerland.[11] In a famous comment, which he subsequently and unsuccessfully sought to withdraw, he observed: 'From the way certain people talk, I sometimes wonder whether Auschwitz isn't located in Switzerland' (quoted in Wiedmer, 2001: 472). In response to this interview, four thousand people, among them well-known writers and intellectuals, published *The Manifesto of 21 January 1997*, which rejected the equation of Swiss interests with commercial or banking interests and argued that Switzerland should urgently examine its national identity and reformulate its history.

*Fragments* was published and read in this highly charged political atmosphere. Wilkomirski's construction of his personal memories closely echoes the reformulation of Swiss national history, suggesting the influence of socially organised representations of the past on individual remembrance. The overwhelming response to *Fragments* undoubtedly emerged, in part, from the revision of Swiss history and identity which Wilkomirski offers to his readers. On seeing, in Switzerland, what he believes to be the concentration camp ovens and barracks, the child observes: 'The camp's still there – just hidden and well disguised' (150) and he unequivocally condemns the Swiss as Nazis: 'Just give them the gentlest of hints that maybe, possibly, you're a Jew – and you'll feel it: these are the same people, and I'm sure of it. They can still kill, even out of uniform' (151). These words take on a specific political resonance in the context of the discussions regarding the extent to which 'Auschwitz' was located in Switzerland. In particular, *Fragments* condemns the Swiss refusal after the war to discuss the Holocaust: 'I grew up and became an adult in a time and in a society that didn't want to listen, or perhaps was incapable of listening' (153). This attitude is powerfully dramatised in the class-room scene, in which the narrator misidentifies William Tell as an SS man, only to find that his tentative descriptions of the concentration camps are dimissed by his teacher as 'drivel' (130). In retaliation, the boy dismisses the story of William Tell, in turn, as 'drivel' (133) in an implicit criticism of Swiss national myth-making and the heroicisation of a past based in legend and folklore.

*Fragments* provides a sharp critique of Swiss society and presents Swiss readers with defamiliarised versions of stock national images, revealing them as they would be seen through the eyes of a refugee child. In the classroom scene, William Tell morphs into the figure of a torturing SS man. In one of the most powerful passages in *Fragments*, the ski lift similarly converts into a death machine. A recurring motif in the text is the child's nightmare, in which the trauma of the concentration camps is relived. Emerging initially on the boy's first night in a Swiss orphanage, the dream repeats itself into adulthood 'like an unstoppable copying machine' (38), and signifies that the experience of the camps cannot easily be left behind. The content of the nightmare is unchanging and concerns a death machine which relentlessly and unstoppably processes the dead; the child awakens with a feeling of despair and an absolute certainty that he cannot escape from a slow and agonising death.

At the foot of the mountain was a hut with a sort of canopy in front. Under the canopy were a lot of coal cars on rails. Some of the cars were full of dead people; their arms and legs stuck out over the edges. A narrow rail track ran straight up to the peak and in under the helmet, into a gaping jawbone with filthy brown teeth. The cars cycled uphill, disappearing into the jaw under the helmet, then cycled back down again, empty. (39)

When the child first encounters a ski lift in Switzerland, it seems to him to be the manifestation of his nightmares and the ski instructor, who attaches pairs of children to the hooks to be carried to the top of the mountain, is cast by the narrator as an 'executioner' (142). The episode acts as a powerful narrative device through which Wilkomirski is able to convey the threats of brutality and anti-Semitism which underlie the seemingly innocent and benevolent surface of Swiss society and to unveil as a lie Frau Grosz's promise to the child that 'Switzerland's a beautiful country' (12).

In this chapter, I have argued that *Fragments* is inseparable from its cultural and political context, and that Wilkomirski's fabricated memories are profoundly imbricated in and influenced by the collective reformulation of Swiss national history. Regardless of the fictionality of Wilkomirski's Holocaust experience, *Fragments* uses the Holocaust past to powerfully indict Swiss political and cultural attitudes to the Holocaust, both in the immediate postwar years and in the present. For Wilkomirski himself, it seems that the controversy regarding his own past and the debates concerning Switzerland's past, are inextricably intertwined. In a statement released to the media on 16 September 1998, Wilkomirski appealed to the Bergier Commission to investigate his past or his own wartime involvement in the Holocaust:

I am asking the Bergier Commission, which is examining Switzerland's relationship with Jews in the 1940's, also to research my early years within the general context of the history of refugee children, including 'Yenish people' (gypsies) in Switzerland. I will give the commission all the information I have, and grant it exclusive and unconditional access to all available documents, including those of the research institute Children Without Identity in Jerusalem. I am asking the Bergier Commission to contact me. (Quoted in Maechler, 2001: 138)

The Bergier Commission rejected Wilkomirski's invitation, arguing that it fell outside of their remit. However, the incident reveals the extent to which the *Fragments* controversy was imbricated in the ongoing crisis of Swiss cultural memory. It also demonstrates the ways in which Wilkomirski deliberately and provocatively intertwines his own claims against the Swiss – that they had issued him with a false birth certificate and 'imposed' an identity on him (154), thereby depriving him of his own history and identity – with the broader claims against the Swiss made by the international Jewish community. *Fragments* reveals the power of the Holocaust as story, not only as it is implicated in the individual imagination or fantasy but also for its formidable authority and influence in contemporary political and cultural discourse. In *Testimony*, Laub tells an anecdote about a Holocaust survivor who remembered seeing the crematorium chimneys of Auschwitz blown up but misremembered the number of chimneys that were destroyed (Felman and Laub, 1992: 59–63). Her testimony was subsequently attacked by historians who regarded her inaccuracy as the sign of a lack of veracity. However, as Laub observes, the woman's testimony powerfully bears witness to the incomprehensibility of any form of rebellion in Auschwitz. The woman's story was not true but it was truthful. *Fragments* is not the true account of a child's Holocaust experiences. The question therefore arises as to whether it nevertheless contains elements of truth in its representation of postwar Switzerland.

The debates in Switzerland in the mid-1990s ultimately concerned the way in which national history is constructed and memory politics are practised. The Swiss government gradually lost its sway over the prevailing self-representation of Switzerland, and various groups contended for the construction of alternative narratives and visions of the past. The stakes were high not only in political and cultural terms but also in relation to financial payouts, the Swiss government eventually agreeing in 1998 to a $1.25 billion settlement, which covered claimants to dormant Swiss accounts, refugees denied Swiss asylum and victims of slave labour. Wilkomirski has written a powerfully imagined intervention into Swiss memory politics which demonstrates that, for the narrator of *Fragments* at least, the nightmare of the Holocaust did not cease with the end of the war but continued and, if anything, worsened, because in Switzerland the memory of the past was silenced and racism and prejudice were hidden or concealed. Wilkomirski's text provides a powerful voice against the claims of conservatives and traditionalists in asserting that Switzerland is *not* a beautiful country and in revealing the extent of the country's implication in the events of the Holocaust.

# Chapter 3

## *'Ground that will remember you': trauma and landscape in Anne Michaels's* Fugitive Pieces

The notion of 'place' occupies a rich and interesting position in contemporary trauma theory, both through Geoffrey Hartman's writing on landscape and place, and through Pierre Nora's influential formulation of *lieux de mémoire* or 'sites of memory'. This chapter seeks to introduce recent work on landscape and trauma as a frame for reading Anne Michaels's *Fugitive Pieces* (1997), which is centrally concerned with the relation between landscape and memory. The process of viewing a landscape is one of careful construction, through which the indifferent or unaccommodating *space* of a site or environment is transformed into a *place* which draws the viewer into its territory. Crucial to this task of conversion is the viewer's location of a proper position or perspective from which to gain access to the landscape. On encountering a particular site, the viewer must find his bearings in relation to it in order to fulfil the demands of landscape. The contemplation of landscape teaches us that what we see is always and necessarily a question of *how* and *from where* we see. The traumas of the recent past profoundly challenge our ability to position ourselves in relation to them or to find our bearings. The question of positioning that landscape evokes can be regarded as crucial within the current discourse of trauma, for all efforts to confront and remember the past must be preceded by a consideration of the perspective from which we, as belated witnesses, view the event. Ulrich Baer elaborates:

> Where is the proper position from which to face this stark truth, and how is this notion of a position related to the experience of place? Prior to all efforts at commemoration, explanation or understanding, I would suggest, we must find a place or position from which we may then gain access to the event. (2000: 43)

Geoffrey Hartman has observed of his own writing, which encompasses critical readings of Wordsworth and his more recent work on trauma and the Holocaust, that it is brought together by his interest in place and its relation to memory and identity. Speaking of his joint fascination with Wordsworth and the Holocaust, Hartman has commented:

> There is a clear separation between these subjects. But once I had engaged with questions the Holocaust raised for me – how do I take this into consciousness, what can I do about it, is this in any way thinkable, is it representable – once I had gone along that path, my interest in Wordsworth's understanding of the memory process did come in. I sensed a loss of memory place, of the Wordsworthian memory place, after the Holocaust. (Quoted in Caruth, 1996b: 645)

For Hartman, one of the key aspects of Wordsworth's originality lies in his conversion of place into 'memory place', so that specific sites and landscapes create a temporal consciousness. In recollecting or describing past states of feeling, Wordsworth is invariably concerned to situate the feeling within a particular place or location. Hartman questions, however, whether the Wordsworthian 'memory places' can be connected with the sites of Holocaust suffering. The concentration camps are clearly fixed in the imagination of survivors and so seem related to Wordsworth's constructions, but Hartman resists this identification: 'it's difficult to think of the camps as being such memory places' (quoted in Caruth, 1996b: 647–8). Survivor accounts often recollect the deportation to a 'non-place' (reinforced by their transportation across long distances) and recount the destruction of a symbolic notion of 'place' that could make sense of their experiences. The former places of Jewish existence destroyed in the Holocaust also cannot be associated with 'memory places' because they lack the dynamism within individual memory of Wordsworth's descriptions. When asked to recall places of origin before the camps, survivors are typically vague in their recollections, while memories which do emerge tend to be fixed or nostalgic in character.

Two notable historians have recently explored the convergence of landscape, memory and the Holocaust: Simon Schama in *Landscape and Memory* (1996) and Martin Gilbert in *Holocaust Journey: Travelling in Search of the Past* (1997). Travelling through the present-day landscapes in which the events of the Holocaust took place, both writers are forcibly struck by the incongruity of the peaceful, pastoral vistas with which they are presented. Driving through Poland, Schama records a sense of shock at the unexpected and almost unseemly beauty of the landscape, the 'rolling, gentle land, lined by avenues of poplar and aspen' (1996: 26). Schama's perplexity relates to a problem of positioning: how can the Holocaust be situated within this landscape in which it has seemingly left no trace and how can Schama, in turn, position himself between the imagined and actual landscapes of the Holocaust? Travelling largely by rail across Germany, the Czech Republic and Poland, Gilbert records in his journal the same incredulity that history has apparently not left its mark on the countryside that rolls past the train windows.

If the Jewish past is seemingly not recorded on the landscape in which it took place, Schama suggests a new way of reading landscape, by removing it from the category of 'nature' and demonstrating the extent to which it is culturally invested. His project rests on the assumption that nature and culture are not mutually exclusive categories. Landscape is always a cultural construction; it is a product of 'imagination projected onto wood and water and rock' (1996: 61). No longer exclusively a phenomenon of nature, landscape is a site that has been modelled by history. Our readings of the landscapes by which we are surrounded always combine inherited memory, factual information, and personal and national politics. Schama's aims in writing *Landscape and Memory* are dual: he seeks to uncover the narratives that always inform our readings of landscapes, whether or not we are aware of them, and he is also concerned with the ways in which our myths of landscape construct cultural institutions and individual and national identities.

Hartman's interest in the convergence of landscape and memory resonates with the work of Pierre Nora, a French historian who supervised the compilation of a seven-volume study on national memory in France. Entitled *Les Lieux de mémoire* ('Realms of Memory', 1998), the work aimed to identify and analyse key sites of memory which have been invested with particular emotive and symbolic significance in the construction of the French national identity. Examples of *lieux de mémoire* include places (the national heritage site at Rheims), symbols (the *tricolor*), monuments (the Panthéon), commemorative dates (14 July), and exhibitions (*L'Exposition coloniale* of 1931). Nora contends that contemporary history has suffered a radical disjunction from the processes and rituals of memory. History is no longer concerned with the relation between past and present but is organised around the principle of preservation. In what Nora terms a 'terrorism of historicised memory' (1989: 14), the fear that the past will disappear leads to an obsessive and indiscriminate preservation of everything. Memory is replaced by the assiduous collection of remains, testimonies, documents, images – an endlessly proliferating construction of archives. Nora argues that such a reliance on the archival trace does not facilitate remembrance, for the storehouse of material remains overwhelms attempts to absorb or recall its contents. On the contrary, the archive replaces or substitutes for remembering:

> Memory has been wholly absorbed by its meticulous reconstitution. Its new vocation is to record; delegating to the archive the responsibility of remembering, it sheds its signs upon them depositing there, as a snake sheds its skin. (1989: 13)

Nora's remarks resonate with the memorialisation of the Holocaust, for a reliance upon the archival trace does indeed dominate the processes of remembrance. The most familiar tropes of the Holocaust are the piles of material remains – hair, suitcases, spectacles, shoes – which were removed from the victims on their arrival at the camps and left behind by the Nazis in their hasty departure. Nora questions whether these traces or residues of the past facilitate or substitute for remembrance.

Nora distinguishes *lieux d'histoire*, associated with the archive and arising from the preservation of the trace, from *lieux de mémoire*, which are sites, material or immaterial, around which the memory of a group or community crystallises itself. Invested with traces of longing and belonging, *lieux de mémoire* form part of a symbolic topography and are crucial to the formation of collective identities. Organised around such sites, memory is a dynamic process through which communities imagine and enact their changing relation to the past. Bound up with ritual enactment, *lieux de mémoire* generate devotional behaviour in a secular age, whether through visiting sites of pilgrimage, maintaining anniversaries or organising celebrations. *Lieux de mémoire* act to record the historically evolving relation of individuals and communities to sites and the associated transmutations of memory and identity. Originating in the sense that there is no spontaneous memory, *lieux de mémoire* deliberately or consciously invest sites with symbolic significance. There must be a human 'will to remember' (1989: 19) in order to transform a material site into a site of memory.

Nora has provided a theoretical basis for James Young's recent work on the memorialisation of the Holocaust. The *lieux d'histoire*, organised around the preservation of the trace, is reflected in

Young's analysis of Holocaust museums. With an emphasis on the display of objects, Holocaust museums evidence a fascination with the preserved relics found in the camps at the time of liberation, which appear as fragments of the event itself. The found objects frequently do not gesture beyond themselves, and consequently the debris of history can be mistaken for an encounter with history itself. Young echoes Nora's concern that a fetishisation of objects replaces the work of memory: the artefacts too often come to represent for us a material form of witness to the past that relieves us of the burden of remembrance:

> At such moments, we are invited to forget that memory itself is, after all, only a figurative reconstruction of the past, not its literal replication [. . .] The fragment presents itself not only as natural knowledge, but as a piece of the event itself. (1993: 127)

Young questions what kind of knowledge is awakened in us by the relics of the camps that have been so carefully preserved. He points out that the piles of belongings, which are so affective for visitors to the museums, recall the Jews primarily through the image of their death. The fragments of lives that these objects represent cannot be connected into a whole and they consequently commemorate not the culture and community of the Jewish people, but rather their absence and status as victims:

> For, by themselves, these remnants rise in a macabre dance of memorial ghosts. Armless sleeves, eyeless lenses, headless caps, footless shoes: victims are known only by their absence, by the moment of their destruction. In great loose piles, these remnants remind us not of the lives that once animated them, so much as of the brokenness of lives. For when the memory of a people and its past are reduced to the bits and rags of their belongings, memory of life itself is lost. (1993: 132)

In memorialising the Jews through the display of relics and artefacts, the museums produce a work of remembrance that mourns the death and absence of the Jews, but does not seek to reconstruct their lives, work and communities.

The *lieux de mémoire* are reflected in Young's writing on Holocaust memorials. In the absence of any tombstones or markers for the dead, the memorial functions as a substitute focus for mourning and remembrance. Young is interested in the memorial as a performative space, in which the visitors who congregate at the site produce its ever-changing meaning and significance. Memorials by themselves are inert and amnesiac; they depend on visitors to invest them with the memory of the past. The memory-work of the visitor acts to fill in gaps and to reassemble meaning, although this is a task that can never be fully completed: 'memory is never seamless, but always a montage of collected fragments, recomposed by each person and generation' (1993: 198). Young argues that the memorial text is produced by the conjunction of the monument and the visitor who invests it with memory and meaning. The memory produced in the memorial space is a perpetual and animated activity, always changing as visitors come and go across the perimeters of the site. The monument continually transforms itself, in alignment with the nature of the memory that it produces:

> For neither time nor its markers ever really stand still. Even as I write, chunks of mortar holding these monuments together crumble and fall away, lichens cover their surfaces, and grass grows high around their bases [. . .] Of course, a monument's meanings were always changing, along with the changing face of the monument itself. (1993: 208)

## The second generation

Anne Michaels was born in Toronto in 1958 and belongs to the generation after the Holocaust. Although she is not a child of survivors, Michaels was nevertheless profoundly affected by the Holocaust, an event she did not experience. Her novel explores the possibility of responsibly representing the imprint of the Shoah on the generation who came after. Like Wilkomirski, Michaels relies on the motif of fragments to represent the Holocaust, so that the novel is pervaded by the notion of a past that has been shattered and broken into pieces. Unlike Wilkomirski, however, Michaels is careful to represent the effect of the Shoah on those who are at a remove from the direct experience of the Holocaust. The novel has two main protagonists: Jakob who is a child in hiding during the war, and Ben who belongs to the second generation. In the childhood experiences of Jakob, Michaels encapsulates Caruth's notion of 'missed' or 'un-claimed experience', a history which cannot be fully perceived as it occurs. Hiding behind a wall of the family home in Poland, Jakob is both present and absent as his parents are killed and his sister, Bella, is arrested in a Nazi raid. If Jakob is haunted by a past that he failed to fully witness, Ben, who belongs to the second generation, is haunted by the unspoken history of his parents which defines his own identity. The trauma is passed down across the generations, and reveals the ways in which we are implicated in each other's traumas. Michaels explores the complex interrelationships between Jakob and Ben so that although there is in life only a tangential connection between them, their histories are inextricably interlinked through a series of corresponding events and submerged images. Ben finds Jakob's journals, unearthing a story that was hidden or buried during the latter's lifetime, while Jakob becomes a surrogate father for Ben, enabling him to address his unresolved relation to his dead parents and siblings. Ben completes the circuit of returns in the novel, so that Jakob returns to Greece, his wartime hiding place, in order to bury Athos and to complete his mentor's writing, while Ben travels to Greece to unearth the journals which comprise Jakob's own hidden or concealed testimony.

Geographically, *Fugitive Pieces* is divided between the old world of Europe and the new world of Canada, in the departure of Jakob and Athos from the Greek island of Zakynthos to live in Toronto after the war. Jakob emphasises the seemingly irreconcilable divisions between the old world and the new, which are embodied for him in his relationship with Alex, who has been filled by her father with romantic visions of Europe. In the company of Alex's friends, Jakob feels painfully out of place. In Canada, he feels separated from Bella, representative of the trauma of the past, and wonders how she will ever find or recognise him there. Ben echoes Jakob's feelings in his description of Naomi. With her 'Canadian goodwill', Naomi cannot intuit or understand the pain of the Holocaust in Ben's family, the European past that has been 'written in blood' (248–9).

Despite the protestations of its protagonists, however, the novel works to undermine the perceived separation or gulf between the two worlds. Jakob spent his childhood in hiding – in the wall of his childhood home in Poland, in the forest of Biskupin, in Athos's clothes as he was smuggled from Poland to Greece and in the sea-chest at Athos's home in Zakynthos. The early part of the novel is structured around recurring patterns of burial and re-emergence, for Jakob's concealment is situated in the context of a Europe filled with Jews in hiding: 'Jews were filling the corners and cracks of Europe, every available space' (45). However, through Ben we learn that the new world does not offer an escape from such a life in hiding. Ben's parents recreate Europe in the new world, so that their Canadian home becomes a 'hiding place' (233). Although survivors depart from the old world, they often cannot leave behind the habits and attitudes ingrained by fear and persecution. The silence of Bella's disappearance resurfaces in Ben's parental home, where the family 'waded through damp silence' (204). In the course of the novel we learn, along with Ben, that this silence is weighted with the unspoken names of Ben's elder siblings who perished in the Holocaust. Far from representing an escape from trauma, departure for the new world often signals a continuation of the past and a perpetuation of the legacy of pain and suffering. On his own arrival in Toronto, Jakob begins to grasp this as he is confronted with a 'ghostly metropolis' (90) and experiences a 'stunning despair' (91).

*Fugitive Pieces* is about the haunting effects of the past, and the narrative is crowded with ghosts: the ghosts of Bella, of Jakob's parents, of Ben's extended family who congregate in the kitchen, of all those who were killed in the Holocaust. The ghosts signify that those who live in the post-Holocaust generation are haunted by the memory of those who died; they are 'possessed' by a history which they did not experience and cannot own. Ellen S. Fine (2001) has noted the profoundly ambiguous nature of ghosts in post-Holocaust fiction. They can be consoling presences who replace the dead and keep the past alive – the ghost of Bella provides the young Jakob with continuity and enables him to cope with his loss and grief. Ghosts can embody the pain which is transmitted from one generation to the next. This is evident in Jakob's sense of being overwhelmed by the multitudes of the dead and his vision of a 'molecular passage' (52) or transmission between the dead and the living, which extends to the second generation so that the dead enter them through their blood. Ben takes up this refrain in his conviction that his parents' past 'is mine molecularly' (280); through his blood, the humiliation and fear that his father endured during the Holocaust has been transmitted to him. Fine also notes that ghosts can represent an attempt to work through the belated trauma that has been inherited. However, Michaels complicates this process in her representation of memory as a 'molecular' inheritance. Echoing Ben, we are compelled to question how it is possible to work through a memory that is transmitted through the very blood and cells of the body.

Redemption or healing, in so far as it is envisaged to be possible, is conceptualised as a process of gathering up dispersed fragments and piecing together the past. *Fugitive Pieces* is profoundly concerned with dispersal: the dispersal of memory, of belongings, of the Jews in exile. Focusing on the piles of possessions belonging to the concentration camp victims, Jakob fantasises the 'power of reversal' (50), imagining that if it was possible to name the owner he or she could be brought back to life. Jakob imaginatively assumes the role of Adam who, according to kabbalistic doctrine, bestowed life on Creation by the power of naming. Lacking any of his parents' possessions, he is unable to transfer to them his vision of 'cloning from intimate belongings' (50). Of Bella's possessions, Jakob has the remembered fragments of music, the fugitive pieces of the novel's title, which fill the haunting and enigmatic silence surrounding her arrest and echo throughout his journal. Jakob notes that sound waves do not die but 'carry on to infinity' (54); if he gathers together the fugitive pieces of music, he can imaginatively restore Bella to life and presence. In his journal, Jakob imagines through sound the life of Bella in the camps; a life which he himself did not experience or witness. He envisages Bella mentally practising Brahms's intermezzos to escape from the horrors of the camp and her own deteriorating physical condition. His imagination abruptly ceases, however, when it confronts the reality of the gas chambers: although the screams of the victims escape through their thick walls, Jakob concludes: 'It is impossible to imagine those sounds' (168). Faced with the reality of the Holocaust, the process of imaginative restoration cannot be sustained.

Ben shares Jakob's attachment to the belongings of the dead. The mountain of shoes belonging to the concentration camp victims metamorphoses for him into the pile of shoes by the door of his parents' home which, even more than a diary, encapsulates for him their lives, retaining after their deaths 'the way they walked, the residue of motion in the worn leather' (265). Once again, however, the promise of life restored through intimate belongings proves to be illusory; packing away the possessions of his parents, Ben is struck by the eerie silence which surrounds him, although he had expected sound to enter their house once they were dead. He is left reflecting not only on the loss of his parents but of the elder siblings he never knew, and on the impossibility of knowing whether the silence in the apartment would have been filled had their names been spoken. Michaels's evocation of the haunting power of the possessions of the dead resonates with Young's description of the memorial efficacy of the artifacts in the camps. Her vision of resurrecting the dead through the objects that they leave behind risks remembering the dead only through their death. Like Young, however, Michaels refuses to accord to intimate belongings the power to restore the past. Despite the touch left behind in the 'knit of atoms' (265), the possessions of the dead cannot return their former owners to life. Michaels echoes Young's conviction that the lives of the dead will indeed 'be lost to subsequent generations who seek memory only in the rubble of the past' (Young, 1993: 133).

## The sedimentation of memory

For Michaels, the fragments of the past are located not in the remnants or belongings of the dead but rather in nature and the landscape. *Fugitive Pieces* is suffused with a pantheistic vision in which nature itself remembers, and the sufferings of the past are registered by and encoded in the landscape. Jakob observes: 'Human memory is encoded in air currents and river sediments' (53). Michaels's imaginative response to the Holocaust explores what meaning is possible in the aftermath of the catastrophe. In writing *Fugitive Pieces*, Michaels renews and revises the kabbalistic tradition in Jewish philosophy. Kabbalism initially emerged as a response to the catastrophe of the expulsion of the Jews from Spain in 1492. Gershom Scholem, the foremost kabbalist scholar in the twentieth century, has argued that kabbalism assumes a renewed significance or urgency in the wake of the Holocaust: 'In a generation that has witnessed a terrible crisis in Jewish history, the ideas of these medieval Jewish esoterics no longer seem so strange. We see with other eyes, and the obscure symbols strike us as worth clarifying' (1965: 2–3). The questions asked by the kabbalists resonate today with renewed force: What is the role or vocation of the Jews in the generations after the catastrophe? What is the meaning of exile? What form might the renewal of hope take? Michaels addresses these questions in *Fugitive Pieces*, which comprises a modern Kabbalah for a highly secular and disillusioned age.

In *Fugitive Pieces*, the Holocaust lacks a landscape and is associated with places of burial (individual or mass graves) or of concealment (ovens, chests, drawers, cupboards, crawl spaces, cracks in walls). The graves and hiding places are negative spaces, raising the question of how the processes of mourning and commemoration can take place. Michaels focuses on the impossibility of properly or ceremoniously burying the dead, because their bodies have been burned, drowned, thrown away. Mourning becomes impossible unless creative and improvised funeral rites emerge, such as Athos's commemoration of the drowned Jews of Crete and Corfu on the shores of Zakynthos. Immediately after the war, the landscape of Greece is severely depopulated and Jakob perceives it as '[a] place so empty it was not even haunted' (61). The landscape of the Peloponnese is 'sorrow darkened' (60) and the ancient tragedies of Greece give way to more recent catastrophes. The grotto at Delphi, the sacred ground of the oracle, finds its contemporary counterpart in the holy ground of the mass graves where the earth 'blistered and spoke' (143). Athos speaks of the need to invest these modern ruins with the significance of ancient sites, arguing that tourists to Greece must now visit the 'burned-out chorios' that remain (70). Athos manifests Nora's 'will to remember', transforming the empty landscapes into commemorative sites for the dead. In writing his book of poems, entitled *Groundwork,* Jakob continues Athos's work. Ben observes of the poems that it is 'as if we hear the earth speak' (209); through his writing, Jakob transforms the hidden or concealed sites of the Holocaust into eloquent places of suffering. In one of the puns of which he is so fond, Jakob's poetry also prepares the basis, or provides the groundwork, for the collective task of remembering and mourning the dead.

Michaels extends beyond Nora, however, in suggesting that the landscape manifests its own 'will to remember'. Athos advises Jakob to seek to be buried in 'ground that will remember you' (76), and Jakob honours Athos's sentiments by burying the latter's ashes at the site of the house on Zakynthos. Ben unequivocally observes: 'everywhere nature remembers' (211). Nature is not only endowed with memory but also contains its own order and wholeness, so that everything is interconnected according to secret and unfathomable laws. Athos observes, quoting the Antarctic explorer Wilson: 'Nature's harmonies cannot be guessed at' (44). If redemption is possible in *Fugitive Pieces,* it is through a fleeting perception of nature's order. Athos's research demonstrates that insight into nature's secrets is based on careful and painstaking study, but illumination or revelation is nevertheless a gift that nature itself bestows: 'But sometimes the world disrobes, slips its dress off a shoulder, stops time for a beat' (175). Athos teaches Jakob of the potential for revelation through closely observing the matter of which the landscape is composed.

Michaels's vision of nature is profoundly influenced by kabbalism, a mystical tradition of Jewish philosophy which is primarily concerned with the role of the Jews in the world and the meaning of the condition of exile. At the heart of kabbalism lies the notion that it is with nature, rather than with God, that the Jews are to be reconciled; material nature, in spite of its fallen state, is the sole source of divine knowledge. Healing or redemption comes through the contemplation of nature, which contains within it the scattered sparks of God's attributes or divinity. Isaac Luria was a particularly influential figure in the history of kabbalism, and Annick Hillger has convincingly demonstrated that his ideas provide important source material for *Fugitive Pieces*. Luria's myth of the world is concentrated in three key symbols: *tsimtsum*, the self-limitation of God; *shevirah*, the breaking of the vessels; and *tikkun*, the harmonious correction and mending of the flaw which came into the world through the *shevirah*. *Tsimtsum* means 'concentration' or 'contraction', and refers to Luria's notion that, in order to make the world, God abandoned a region within Himself, so that the first act of Creation became a gesture of hiding or withdrawal. Instead of turning outwards, God contracts his essence and becomes more and more hidden. For Michaels, the world during and after the Holocaust is a world of hidden spaces, which is characterised by acts of concealment and withdrawal. She portrays the history of the Jews as a series of exiles and banishments, during which the Jewish people confine or contract themselves into negative spaces. The Holocaust is the most recent in a long history of such catastrophes; directed by the Nazi policy of 'anti-matter' (165), it aims to reduce the Jews to a state of absence or negative being.

The *shevirah* translates as the 'breaking of the vessels', and represents a decisive moment in the history of Creation. The first created being was *Adam Kadmon* and divine lights or *Sefiroth* burst forth from his eyes, ears, nose and mouth. In the creation of finite beings, special vessels or bowls were emanated which contained or held the lights. However, the bowls proved to be too fragile to contain the *Sefiroth* and were broken and shattered. The fragments of the vessels scattered throughout Creation and some of them retained sparks of the holy light; Luria speaks of two hundred and eighty-eight in total. Michaels's 'fugitive pieces' refer to the scattered fragments of the vessels, dispersed throughout the world and diffused into matter. *Tikkun* is the process of salvation or redemption which is achieved through reintegrating the original whole. The nature of *tikkun* is the chief concern of Luria's philosophy. The process by which God creates the world and reveals Himself is, in part, dependent on man's agency. It is the task of man to devote himself to restoring the original harmony by gathering together or reassembling the divine sparks or fragments. Luria's vision is deeply concerned with the condition of exile: nothing is in its proper place, all of nature is a being in exile, and there is a need for everything to be led back and redeemed. Luria also seeks to explain the exiled condition of the Jews: there is a need for the Jews to be scattered or dispersed throughout the world in order to retrieve the pieces of the broken vessels. Scholem explains: 'In the course of its exile Israel must go everywhere, to every corner of the world, for everywhere a spark of the *Shekhinah* [God's presence] is waiting to be found, gathered, and restored' (1965: 116). The condition of exile is, for Luria, a necessary stage in the historical process which leads towards redemption.

Young (1993) has pointed out that the gathering of fragments is central to the process of Holocaust memorialisation, particularly in Poland. Of Jewish life and death in Poland, only fragments remain – remnants of religious artifacts, synagogues, tombstones. The remains of the shattered past are 'retrieved piece by jagged piece' (185), gathered together and consecrated. Assembled as memorials to the dead, the fragments of gravestones are arranged in order to display their fissures or brokenness, for 'in this way, broken tombstone monuments commemorate their own fragility, gather and exhibit the fragments *as* fragments, never as restored wholeness' (185). For Young, the fragments themselves are inert and amnesiac; it is human memory that converts the mosaic of fragments into a commemorative structure: 'Mind pours itself into the gaps between fragments, like so much mortar, to bind the remnants together' (198). In contrast, Michaels accords her fragments a monadological significance; each contains a divine spark and the presence of the whole can be discerned within it, such is the interrelation or interpenetration of nature. For Young, even when the fragments are gathered together, it is 'destruction' which inevitably remains (185). For Michaels, how-ever, the gathering of the fragments carries a redemptive import and leads to a fleeting or momentary illumination or revelation. Jakob's inspiration in gathering together the fugitive pieces of Bella's music is her piano-playing, which is itself an act of memorisation. Bella's slow and painstaking process of accumulation culminates in a moment of grace and truth: 'I was lost; no longer aware of a hundred accumu-lated fragments but only of one long story' (138). Ben echoes Jakob, in his own description of the process of illumination as slow accu-mulation and sudden revelation: 'Truth grows gradually in us, like a musician who plays a piece again and again until suddenly he hears it for the first time' (251). The fugitive pieces coalesce to act as a mode of revelation and to bestow a momentary vision of wholeness.

Schama has argued that landscape is profoundly imbricated in the processes of memory and imagination. Although we are accustomed to separate nature and human perception into two realms, they are, in fact, indivisible: 'Before it can ever be a repose for the senses, landscape is the work of the mind. Its scenery is built up as much from strata of memory as from layers of rock' (1995: 6–7). He breaks the landscape down into its component parts – wood, water and rock – in order to analyse the ways in which matter is permeated by memory and the collective imagination. Michaels echoes Schama in describing landscape as the gradual sedimentation of memory: 'A narrative of catastrophe and slow accumulation' (48). Memory is encoded in natural forms and diffused in the molecules of matter. Athos seeks to study closely the components of nature and, like Schama, he breaks the landscape down into wood, water and rock in order to uncover the history or memory which is embedded within them. The kabbalistic divine sparks dispersed through nature are secularised by Michaels into the fugitive pieces of memory, and Athos fulfils the task of gathering and piecing together these fragments.

Wood is Athos's particular area of specialisation; as a Greek archaeologist, he is expert in its preservation and conservation. Hillger (1999: 32) points out that the Greek word for 'matter' (*hyle*) originally designated wood and that, as a specialist in wood, Athos is expert in analysing or preserving matter itself. Athos's expertise is the reason for his presence in Biskupin: he has been brought into the archaeological project to preserve the wooden structures of the buildings at the prehistoric or Iron Age settlement. He preserves the matter which the Nazis are intent on destroying, because the history that is encoded within does not accord with their own ideology. His rescue of Jakob comprises an analogous act of preserving that which the Nazis would destroy or murder; Athos's rehabilitation of the profoundly traumatised boy is accordingly described in terms of his work: 'Athos replaced parts of me slowly, as if he were preserving wood' (144). Athos teaches Jakob the mysteries of wood or passes on to him the secrets that he himself has learnt. As a young child, Athos was taught an important lesson by an old Jew: 'The great mystery of wood is not that it burns, but that it floats' (28). Athos tells Jakob the story which was related to him by the Jew concerning a ship that sunk into oblivion only to surface after its cargo of salt had dissolved. Jakob himself surfaces from the bog at Biskupin and embodies the process of survival which is the burden or import of the Jew's story: the wonder is not that Jakob's family were lost or devoured in the flames of the Holocaust, but rather that the child can live on. On his departure from Greece, Jakob has a vision of Athens as a similarly improbable survivor of the war: out of the flaming sunset, he sees the city floating on the horizon and hears the voice of Bella whispering to him: 'It's the mystery of wood' (86).

Athos's slow and patient attentiveness acts as a model for recovery and healing in the novel, and contrasts with Alex's desire for Jakob to suddenly change now that he has reached the new world of Canada: 'Alex wants to explode me, set fire to everything. She wants me to begin again' (144). Ben, in contrast, intuits or understands the secrets of wood in his observation that trees hold their own history within them for those who know how to read it: 'In their rings we read ancient weather – storms, sunlight, and temperatures, the growing seasons of centuries' (211). However, it is not only the weather that trees record; Ben suggests that they also preserve the memory of events that they have witnessed: 'A forest shares a history, which each tree remembers even after it has been felled' (211). During the Holocaust, mass shootings and burials took place in forests across Europe, and forests were planted by the Nazis in order to conceal the sites of mass graves and concentration camps. Ben implies that the trees actively remember and record the past. He reflects the kabbalistic view of nature as composed of monadological fragments, so that it is possible to read the memory of the Holocaust, or to find the fugitive pieces of the past, in seemingly insignificant places.

If Athos is an expert in the preservation of wood, his Greek inheritance links him to the sea: 'But like most Greeks, he rose from the sea' (19). His father's family have been mariners stretching back to the eighteenth century, and he teaches Jakob the family trading routes, giving him a substitute history or genealogy for the one that he has lost. The sea is capable of human memory and desires; Jakob tries to imagine the thoughts of the sea and concludes that: 'It's longing that moves the sea' (75). Like the trees of the forest, the sea holds its own painful memories of the Holocaust and bears witness to those who were lost. Athos and Jakob learn on Zakynthos of the fate of the Jews of Crete and Corfu, who were rounded up by the Nazis and crowded onto boats which were deliberately sunk, drowning all on board. Before leaving for Toronto at the end of the war, Athos and Jakob hold a ceremony to commemorate and lay to rest the Jews who were drowned. The dead merge in Jakob's imagination with his own family, who were also deprived a proper burial. Jakob visualises his parents in the clear, blue light under the waves and imagines that Bella has risen to the surface of the sea. In Jakob's fantasies, the bones of the dead, washed clean by the tides, are brought like driftwood onto the shore; only the skulls remain in the sea as evidence of the crime. The memory of the past will never fade from these skulls, which preserve the secrets of those who died as a lasting testimony: 'Burned into the bone, last thoughts line the skulls' (77).

If the sea mourns those whose grave is the ocean floor, then the water-logged ground of Biskupin acts as a metaphor for the accumulation or sedimentation of memory over time. The work of the archaeologists reveals that the process of memory is a slow and patient uncovering of layers. Jakob suggests that imagining oneself into the past requires a comparable technique of immersion: 'I spent hours in other worlds then surfaced dripping' (29). The layerings of memory are not confined to the old world; unexpectedly, the new world contains its own strata and sedimentations. Athos and Jakob immerse themselves in the geological past of Toronto, imagining the subtropical salt sea which was once there. For Ben, the processes of sedimentation are connected to the Humber River and the shards of crockery that are lodged in the river bed. These fragments testify to the recent catastrophe of the flood, which is inextricably linked in Ben's imagination to the violence of tornados. Through his mother's associations, the tornados are, in turn, connected with the Holocaust.[1] As a child, Ben gathers together pieces of the broken crockery and preserves them but he observes, signalling his own dilemma as a child of the second generation: 'I didn't find anything I remembered' (253). Ben's archaeological excavations mirror Athos's work and reveal that the fugitive pieces of memory are indeed scattered throughout the world, echoing the diasporic condition of the Jews themselves.

The process of sedimentation also acts as a more ominous metaphor for covering over or erasing the past. Biskupin is an area which is silting up, preserving the traces of the past; but it also means that the landscape is solidifying or stultifying. If memory is, for Michaels, a fluid and creative process in which the past is open to interpretation, Biskupin is a site where attempts were made by the Nazis to impose one meaning or reading on the past. For Michaels, this means that memory itself is silting up: 'History is the poisoned well, seeping into the groundwater' (161).[2] The sediment of the past also threatens to stultify the development of Jakob himself, who is silted up with his own grief and loss. It is only with Michaela that he finally feels free of the past: 'The river floods. I slip free the knot and float, suspended in the present' (188). Michaels gestures towards the need to maintain a balance between preserving the past and becoming silted up or clogged with memory. History needs to be flooded with memory, so that its narrative does not solidify. In Michaels's eloquent image, memory acts as a watermark on history, which both leaves its trace or imprint on the recounting of the past and marks the point at which floating becomes sinking or life is cut short by death.

The final element of which the landscape is composed is rock. Athos's love is paleobotany, and he teaches Jakob that rock contains not only the history of the earth but also 'the history of men' (32). Jakob learns that stones are invested by men with the power 'to hold human time' (32). Stones such as temples, cairns, standing stones and gravestones act as markers of commemoration and consecrate the sacred or the divine. James Young points out that the symbolic and commemorative power of gravestones was recognised by the Nazis, which resulted in them becoming targets for destruction:

> In wiping out a people, the Nazis not only destroyed those who would have preserved the memory of past generations; they also took pains to obliterate the spaces where the murdered might be remembered. Some of the oldest cemeteries [. . .] were literally scraped off the face of the earth. In other instances – recalling the treatment of Jews at the hands of Germans – the tombstones were machine-gunned, clubbed into pieces by sledgehammers, ground into dust. Or the *matzevoth* [gravestones] were put to work: uprooted, carted off, and used to pave roadways, sidewalks, and courtyards. (1993: 189)

Jakob recites a litany of the humiliation of stones through Nazi abuse: the smashing of Jewish gravestones; the use of Jewish tombstones for Polish pavements; the torture of the prisoners in the limestone quarries at Golleschau, who had to haul huge blocks of stone endlessly, so that the weight of the rock in their arms became the burden of their own lives. Limestone is accorded a particular significance in the novel, and it is a rock for which Athos has a special affection. Rich in fossils, it preserves the traces of the past, forming a 'crushed reef of memory', and in the slow transformation of the dead into stone, it reveals the gradual processes of change that characterise 'organic history' (32). Athos draws Jakob's attention to the limestone in the city of Toronto, revealing that the dispersed traces of the past lie even at the urban heart of the new world. The fossils embedded in the limestone comprise an alternative manifestation of the fugitive pieces of the past, and Jakob's description of them reveals that they are indeed scattered to the very furthest reaches of the world: 'I learned that fossil elephants were found in the Arctic, fossil ferns in Antarctica, fossil reindeer in France, fossil musk ox in New York' (30).

The other rock to which particular significance is attached in the novel is salt. Salt is important to Athos as a signifier of Greece: 'The element that reminded him most of his country' (114). Salt is the reason for the move to Canada: the invitation to Athos resulted from the explorer, Debenham, hearing him lecture on salt during the war.

Athos teaches Jakob the magic of salt, which is associated with the story of the cargo of salt dissolving in the ship's hold, allowing the boat to surface. The story suggests that salt is a catalyst of the process of survival. More specifically, salt symbolises in the novel human desire or yearning. Ben's introduction to Athos's thought was through his book on salt. In his work of lyric geology, Athos describes with passion the yearning of all created elements; for him, even rock or stone can weep and desire: 'Dramatic and slow earth events [. . .], all an evolution of longing' (209). Athos correspondingly understands salt in terms of a 'desirous ionic bond' (80). He entitles his book *A Covenant of Salt*. For Jakob, this refers to the covenant made by an Inuit hunter with his prey. Once he has caught a seal, the hunter pours a libation of water into its mouth, for the seal, living in salt water, is perpetually thirsty. Jakob reflects that he must honour his own covenant to Athos and Bella, to resolve his 'perpetual thirst' by learning 'to make love necessary' (121). It will take Jakob most of his life before he is able to fulfil his covenant with the dead and to uncover the true meaning of desire.

Athos's title also carries broader implications, however. In Judaism, salt is the symbol of the eternal nature of God's covenant with Israel. The book of Numbers states: 'it is a covenant of salt for ever before the Lord' (Numbers, 18: 19), while the book of Chronicles declares: 'The Lord God of Israel gave the Kingdom over Israel to David forever, even to him, and to his sons by a covenant of salt' (2 Chronicles, 13: 5). On Friday nights, Jews dip the Sabbath bread in salt in order to symbolise and keep alive the covenant between God and his people. Through Athos's title, Michaels gestures towards the diaspora of the Jews and the promise of redemption. Salt is essential to preservation and Jakob associates Athos's work on salt with his writing on peat, both of which preserve the traces of the past. However, salt also warns of the dangers of memory. Jakob speaks of Athos's 'backward glance', which gives him a 'backward hope' (101), but there are hazards in immersing oneself too deeply in the past. Athos's backward glance recalls Lot's wife, who was petrified by looking back into a pillar of salt and stands as a powerful warning to those who would risk 'stirring up historia' (103).

In *Fugitive Pieces*, Michaels develops a distinctive vision of nature and the landscape. Nature is both humanised and consecrated, and the elements of the landscape manifest their own will to remember or contain within themselves the traces of past trauma and suffering. Athos seeks to break the landscape down into its component parts, and to reveal the secrets that are embedded in the various elements of nature. The Kabbalah acts as an important influence on *Fugitive Pieces*, both in its vision of nature as containing the mysteries of redemption and healing, and in its conviction that, in the wake of the catastrophe, it is necessary to probe the condition of suffering. In Michaels's secularised Kabbalah, nature does not contain divine sparks but rather the shards of a broken or shattered past. Michaels explicitly refers to the Kabbalah in Jakob's reflection: 'We look for the spirit precisely in the place of greatest degradation. It's from there that the new Adam must raise himself, must begin again' (167). It is not divine revelation but insight into the processes of humiliation that Athos, Jakob and Ben seek. Wordsworth's Romantic vision of a pantheistic nature also informs Michaels's novel. For Wordsworth, nature is responsive and can help to absorb the shock of trauma.[3] Although Hartman remains cautious about whether Wordsworth's poetic vision of nature can be sustained after the Holocaust, Michaels's writing tentatively revives the notion of a reciprocal and potentially healing bond between man and nature.

There are, however, a number of problems raised by Michaels's text. Nicola King has expressed concern regarding Michaels's tendency to give human memory natural forms, arguing that the eliding of the human with the geological or the biological potentially draws attention away from the subject of the Holocaust. For King, Michaels's mystification suggests a false consolation and her metaphors fail to 'acknowledg[e] the impossibility of fully restoring the past, and the dead' (2000: 148). Ethical and political problems emerge out of Michaels's treatment of the question of redemption, which is inevitably invoked by her kabbalistic framework. Does Michaels feel that redemption is possible? If so, what form will this take, and is this vision appropriate to a work of (post-)Holocaust fiction? What is the relation between Michaels's version of redemption and the state of Israel? Although Michaels's use of the kabbalistic framework invokes Israel as a potential aspect of post-Holocaust redemption, she does not explicitly address this issue in the novel. Jacqueline Rose points out that anyone who attributes 'religious meaning' to anything 'in the natural [. . .] domain' risks 'deification of the nation and fetishism of the land' (1996: 25). Rose's observation suggests that the question of Israel inhabits Michaels's writing as an underlying and insufficiently addressed subtext of the novel, and reminds us of Schama's insistence that the myths of landscape are not entirely separable from the construction of national identities. Michaels's view of redemption is also intimately connected to the philosophy of Walter Benjamin, and is profoundly influenced by his writing on historical materialism. In Benjamin's messianic view of history, a contemplation of the endless catastrophe of the past offers the potential for fleeting or momentary illumination. Benjamin was a lifelong friend of Scholem and was strongly influenced by the latter's work on the kabbalistic tradition. He believed that kabbalism could be renewed in a secular context, and I will demonstrate in the following pages that Michaels incorporates into *Fugitive Pieces* significant aspects of Benjamin's thought concerning the nature of redemption, and revives or renews his project of writing a secular Kabbalah for the modern age.

## The history of matter

Athos and Jakob share a common interest in the 'history of matter' (119). Through this phrase, Michaels gestures towards Benjamin's 'historical materialism', which he most famously articulated in his elusive and fragmentary text, 'Theses on the Philosophy of History'. Benjamin contests the myth of historical progess and advances a construction of history which looks backward rather than forward. He argues that the genuine historian, the historical-materialist, contemplates a vision of history as perpetual catastrophe. The past is broken and discontinuous, shattered so that only fragments, debris and detritus remain, and Benjamin's 'angel of history' stands as a forlorn witness to the catastrophic course of human events.

> This is how one pictures the angel of history. His face is turned toward the past. Where we perceive a chain of events, he sees one single catastrophe which keeps piling wreckage upon wreckage and hurls it in front of his feet. The angel would like to stay, awaken the dead, and make whole what has been smashed. But a storm is blowing from Paradise; it has got caught in his wings with such violence that the angel can no longer close them. This storm irresistibly propels him into the future to which his back is turned, while the pile of debris before him grows skyward. This storm is what we call progress. (1973: 259)

In the face of history as catastrophe, the role of the historian is to gather together and compose the fragments of the past, with a view to moving beyond an immersion in the past, in order to discern how the past appears in the present, the nature of its contemporary significance. For Benjamin, the past is always open to (re)construction, (re)interpretation and (re)appropriation. The historical-materialist

67

carefully and painstakingly compiles the fragments of the past into a mosaic, which replaces the linear narratives of the conventional historian. Just as the whole design of the mosaic is revealed once the last fragment has been put in place, so the fleeting and ephemeral moment of illumination is bestowed only when past and present have been pieced together and a constellation is suddenly formed between the two. The moment of revelation stops the flow of thought and acts as a sign of revolutionary chance or potential. In the coming together of past and present, a dialectical image is formed which reveals that which was previously invisible or inconspicuous in the past. Often it is the most seemingly insignificant phenomena, the waste products or detritus of history, which resonate with the present, causing the past to suddenly come alive. In Judaic thought, every moment contains its own revolutionary or messianic potential. Benjamin observes that for the Jews, 'every second of time was the strait gate through which the Messiah might enter' (1973: 266). In order to reflect the Jewish conception of history, Benjamin divides time into two distinct but interrelated registers: secular history comprises the sequence of catastrophic events that mark human time without fulfilling it, while in revolutionary 'now-time', or *Jetztzeit*, every moment is filled with the anticipation of and potential for redemption.

Athos resembles Benjamin's angel of history in his contemplation of a 'narrative of catastrophe and slow accumulation' (48). He shares not only the angel's 'backward glance' but also his 'backward hope', his belief in the redemptive power of the past: 'Redemption through cataclysm; what had once been transformed might be transformed again' (101). Athos, Jakob and Ben share a fascination with the moment of cataclysm, which comprises a 'gradual instant' (140) filled with redemptive potential. Throughout *Fugitive Pieces*, time is collapsed into two registers and the refrain echoes across the novel: 'Every moment is two moments' (138). History is finished and closed, while memory holds the past open to the possibilities of the future: 'History is amoral: events occurred. But memory is moral; what we consciously remember is what our conscience remembers' (138). Benjamin argues that if the past is open to the influence of the future, then the historian should have the gift of 'fanning the spark of hope in the past' (1973: 257). For Jakob, likewise, every moment in the past, 'no matter how casual, how ordinary – is poised, full of gaping life' (19). The power of the commonplace means that every scrap of the past must be accorded importance, especially those things that seem to hold the least significance. The materials on which memory works

in the novel range from the apparently insignificant to the momen-
tous, and no distinction is made between the two. In not distinguishing between major and minor events, Michaels's protagonists act in
accordance with Benjamin's dictum: 'nothing that has ever happened should be regarded as lost for history' (1973: 256).

If redemption is possible in *Fugitive Pieces*, then it is the 'redemption
of tragedy' (120). The past cannot be restored, nor can the dead be
raised to life in a secular version of the apocalypse; but the lives and
loves of the forgotten and nameless dead can be salvaged and
recorded through a (com)passionate mnemonic investment. Benjamin's critique of historical progress comprises a provocative call to
remember the hopes and struggles of those who have been silenced
in the past. For Benjamin, it is neccessary to 'brush history against the
grain' (1973: 259), because it holds an implicit but unspoken pact
with the powerful. History is always written from the viewpoint of the
victor, and even the dead are not safe from having their lives
rewritten in the interests of the enemy: 'Whoever has emerged
victorious participates to this day in the triumphal procession in
which the present rulers step over those who are lying prostrate'
(1973: 258). History is made in the image of those who have conquered; hence its characterisation as progress. Culture is also deeply
implicated in the course of catastrophic history; cultural treasures are
the spoils of war and the process of their production is invariably one
of oppression and exploitation: 'There is no document of civilization
which is not at the same time a document of barbarism' (1973: 258).
The historical-materialist must work with an awareness of the taint-
edness of cultural treasures, and dissociate himself from them as
much as possible. He does not ransack the past for trophies or booty.
Rather, like a ragpicker, he salvages its waste or detritus for fragments
and scraps that may speak of forgotten lives. The interruption of
history carries a political dimension; in the dialectical image, past and
present illuminate each other to reveal a previously occluded and
unrecorded history. The historian assumes the role of a redeemer,
who recuperates and bears witness to the sufferings of the oppressed
and conquered.

*Fugitive Pieces* is concerned with salvaging the 'buried treasure'
scattered across Europe, which is valuable for the vanished lives that it
witnesses and recalls: 'A scrap of lace, a bowl. Ghetto diaries that have
never been found' (40). The most significant buried treasure in the
novel is the prehistoric settlement at Biskupin. The site of a two-
thousand-year-old civilisation, Biskupin provides evidence of rich

cultural activity in the Iron Age. As an archaeological site, Biskupin exemplifies Benjamin's notion that history is always (re)written by the victors or conquerors. For Polish archaeologists, Biskupin provided evidence of an advanced and highly organised (non-Germanic) culture whose inhabitants had left because of natural causes. The settlement became a focus of attention for the Nazi occupiers in Poland, and SS excavations of the site took place between 1940 and 1942. Himmler's *Ahnenerbe*, the Bureau of Ancestral Inheritance, was founded specifically to (re)interpret history according to theories of German racial supremacy. The *Ahnenerbe* revised the previous archaeological findings, arguing that the settlers at Biskupin had been driven out by the violent southward expansion of the Germanii which, in turn, provided evidence of the military, physical and racial superiority of the Germanic race. In *Fugitive Pieces*, Athos is part of the Polish archaeological team uncovering the history of the settlement at Biskupin. Following Jakob's emergence from the peat, Athos leaves the site to smuggle him back to Greece. Shortly after his departure, the Nazis occupy Biskupin, destroy the artefacts, bury the excavations in sand and murder the archaeologists, either shooting them in the forest or sending them to Dachau. Jakob's appearance saves Athos's life, just as Athos rescues Jakob.

Michaels acknowledges as source material for her writing on Biskupin *The Politics of the Past* (1994), edited by Peter Gathercole and David Lowenthal. This volume articulates a Benjaminian view of history, which comprises a highly partisan activity. Gathercole paraphrases Benjamin: 'those in power often write accounts of the past to justify the status quo. What has actually taken place, an amorphous ragbag of happenings and attitudes, becomes in the eyes of its interpreters the logical and smoothed-out antecedent of things as they now are' (1). For Gathercole, archaeology can assume a political role in contesting and complicating the narratives that emerge and recuperating alternative versions of the past: '[A]rchaeology can help to ensure that history is not written only by the winners' (1). In *Fugitive Pieces*, Athos writes an account of Biskupin which aims to excavate an alternative history of the site. *Bearing False Witness* recovers the stories of two groups of historical victims: the Iron Age settlers whose history has been overwritten or occluded, and Athos's archaeological colleagues at Biskupin who were murdered and whose findings were lost. His dedication to the book reveals that Athos seeks to restore significance to the lives of his friends by preserving a record of their work. The book absorbs all of Athos's strength and remains unfinished at his death. Jakob completes the work, compiling Athos's notes and translating the volume into Greek. Athos and Jakob both take on the role of historical-materialist, brushing history against the grain in order to reveal its pact with the powerful and to commemorate the nameless and forgotten dead.[4]

Jakob emerges from the excavations at Biskupin covered in mud, surfacing as the '[a]fterbirth of earth' (5). He merges in identity with those whose bodies have been preserved for millennia in peat bogs: 'I squirmed from the marshy ground like Tollund Man, Grauballe Man' (5). Michaels's imagery echoes the poetry of Seamus Heaney whose most famous poems, 'Tollund Man' and 'Grauballe Man', were inspired by the bog bodies excavated in Scandinavia. In particular, Heaney's poems originated from his encounter with P. V. Glob's *The Bog People* when it was first published in translation in 1969. Glob argues that the preserved bodies of men and women in the bogs of Jutland, which date from early Iron Age times and met with violent deaths, were the victims of ritual sacrifice to the goddess of the ground in order to ensure fertility in the spring. He observes that the victims have won a posthumous victory, for it is their bodies that have been preserved in the peat, so that they outlast their killers and, recuperated through archaeology, bear witness to their crimes:

> Young and old, men and women, met their ends by decapitation, strangulation, cutting of the throat, hanging and drowning. Very probably they suffered torture, mutilation, and dismemberment before they died. Yet these are the ones the bogs have preserved as individuals down to our own day, while all their relatives and contemporaries from the eight centuries of the Iron Age have totally vanished or at the most only survive as skeletons in their graves. (Glob, 1969: 144)

The year in which Heaney read Glob's history of the bog bodies also marked the onset of the sectarian killings in Ulster, and the peat bodies resonated with the violent reality of the present-day political situation. Heaney's poems provide a constellation of past and present, or deploy the past as a means of confronting and reflecting on the present. Discussing his bog poems, Heaney has observed that the language of poetry responds more readily to the peat bodies than to the present-day victims of violence:

> My emotions, my feelings, whatever those instinctive energies are that have to be engaged for a poem, those energies quickened more when contemplating a victim, strangely, from 2,000 years ago than they did from contemplating a man at the end of the street being swept into a

plastic bag [. . .] Now there is of course something terrible about that, but somehow language, words, didn't live in the way I think they have to live in a poem where they were hovering over that kind of horror and pity. (Quoted in Parker, 1993: 105)

Heaney's bog poems have been criticised for an aestheticisation of brutality and violence which distracts from the reality of the present-day killings. Similar criticism has been levelled at *Fugitive Pieces*. I have noted Nicola King's observation that in drawing on archaeological and natural imagery, Michaels aestheticises the Holocaust and distracts the reader from its reality. In gesturing towards Heaney, Michaels signals a poetic dilemma in which language 'lives' in contemplating violence at a historical remove. The challenge is to bring the past into constellation with the present, so that the remnants of history are not inert but assume a living force and a significant relation to contemporary events. Michaels signals the risks of her own aesthetic strategy in Jakob's observation: 'To go back a year or two was impossible, absurd. To go back millennia – ah! that was . . . nothing' (30). For the traumatised boy, prehistory provides a refuge from the recent catastrophe of the Holocaust; one of Jakob's (and Michaels's) key tasks in the novel is to bring the two histories in relation to each other and to make sense of his identity as both Holocaust survivor and '[b]og-boy' (5).

Athos's understanding of the bog bodies resonates with Glob's writing. He observes that the preserved bodies of the victims testify against their killers which, in turn, underlines the importance of his own work of recuperation: 'thus they outlast their killers – whose bodies have long dissolved to dust' (49). As a '[b]og-boy' himself (5), Jakob bridges past and present, and the peat graves merge with the mass graves of the Holocaust. If Athos's work as archaeologist is to uncover the past, it is Jakob's task to imaginatively give voice to the sufferings of the dead; in his poetry, he makes 'the earth speak' (209). Ben encounters photographs of the bog people in the *National Geographic* and in his response, there is a notable shift from archaeology to biography: 'The faces [. . .] were the faces of people without names [. . .] It was my responsibility to imagine who they might be' (221). Ben assumes the role of the historian as witness or redeemer, recovering the lives of the forgotten or nameless dead from the grave. He derives comfort from the preservation of the bog bodies, which differs from the rapidly decomposing bodies of the Holocaust victims. There is a restfulness about these bodies, which are covered with a blanket of peat. Ben's challenge, like that of Jakob, is to find a constellation between the distant and more recent past, to bear witness to and lay to rest the dead of the Holocaust.

Michaels also refers in the novel to the archaeological excavation at Lascaux, a series of caves in the Dordogne where Neanderthal paintings were first discovered in 1940. Michaels juxtaposes the beauty of Lascaux with the murders that were simultaneously taking place in Auschwitz: 'While a worker in the French cave remarked, "What a delight to listen to Mozart at Lascaux in the peace of the night," the underworld orchestra of Auschwitz accompanied millions to the pit' (143). The refrain that sounds throughout the novel, '[e]very moment is two moments' (143), assumes a new significance as Michaels contemplates the unfathomable simultaneity of horror and beauty. The passage assumes a metatextual significance, as Michaels reflects on the consequences of juxtaposing the aesthetic with the violent, which forms the heart of her own writing style. Michaels suggests that the incomprehensibility of the Holocaust lies partly in the terrible inextricability of horror and aesthetics which cannot easily be reconciled or resolved.[5]

The archaeological motif is central to *Fugitive Pieces*, reflecting the Benjaminian project of salvaging and recording the histories of those who were murdered and recovering the stories of those who lie in nameless graves. I have argued that Michaels draws on a variety of sources, both archaeological and poetic, to merge the buried traces of the distant past with the mass graves of the Holocaust, and to reflect on the relation between past and present, and the issues of aesthetics and distancing that are necessarily involved in representing the Holocaust. Michaels's most explicit merging of histories arises in Jakob's observations on the buried realm of the dead, who wait to surface from the grave: 'The place where all those who have uttered the bony password and entered the earth wait to emerge' (49). The underlying imagery in the passage is apocalyptic or messianic: the dead will 'emerge' from their graves with the coming of the Messiah on the day of redemption. Influenced by Benjamin, however, Michaels envisages a secularised version of messianism, in which the stories of the dead emerge from the fabrications and falsifications under which they have been buried and it is their histories, rather than their lives or souls, that are redeemed from the grave. Michael Rothberg observes of the contemporary relevance of Benjamin's theory of history:

In this post-Holocaust and post-Marxist period, Benjamin's messianic historian has become an encoder and decoder of constellations that bear witness to the traumatic legacies of modern historical extremity. For better or worse, the expectation of revolution has given way to the more modest, if still elusive, goal of working through – instead of repetitively acting out – the traumas of the past. (2000: 11)

I have argued that Michaels's vision of redemption is based on salvaging and recording the stories of the victims of trauma. She absorbs into her novel an influential contemporary reworking of Benjaminian messianism that emphasises the role of secondary or belated witnessing, and the necessary implication in trauma of the post-Holocaust generation(s).[6]

## The work of naming

In *Fugitive Pieces*, Athos and Jakob are both explicitly identified with kabbalism. Athos compares a sonnet to 'the linguistic investigations of the kabbalists' (100), while Jakob, reflecting on his own writing, observes: 'I'm a kabbalist only in that I believe in the power of incantation' (162–3). In these references, Michaels gestures towards the kabbalistic conception of language. In kabbalism, God's name was regarded as being the highest concentration of divine power. The Torah was both the site of God's revelation of Himself and an unfolding of the divine language or essence. Kabbalists held a mystical view of the Torah, which was used for purposes of magic and incantation. The text of the Torah was considered to contain secret combinations of letters which could not be divined by human eyes but revealed to God the mysteries of Creation. The scrolls of the Torah were observed with the utmost care; a scroll would be rejected for use in the synagogue if it contained a single letter too few or too many. For the kabbalists, language carried tremendous destructive power: the alteration of one letter in the Torah could potentially destroy the world. However, language also held the power to bestow life, as revealed in Adam's naming of Creation.

In *Fugitive Pieces*, Jakob undergoes a kabbalistic education, learning both the destructive and the restorative powers of language. He learns quickly that '[a] single letter was a matter of life and death' (78). In occupied Greece, the *graffitos* risked their lives to write a single letter; if they were caught by the Germans, they were executed on sight. Jakob also learns the importance of each individual letter from his experience of persecution; a single letter on a passport could mean the difference between life and death. The power of naming can, likewise, bestow life or death on that which is named. The Nazis refused to recognise or to name the Jews as human, and rapidly became unable to distinguish between name and referent: 'Humans were not being gassed, only "figuren"' (165). The act of naming also carries significant creative or life-giving potential. Jakob inadvertently saves himself by absorbing Bella's name which he intends to pass on, in turn, to the next generation. Ben learns that his name derives from his parents' desire to save him from the fate of his elder siblings and to give him a chance of life: 'They hoped that if they did not name me, the angel of death might pass by. Ben, not from Benjamin, but merely "ben" – the Hebrew word for son' (253). As a child, Jakob learns Greek and seeks to rid himself of his painful past by absorbing the language. Athos teaches him, however, that Greek carries a memorial weight and 'contain[s] the ancient loneliness of ruins' (21–2). It is only once Jakob arrives in Canada that he discovers in English 'an alphabet without memory' (101), a language that is strong enough to carry his experience. Jakob's writing seeks to isolate the cause of language's brokenness, to undertake the work of repair and to 'restore order by naming' (111). Jakob assumes the role of a second Adam, seeking to undo the consequences of the Fall which, according to kabbalistic doctrine, caused the initial breach between word and referent.

Scholem observes that if the letters of the alphabet and the combinations of letters in the Torah have secret, mystical power, then certain rabbis can harness this potential for the purposes of magical creation. In particular, the kabbalists could use the principles of combination, grouping and word formation in order to create the figure of the golem. 'Golem' is a Hebrew word which appears only once in the Bible and probably means amorphous or unformed.[7] From the twelfth century, the word appears in a number of kabbalistic texts and refers to a man-like creature which is modelled by men out of clay or earth and called into life by the mystical combination of letters inscribed on his forehead. The letters spell out the word *emeth* and if the initial letter or *aleph* is erased, the figure will immediately crumble to dust. The most famous golem was created by Rabbi Judah Loew of Prague, who was a widely revered kabbalistic teacher, and the legend of the golem is popularly associated with his name.

In her description of Jakob's emergence from the bog, Michaels refers to him as a 'golem' (12). Athos, by analogy, assumes the identity of Rabbi Loew who moulds or forms Jakob. Scholem notes that in the legend of the golem there is an emphasis on being 'buried in the earth as *materia prima* and ris[ing] up out of it', which acts as 'a symbol of rebirth after death' (1965: 198). Jakob's surfacing from the mud symbolises his second birth but, like the golem, he is marked with the indelible sign of death. Michaels symbolises, through the figure of the golem, the lasting traumatic legacy of the Holocaust which extends as far as the third generation. When Ben imagines having a child, he visualises the mystical letters on the forehead of the golem which merge with the concentration camp number tattooed on the wrist. The child is indelibly inscribed with the mark of the camps: 'I can't stop the writing on its forehead from growing as the child grows' (280). The legacy of the Holocaust is passed on to succeeding generations, and Ben articulates a powerful sense of helpessness and passivity in the face of such lasting trauma.

The act of naming is, above all, significant in the novel as a mode of commemoration. In his determination to call his child Bela/Bella, Jakob follows Jewish tradition in naming the living after a dead family member. However, he also risks placing the burden of the past onto his child, creating what Dina Wardi has termed a 'memorial candle'. For Wardi, this term designates a child of survivors who is

> given the special mission of serving as the link which on the one hand preserves the past and on the other hand joins it to the present and the future. This role is generated out of the need to fill the enormous vacuum left behind by the Holocaust. (1992: 6)

The act of naming is crucial to designating a child as 'memorial candle'; in giving a child the name of one or several family members who have perished, the parent transmits a (conscious or unconscious) message that the child is invested with all the memories and hopes of those who did not survive. Jakob's decision thus assumes an ambiguous significance, simultaneously commemorating the dead and risking the transmission of the Holocaust trauma into the next generation.

Elsewhere in the novel, Michaels indicates that the act of naming is inflected in different ways by history and memory. History invests names with a documentary significance and the records of history are often lists of names. History is complicit with the powerful: national censuses enabled the Nazis to round up the Jews in occupied territories, names were registered in ghettos and at deportation centres, the files of the concentration camps recorded lists of the dead: 'History is the Totenbuch, The Book of the Dead, kept by the administrators of the camps' (138). Memory, however, imparts to the act of naming a commemorative significance that counteracts the anonymity of the mass graves. Memorial naming both preserves a record of the dead and consecrates the moment of death itself: 'Memory is the Memorbucher, the names of those to be mourned, read aloud in the synagogue' (138). James Young points out that the first memorials to the Holocaust were not of stone but took the form of memorial books, which remembered the lives of those who had been lost and commemorated the destruction of the European Jewish communities. These books acted as symbolic tombstones or substitute graves for those who had no bodies to bury and no ashes to inter:

> The scribes hoped that, when read, the Yizkor Bikher [memorial books] would turn the site of reading into memorial space. In need of cathartic ceremony, in response to what has been called 'the missing gravestone syndrome', survivors thus created interior spaces, imagined grave sites, as the first sites for memory. Only later were physical spaces created. (1993: 7)

Young makes clear that the first *lieux de mémoire* of the Holocaust were literary or textual. In *Fugitive Pieces,* Jakob's writing seeks to provide a memorial book for the dead, supplementing Athos's ceremony of mourning on the shores of Zakynthos with imagined grave sites, and creating for himself and his readers the interior spaces in which grief can emerge.[8] The figure of the memorial book assumes a central significance in *Fugitive Pieces,* drawing together the various strands of the text. It fulfils the Benjaminian imperative to preserve a record of the dead and to recuperate the memory of the nameless and forgotten. It secularises the kabbalistic emphasis on Adam's bestowal of life through naming, so that the historian or writer bestows on the dead an afterlife through memory. Young makes clear that the memorial book also looks backward in order to move forward, so that the dead are witnessed in order that they may be laid to rest. In *Fugitive Pieces,* Michaels has written her own 'memorial book' to the Holocaust victims, which provides the dead with rhetorical burial sites in the interior spaces of her readers' imagination and memory. The novel reflects Hartman's sense that there has been a loss of 'memory place', for it creates the site of reading as a substitute memorial space for physical or geographical places.[9] Michaels, like Nora and Young, reminds us that memory is not indigenous to a (rhetorical or literal) place, but must be created through the ongoing intervention of human agents and through a will to remember. The above quote from Young also suggests that Michaels's novel, conceived as a memorial book, forms the first stage in a process of working through. In *Fugitive Pieces*, Michaels questions how the post-Holocaust genera-tion can position themselves in order to gain access to the event, and how the notion of position is related to the experience of place. As Baer (2000) points out, these fundamental questions lie at the heart of, and provide the basis for, all subsequent attempts at commem-oration, explanation and understanding.

# Part II

## *Style*

# Introduction to Part II

The past two decades have witnessed an increasing fascination with history and memory in literary studies. Contemporary historical studies have simultaneously engaged with questions of narrative and memory, which have traditionally been regarded as the preserve of literature. Historians have been concerned with the effect of trauma on the collective construction of the past and the ways in which that past is remembered in the present. The rise of trauma fiction in recent decades is inseparable from the turn to memory in literary and historical studies. I have suggested in the Introduction to Part I that trauma fiction effectively articulates several issues that contribute to the current interest in memory: the recognition that representing the past raises complex ethical problems; the challenge posed to conventional narrative frameworks and epistemologies by belated temporality; the difficulty of spatially locating the past; and the hitherto unrecognised cultural diversity of historical representation. Many contemporary novelists, including those whose work forms the basis of this study, base their writing on extensive research in the field of trauma. However, trauma fiction also emerges out of an ongoing public discourse of memory as trauma theory becomes part of the ideology of history. In particular, trauma fiction arises out of and is inextricable from three interrelated backgrounds or contexts: postmodernism, postcolonialism and a postwar legacy or consciousness.

At first glance, postmodernism seems to work against the contemporary emphasis on history and memory, for it advances the notion of an amnesiac culture based on images and simulations, and suggests that the role of memory has been superseded in our time. However, as Roger Luckhurst (1999: 83) has pointed out, postmodernism's emphasis paradoxically overlaps with the work of recent memory theorists. Pierre Nora insists that our current 'era of commemoration' is also characterised by an unprecedented degree of forgetfulness: 'We speak so much of memory because there is so little of it left' (1989: 7). Likewise, Andreas Huyssen suggests that '[m]nemonic fever' is paradoxically attributable to 'the virus of amnesia that at times threatens to consume memory itself' (1995: 7). Memory and forgetting do not oppose each other but form part of the same process. In the face of mounting amnesia, there is an urgent need to consciously establish meaningful connections with the past. Postmodernist fiction is part of this memory project. Its innovative forms and techniques critique the notion of history as grand narrative, and it calls attention to the complexity of memory. Trauma fiction emerges out of postmodernist fiction and shares its tendency to bring conventional narrative techniques to their limit. In testing formal boundaries, trauma fiction seeks to foreground the nature and limitations of narrative and to convey the damaging and distorting impact of the traumatic event.

Postcolonialism has drawn attention to the ways in which contemporary cultural works are influenced and shaped by the complex legacies of colonialism. It recognises that history represents an investment by groups or ideologies in specific power formations. Postcolonial fiction has often sought to replace the public and collective narrative of history with an interior and private act of memory. Memory counters or resists the ways in which history elides difference and forgets the heterogeneous. Postcolonial novelists seek to rescue previously overlooked histories and to bring hitherto marginalised or silenced stories to public consciousness. Trauma fiction overlaps with postcolonial fiction in its concern with the recovery of memory and the acknowledgement of the denied, the repressed and the forgotten. Toni Morrison innovatively draws on the discourse of trauma to counter the emotional and cognitive resistances to remembering the African-American experience of slavery. In *Beloved* and *Jazz*, she presents the trauma of slavery to a culture which has long resisted its acknowledgement, and she describes her novels as a public form of memory or anamnesis: '[*Beloved* is] about something the characters don't want to remember, I don't want to remember, black people don't want to remember, white people don't want to remember' (quoted in Henderson, 1991: 83). Morrison provides a literary model for contemporary novelists, many of whom use scenes of recollection and witnessing to highlight the selective amnesia of collective and public history. History is reconfigured through the trope of memory and formerly unprivileged voices are given their say. In allowing the (politically and psychologically) repressed to surface to consciousness, trauma fiction makes a significant contribution to rethinking the ethics of historical representation.

Contemporary fiction is obsessed with the representation of war and its effects. The trauma of the First World War is explored in Pat Barker's recent fiction and in Sebastian Faulks's *Birdsong* (1994). The Vietnam War is compulsively reworked in the fiction of Tim O'Brien. It is the Second World War, however, and especially the Holocaust, that dominates and overwhelms the contemporary imagination. Ghosts of murdered Jews haunt the succeeding generation in Anne Michaels's *Fugitive Pieces*. Caryl Phillips's *The Nature of Blood* locates the Holocaust in a long history of European racism. W. G. Sebald's fiction obsessively but indirectly evokes the history of the Holocaust. Nicola King justifiably notes of the prevalence of the Holocaust in recent fiction: 'The Holocaust remains a contemporary concern [. . .] because the event itself has come to represent a rupture in historical continuity, problematising the relationship between past and present' (1999: 94). In the face of this 'rupture', trauma fiction shares trauma theory's epistemological belief that the Holocaust is not knowable through traditional frameworks of knowledge and that it cannot be represented by conventional historical, cultural and autobiographical narratives. The Holocaust past, that is to say, cannot be narrated in an objective mode without omitting all that is most significant to understanding its power over the present. Both trauma theory and trauma fiction are committed to exploring new modes of referentiality, which work by means of figuration and indirection.

If trauma fiction is effective, it cannot avoid registering the shocking and unassimilable nature of its subject matter in formal terms. As Sue Vice observes, the features of trauma fiction are the same as in other novels: intertextuality, the narrator, plot and story. Because of the subject matter, however, these standard features are 'brought to their limit, taken literally, defamiliarized or used self-consciously' (2000: 4). As Hartman (1995: 547) points out, trauma fiction problematises its own formal properties, at the levels of reference (what relation does the narrative bear to reality?), subjectivity (can the traumatised subject still say 'I' in a way that has meaning?) and story (does the character control the 'plot', or is he or she controlled by it?). Trauma fiction often demands of the reader a suspension of disbelief and novelists frequently draw on the supernatural, as for example in *Another World, Fugitive Pieces, Beloved* and *Jazz*. Alternatively, the realist novel is troubled by coincidences and fantastic elements which lurk just beneath the surface, a technique that is used to powerful effect by Sebald. These disruptions of the real signal to the reader that there has been a rupture of the symbolic order. The real can no longer appear directly or be expressed in a conventional realist mode. Michael Rothberg (2000) has coined the term 'traumatic realism' to describe the range of innovative formal devices which are used in narratives of trauma to try to make us believe the unbelievable. Rothberg argues that traumatic texts, including trauma fiction, search for a new mode of realism in order to express or articulate a new form of reality. Faced with 'the demands of extremity' (2000: 14), writers of trauma narratives push the realist project to its limits, not because they have given up on knowledge but in order to suggest that traumatic knowledge cannot be fully communicated or retrieved without distortion.

The second half of this volume seeks to elaborate a structural approach to trauma fiction which emphasises recurring literary techniques and devices. I have argued above that trauma fiction relies on the intensification of conventional narrative modes and methods. There are, however, a number of key stylistic features which tend to recur in these narratives. These include intertextuality, repetition and a dispersed or fragmented narrative voice. Novelists draw, in particular, on literary techniques that mirror at a formal level the effects of trauma. Although I aim, in what follows, to indicate the literary features that regularly occur in trauma fiction, it is not my intention to provide a generalisable set of rules which determine in advance the approach to any particular text. I am not claiming, that is, that these literary techniques necessarily appear in a given work of trauma fiction. My readings seek to remain attentive to the nature of trauma itself, which refuses abstractions and remains tied to the specificity of terms, figures and conceptual movements that differ from text to text. As Caruth has pointed out, there can be no single approach to these narratives: '[we face the] difficulty of listening and responding to traumatic stories in a way that does not lose their impact, that does not reduce them to clichés or turn them all into versions of the same story' (1995: vii).

Many works of trauma fiction foreground the literary device of intertextuality. In *Image-Music-Text* (1977), Roland Barthes evocatively described the multiplicity of the text, which comprises a momentary convergence of a wide range of intertexts: 'citations, references, echoes, cultural languages [. . .] antecedent or contemporary' (160). Barthes's description of intertextuality implicitly allies it with the act of memory. As Peter Middleton and Tim Woods point out, the relation of the text to its intertexts resonates with the way 'traces of the past emerge in the present as textual echoes, determinations and directions' (2000: 84). Intertextuality can suggest the surfacing to consciousness of forgotten or repressed memories. In *Jazz*, Morrison consciously evokes this aspect of intertextuality, referring to the figure of Beloved in her description of Wild in order to suggest that the former was not exorcised at the close of the previous novel and has returned to haunt succeeding generations. Through intertextual reference to her own fiction, Morrison reveals that the trauma of slavery has not been laid to rest but resurfaces in the lives and actions of the protagonists. She signals the haunting power of a traumatic past which can be readily identified by the attentive reader but remains beyond the reach or grasp of the characters themselves.

In Chapter 4, I argue that intertextuality can also evoke a literary precedent which threatens to determine or influence the actions of a character in the present. The protagonist seems bound to replay the past and to repeat the downfall of another, suggesting that he is no longer in control of his own actions. In *The Nature of Blood*, Caryl Phillips's Othello echoes Shakespeare's eponymous hero in journeying to Cyprus with his new bride. The reader is left to determine from the evidence in the novel whether he will repeat the tragic mistakes of his predecessor. In *Another World*, Barker's intertextual references to Henry James's *The Turn of the Screw* similarly suggest that Miranda is fated to repeat the actions of James's governess, suffocating the young boy who is left in her charge. Through Nick's intervention, however, Miranda is prevented from murdering Jasper and the ghosts of the past are exorcised. In returning to canonical texts, novelists evoke the Freudian notion of the repetition-compulsion, for their characters are subject to the 'plot' of another('s) story. Novelists can also revise canonical works, however, reading them against the grain and providing a new perspective on familiar texts. Trauma fiction overlaps with postcolonial fiction in its use of intertextuality to allow formerly silenced voices to tell their own story. Phillips rewrites the story of Othello from his own viewpoint, thereby revealing the racial insecurities that underpin his actions. For Phillips, Othello's tragedy is not determined by Iago but by the Venetian society which simultaneously exploits and rejects him. The intertextual recovery of hitherto marginalised voices signals the ethical dimension of trauma fiction, which witnesses and records that which is 'forgotten' or overlooked in the grand narrative of History.

One of the key literary strategies in trauma fiction is the device of repetition, which can act at the levels of language, imagery or plot. Repetition mimics the effects of trauma, for it suggests the insistent return of the event and the disruption of narrative chronology or progression. Many writers, including Barker, Morrison and Sebald, repeat key descriptions or episodes from one novel to another, and this technique both suggests an underlying trauma and implicitly critiques the notion of narrative as therapeutic or cathartic. Freud's work on the uncanny reveals that even apparently innocuous daily objects and incidents can be drawn into an atmosphere of trauma. Through repetition or correspondence, the simplest event can be invested with a symbolic aura. In Chapter 5, I argue that Sebald's writing is based on precisely such uncanny intensification. Descriptions and photographs of railway stations or smoking chimneys insistently recur in his novels and reveal the extent to which the Holocaust permeates our everyday lives and consciousness. Dates and numbers repeat within and between novels, especially 18 May, the date of Sebald's own birthday. Prompted by the narrator's reflections, the reader questions whether there is an underlying pattern or design lurking unseen behind these convergences and coincidences. Sebald's writing explores the critical vestiges of Romanticism, questioning whether the traditional concepts of providence and fate still have any validity or whether they have, in the words of Hartman, 'lost their artistic as well as occult potential, and yield[ed] to more secular ideas of traumatic stress and repetition-compulsion' (1995: 545). Following LaCapra, I question whether Sebald's writing uncomfortably conflates concepts of fate and providence with the discourse of trauma, in a mode which seeks to 'transvalue the traumatic into an occasion for the sublime' (LaCapra, 2001: 190). At the very least, Sebald reminds us that there are some aspects of knowledge which remain beyond our grasp and he demonstrates that our understanding can still be made to sense its limit.

Repetition is inherently ambivalent, suspended between trauma and catharsis. In its negative aspect, repetition replays the past as if it was fully present and remains caught within trauma's paralysing influence. It corresponds to LaCapra's notion of 'acting-out' and

Freud's conception of melancholia, pathological responses to loss which seek to incorporate the other into the self as an act of preservation. Repetition can also work towards memory and catharsis, however. In this aspect it relates to LaCapra's concept of 'working-through' and Freud's notion of mourning. It represents the discharging of emotion cathected to loss and the subsequent reformulation of the past. LaCapra draws on the concept of 'working-through' to describe the role of literary texts in representing trauma, arguing that writing necessarily implies some distance from trauma and is an inherently curative process. LaCapra's emphasis on narrative as cure echoes Freud's claim in *Studies on Hysteria* (1895) that '*each individual hysterical symptom immediately and permanently disappeared* [. . .] *when the patient had described that event in the greatest possible detail and had put the affect into words*' (Freud and Breuer, 1991, III: 57; italics in original). LaCapra also draws on Pierre Janet's distinction between 'traumatic memory' and 'narrative memory' (1910–25). Traumatic memory is inflexible and replays the past in a mode of exact repetition, while narrative memory is capable of improvising on the past so that the account of an event varies from telling to telling. For Janet, the conversion of traumatic memory into narrative memory represents the process of recovery from trauma.

In Chapter 6, I argue that the conceptualisation of literature as a mode of 'working-through' entails its own potential risks. As Nicola King points out, there is a danger that too narrativised, too definite an account of trauma may paradoxically act as 'a *defence* against memory, or destroy its very possibility' (1999: 97). Jean-François Lyotard warns that writing must not forget the challenge that trauma poses to representation: 'Narrative organization is constitutive of diachronic time, and the time that it constitutes has the effect of "neutralizing" an "initial" violence' (1990: 16). In a similar vein, Caruth has expressed concern that the narrative of trauma should not lose the shocking force of its impact: 'The danger of speech, of integration into the narration of memory, may lie not in what it cannot understand, but in that it understands too much' (1995: 154). In the light of these expressions of caution, I argue that literary fiction offers the flexibility and the freedom to be able to articulate the resistance and impact of trauma. While traditional literary realism may not be suited for rendering traumatic events, I have argued that the more experimental forms emerging out of postmodernist and postcolonial fiction offer the contemporary novelist a promising vehicle for communicating the unreality of trauma, while still remaining faithful to the facts of history.

Chapter 6 analyses two key works of recent fiction which draw on the forms of jazz in order to suggest the passage from trauma to recovery. Toni Morrison's *Jazz* (1992) and Jackie Kay's *Trumpet* (1998) each circle around the central trauma of a death. *Jazz* represents the protagonists' attempts to come to terms with Joe Trace's murder of Dorcas and Violet's subsequent attack on her corpse. In *Trumpet*, Joss's family struggle to come to terms with the posthumous revelation that Joss was a woman pretending to be a man. Morrison and Kay suggest, through their evocation of jazz, that the process of recovery is a form of improvisation in which the story of the trauma is told and retold in different ways and from different perspectives. The possibility of making and remaking suggested by jazz enables trauma to be assimilated by the characters, so that the past is not a broken record but sustains the possibility of hope and recovery. I argue that in both novels the significance of jazz lies not only in improvisation, but also in the passing of the refrain from one musician to another. The narrative voice is dispersed or fragmented so that each of the protagonists takes up the story, adding to it his or her individual perspective. The multiplicity of testimonial voices suggests that recovery is based on a community of witnesses. Through the compassionate sharing of the story, trauma resolves itself into new forms and constellations. Although the emphasis in these novels is on 'working through', the novelists nevertheless remain attentive to the resistance and shock of trauma. The absence of the dead remains inviolable and forms the central silence around which the narratives circle but which they cannot finally redeem. The techniques of jazz are also incorporated into Caryl Phillips's *The Nature of Blood*. Here, the narrative voices of Othello, Eva and Stephan Stern echo each other, offering different historical perspectives on European racism. The individual stories converge to reveal a long and bloody history of racism in Europe which has not been sufficiently recognised, and which acts to counter the notion that the Holocaust is a unique and incomparable event.

# Chapter 4

## *Othello in the ghetto:*
## *trauma and intertextuality in*
## *Caryl Phillips's* The Nature of Blood

This chapter seeks to explore intertextuality as a key stylistic device of trauma fiction. The term represents the notion that every text constructs itself as a tissue of quotations, absorbing and transforming material from other texts. In this broad definition, textuality is necessarily also intertextuality. Intertextuality is also used in a more specific sense to refer to the particular set of plots, characters, images or conventions which a given text may bring to mind for its readers. As Judie Newman has pointed out in *The Ballistic Bard* (1995), many postcolonial writers have consciously used sustained intertextuality in their novels in order to revise literary classics and to take possession of their own stories. Intertextuality powerfully mimics and dramatises the political process, whereby those who were formerly colonised reclaim their own realities. In what follows, I will outline the characteristic features of intertextuality and suggest the ways in which it is equally suitable for the purposes of trauma fiction. I will discuss intertextuality with particular reference to Caryl Phillips's 1997 novel *The Nature of Blood*.

If intertextuality is deployed in a sustained manner in a work of fiction, the story that results will already be familiar to the reader from the original version on which the novelist draws. This can give a strong impression that a character in a novel is repeating the actions of a previously encountered story, that the reader knows in advance the end which is to come, and that the decisions and fate of the character are predestined from the outset. The motif of an inescapable trajectory or fate, which the novelist can produce through intertextuality, bears comparison with Freud's elaboration of the repetition-compulsion in 'Beyond the Pleasure Principle' (1991, XI). Freud is fascinated with the pattern of suffering that characterises the lives of certain individuals, so that catastrophic events seem to repeat themselves for those who have already passed through them. These repetitions are notable because they do not seem to be motivated by the individual, but appear as if they were the result of possession by fate.

In *The Nature of Blood*, Phillips retells the story of Othello from the general's own perspective. The power of this section of the novel derives from the reader's foreknowledge of what is to come. Phillips cuts short Othello's story, narrating only the events up to and including his arrival on Cyprus. The reader is therefore forced to decide, from the evidence in the novel, whether Phillips's Othello will indeed (re-)enact the events of the play to their dreadful conclusion, or whether he has achieved sufficient insight and self-awareness to act differently. I will argue that Phillips's Othello is indeed doomed to repeat the pattern of Shakespeare's play, but that it is Venetian society, rather than the influence of Iago, which is the determining factor in his downfall. In *Another World*, Barker's intertextual reference to *The Turn of the Screw* likewise suggests that Miranda is fated to repeat the actions of James's governess and suffocate the child in her charge, so that the past is caught in a seemingly inescapable repetition-compulsion.

Intertextuality can gain powerful effects through repetition. However, it can also enter into a productive critical dialogue with literary classics which makes new meanings possible. John McLeod observes of the potential for an intertextual novel to depart from its source: 'A re-writing takes the source-text as a point of inspiration and departure, but its meanings are not fully determined by it' (168). By departing from the source text, intertextual fiction can suggest that the past is not necessarily always fated to repeat itself, but that alternative futures can be posited and played out. Intertextuality is thus, like trauma, caught in a curious and undecidable wavering between departure and return. The intertextual novelist can enact through a return to the source text an attempt to grasp what was not fully known or realised in the first instance, and thereby to depart from it or pass beyond it. Trauma fiction overlaps with postcolonial fiction in the novelist's challenge or resistance to the representations of marginalised or oppressed peoples or cultures in the source text. Classic literary works have frequently constructed (unintentionally) racist or stereotyped depictions of colonised cultures. The novelist's return to the source text can enable us to grasp a latent aspect of the text, and at the same time to depart from it into an alternative narrative construction.

Intertextual resistance can also take the form of critical dialogue with the author of the source text. In *The Nature of Blood*, Phillips resists the racism implicit in Shakespeare's portrait of Othello and demonstrates that the racist attitudes of the Venetians shape Othello's tragedy. The novelist can also challenge the source text by repossessing the voices of characters who have previously been marginalised or silenced. This technique clearly overlaps with postcolonial fiction, which seeks to reconstruct history, especially European history, from the point of view of those who have been marginalised or written out of the story. In psychoanalysis, that which is repressed will inevitably and disturbingly return to haunt the present. The uncanny or *unheimlich* experience occurs when that which has been marginalised or forgotten appears before us. The grand narratives of history, which are frequently constructed on the basis of exclusion, are haunted by those who have been written out or erased. McLeod observes: 'At the limits of conventional knowledge, these figures return as disruptive "unhomely" presences that cannot be articulated through existing patterns of representation' (2000: 220). These uncanny presences have the potential to disrupt the binary logic on which colonialist, nationalist and patriarchal narratives depend. Intertextual fiction gives voice to these unrealised presences, and can powerfully disrupt received modes of thinking. Such writing assumes responsibility for those who were previously unrepresented. The silenced voices articulate their own stories and bear witness to their former historical and cultural exclusion.

Intertextuality is profoundly disruptive of temporality. Judie Newman observes of its disjunctions: 'intertextuality is achronological and anachronistic, inviting us to consider (in David Lodge's phrase) the influence of T. S. Eliot on Shakespeare' (1995: 6). Newman points out that such atemporality is crucial to the postcolonial project of disrupting the grand narratives of history, which are based on temporal order and chronological sequence. In *A New World Order* (2002), Phillips discusses his own writing in similar terms, allying his experimentation with time and his disruption of conventional narrative order with a corresponding disruption of 'national continuity' (292). However, such temporal disruption also resonates with the symptomatology of trauma. For Caruth, trauma is defined by 'the peculiar, temporal structure, the belatedness, of historical experience', which is 'fully evident only in connection with another place, and in another time' (1995: 8). Caruth's phraseology is richly suggestive for intertextual fiction. Writing in another place and at another time, the modern novelist is able to make fully evident that which was only partially available to the author of the source text. Writing from a contemporary perspective, Phillips can draw out of *Othello* issues of racial, national and cultural identity which may not have had the same cultural inflections for a Renaissance audience.

Intertextual writers necessarily produce works which are highly self-conscious and self-reflexive. Newman observes that intertextual fictions are 'novels about novels, which problematise the relation of fiction to the world' (1995: 4). For the postcolonial writer, Newman argues, such self-consciousness can make a powerful political point: 'Whereas the British writer can merge with his or her society, since that society has, in a sense, appropriated reality, the postcolonial writer must avoid any loss of self-awareness. Postcolonial writers are therefore often at their politically sharpest, when they are also at their most "literary"' (1995: 4). Such a postcolonial strategy is certainly relevant to Phillips's fiction. The multiple reference points of his writing, which mingles European, African and Caribbean influences, signal to the reader that the novels cannot be fixed or identified as belonging to any one literary tradition or home.

In the context of trauma fiction, however, the self-conscious literariness of intertextual writing can serve an altogether different purpose. Modern novelists who represent in their fiction traumatic events of which they have no first-hand or personal experience often feel an undeniable sense of discomfort and unease. A self-conscious use of intertextuality can introduce reflexive distance into the narrative and, to repeat the words of Newman, problematise the relation of fiction to the world. In *The Nature of Blood*, Phillips includes in Eva's narrative intertextual references to Anne Frank's *Diary of a Young Girl* and Cynthia Ozick's *The Shawl*. His representation of the Holocaust is self-consciously filtered through literary sources. I will argue that Phillips's self-reflexiveness in Eva's narrative reflects his desire to comment on the African-American politics which, he feels, separate him as a black writer from Jewish experiences and concerns. Even as his self-conscious literariness suggests his own distance from the reality of the Holocaust, his evocative and moving rendering of Eva's story simultaneously attests to the power of the sympathetic imagination. In a gesture that mirrors Stern's actions at the close of the novel,

Phillips seeks to overcome the isolation of individualism and to imaginatively reach 'across the years' (1997a: 213).

As a result of its extreme literariness, intertextual fiction highlights the role of the reader. McLeod observes: 'A re-writing often implicates the reader as an *active agent* in determining the meanings made possible by the dialogue between the source-text and its re-writing' (2000: 168). The intertextual novel constructs itself around the gap between the source text and its rewriting, and depends on the reader to assemble the pieces and complete the story. Bénédicte Ledent has commented of *The Nature of Blood* that it is a text which 'encourage[s] the reader to *produce* meanings' (2002: 115). Like all novelists who employ intertextuality, Phillips relies on the reader to find his own way through the novel's maze-like structure and to unravel the references in order to make sense of the narrative.

Intertextuality does not necessarily refer to an external source of reference but can operate within a single corpus or body of work. A writer's fiction can act in dialogue with its own precedents, whether plays, novels, poems or critical essays. In trauma fiction, this can create across an author's work a sense of endless repetition, as if the writing is haunted by an inarticulable force, which can neither be named and confronted nor passed beyond. This strategy is exemplified by W. G. Sebald, who relentlessly deploys images that powerfully but obliquely suggest the presence of the Holocaust. Phillips also uses this technique, although Ledent observes that he seeks to suggest both repetition and change: 'the aim of the author is to make the reader see the same elements, the same well-known stories, from new angles' (2002: 154–5). I will argue that there is a particularly close intertextual relation between *The Nature of Blood* and Phillips's earlier collection of essays, *The European Tribe* (1987). Read in conjunction, the two texts work through the same themes and concerns and shed light on each other. Most famously, Toni Morrison uses the technique in *Jazz* to interrogate the possibility of recovery from trauma. Identifying *Jazz* as a sequel to *Beloved*, Morrison encourages the reader to interpret the later work in intertextual relation to the former by suggesting that Wild is a (re)incarnation of Beloved. I will argue in Chapter 6 that *Jazz* hovers between repetition and departure, exemplifying the ambivalence and ambiguity of trauma.

In the above discussion, I have sought to demonstrate that intertextuality represents a key literary device in trauma fiction. Although the technique is widely used by postcolonial novelists, I have suggested that it nevertheless assumes new meaning and significance in the context of trauma. Its uses are multi-faceted and highly flexible. If the novel closely follows the source text, intertextuality can be used to evoke the sense that a character is following an inescapable trajectory or is caught in a repetition-compulsion. If the source text is considerably revised, the novelist can highlight trauma as a mode of departure and suggest the possibility of change or progression. In stylistic terms, intertextuality allows the novelist to mirror the symptomatology of trauma by disrupting temporality or chronology, and to repossess the voices of previously silenced characters, enabling them to bear witness to their own exclusion. Intertextuality can reflect the dilemma of the novelist who represents traumatic experiences which he or she has not witnessed, or it can highlight the role of the reader who acts to fill in the gaps of the text and to actively assemble meaning. In what follows, I aim to demonstrate the effectiveness of intertextuality through a close reading of *The Nature of Blood*. In the novel, Phillips explores the trauma of European history and the text, along with the rest of Phillips's writing, comprises a key contribution to the emergent genre of trauma fiction.

## The extravagant stranger

In *The European Tribe*, Phillips describes his first encounter with the city of Venice, explaining that he found himself curiously unable to respond to the aesthetic and cultural treasures which surrounded him: 'I felt nothing' (1987: 128). He compares his own (lack of) response with the feelings which he imagines Othello to have experienced on his first arrival in the city:

> Unlike Othello, I am culturally of the West. I stood on the Rialto and thought how much more difficult it must have been for him, possessing a language and a past that were still present. Nothing inside me stirred to make me rejoice, 'Ours is a rich culture', or 'I'm a part of this'. (1987: 128)

Phillips's response to Venice is determined by his underlying sense of its 'Eurocentric and selfish history' (1987: 128). In *The Nature of Blood*, Venice is the setting for two of the stories that Phillips relates: his rewriting of *Othello* and his rendering of the history of the Jews of Portobuffole. In each story, Phillips seeks to explore the experiences of those who were culturally marginalised, excluded from the mainstream of Venetian society. He aims to document an alternative history of the city. Phillips's choice of Venice as a setting not only allows him to repossess the marginalised voice of Shakespeare's Othello, but also to address the derided and excluded figure of Shylock in *The Merchant of Venice.*

Phillips's fictional rendering of the story of Othello was preceded by a critical essay on Shakespeare's play, published in *The European Tribe.* As J. M. Coetzee has noted, the essay evidences a degree of conceptual confusion. Phillips veers between viewing Othello as 'a real-life historical person on whom Shakespeare is reporting' and as 'a character in a play who is misinterpreted by actors insensitive to the psychic baggage that an ex-slave must bring with him' (1997: 40). Despite its weaknesses, however, Phillips's essay provides valuable insight into his subsequent treatment of Othello in *The Nature of Blood.* Ironically entitled 'A Black European Success', the essay argues that Othello's preoccupation with proving himself the equal of his Venetian masters and his anxious desire to integrate into Venetian society derive from his failure to come to terms with his own former slavehood. Phillips designates Othello's profound insecurity, origi- nating in his troubled sense of his own slave past, as 'the true nature of [his] psychological anguish' (1987: 45). Othello is a military man, a man of action. He is not a thinker, and at times lacks insight into his own situation. In itself, this is not enough to bring about his downfall. However, when this is combined with the hypocrisy and racism of Venetian society, Othello's fate is sealed. Phillips observes of his tragic downfall: 'It is not a "flaw" in the man, it is what you have made him into. [. . .] [T]he pressures placed upon him rendered his life a tragedy' (1987: 46).

Before we meet Shakespeare's Othello, we learn that he is an indisputably great general and military leader, but within the opening scenes we also hear him called 'the thick lips' (I, i, 66), 'an old black ram' (I, i, 88), 'the devil' (I, i, 91), 'a Barbary horse' (I, i, 111–12), 'a lascivious Moor' (I, i, 126) and an 'extravagant and wheeling stran- ger' (I, i, 136). He is accused of 'making the beast with two backs' (I, i, 116–7) with Desdemona and of drawing her to his 'sooty bosom' (I, i, 70) using 'foul charms' (I, ii, 73). Those who abuse him include a Venetian gentleman, a senator and his own trusted Ancient, Iago. It is clear from the outset that, in spite of his capabilities, Othello's position in Venice is insecure and constantly threatened. He is made continually aware that his origins do not match the honours that are heaped upon him, and the colour of his skin acts as the indisputable visible marker of his difference. Phillips observes that throughout the play, Othello works within the parameters of an uncertain authority:

'Life for him is a game in which he does not know the rules' (1987: 47). He lacks a close friend or confidant who can explain to him the baffling complexity of Venetian society. Othello therefore seeks the quickest route to social acceptance, namely marriage. He wins the hand of Desdemona and secretly marries her and shortly after he wins the approval of the Venetian nobility, although they act with political expediency for they need Othello to sail to Cyprus and defeat the invading Turks. For Phillips, it is at this point in the play that Othello's doom is sealed for he begins to relax, especially once the Duke himself has given his approval of the marriage. He observes: 'It is now that the tragedy commences. But it can do so only because it is precisely at this moment of "triumph" that Othello begins to forget that he is black' (1987: 48).

On his arrival in Cyprus, Othello displays a new-found confidence and tranquillity. However, Phillips notes that he remains troubled by the problems which haunted him in Venice: 'there still exists an impulsive and insecure man who can best express himself in terms of physical violence, which is [. . .] the first refuge of the desperate' (1987: 49). For Phillips, the events of the rest of the play unfold inevitably from this point. Othello dismisses Cassio and appoints Iago to his post because of his need for a friend in his perplexing and confusing social surroundings. His increasing insecurity and suspicion render him vulnerable to Iago's influence. His readiness to resort to violence on the flimsiest of material evidence ends in the terrible murder of Desdemona. If Othello is finally abandoned in the play it is not, as he suspects, by his wife but by Venetian society. However, Phillips also makes clear that Othello carries some of the blame for his own downfall in presuming that he could leave behind him his African background: 'From what we are given it is clear that he denied, or at least did not cultivate his past. He relied upon the Venetian system, and ultimately he died a European death – suicide' (1987: 51). Othello's failure to establish or maintain a peer group means that he has no means of reinforcing his identity and is left entirely alone. Phillips concludes his reading of the play with the fateful observation: 'He has to play by Venetian rules, and historically the dice are loaded against black men in the European arena' (1987: 50).

Phillips's treatment of the Othello story in *The Nature of Blood* is elliptical to the point that he does not even name his speaker, but his earlier reading of Shakespeare's play sheds light on the novel. Phillips creates an intertextual patterning across his own writing, so that the reader is encouraged by the oblique and truncated narrative in the novel to search for its significance in the critical work. Phillips revises Shakespeare's *Othello* in two main areas: the omission of Iago, and the decision to end the story with Othello's stay on Cyprus. Iago's absence enables Phillips to focus on Othello's internal conflicts and dilemmas, and the insecurities that arise from his own unresolved past. The removal of Iago also allows Phillips to emphasise that racism and prejudice are not tied to an individual, but are endemic within Venetian society. This point is amplified through Phillips's portrayal of the Venetian treatment of the Jews, both in the Ghetto and in the trial of the Jews of Portobuffole. The omission of Iago from the novel opens up an intertextual dialogue with the source text, in which Phillips challenges Shakespeare's treatment of racism and its effects.

Iago is not entirely absent from Phillips's narrative, however. The doge grants that the general's wife should be allowed to accompany him to Cyprus, and Othello entrusts her safety to his 'Ancient'. Although Iago has not yet entered the story, he is waiting in the wings ready to take his part in Othello's downfall. Phillips's decision to end his narrative with the arrival on Cyprus has met with differing critical responses. For Marina Warner, Shakespeare's tragedy 'necessarily throws its long shadow' over Phillips's novel and 'the reader cannot dare to hope for a happy ending' (1997: 23). For Bénédicte Ledent, however, Phillips's withholding of the conclusion holds an altogether different significance: 'Shakespeare's ending is not only suspended but cancelled, as though superseded by the potential for interpretive revision' (159). In the context of trauma fiction, Phillips's gesture assumes significance on its own terms. By leaving the story incomplete, Phillips suspends Othello between repetition and change. His narrative mimics the undecidability between departure and return which is inherent to trauma. It is up to the reader to determine whether Phillips's Othello is doomed to repeat the same mistakes and errors of judgement as Shakespeare's protagonist, or whether he can indeed avoid the fate that he is seemingly predestined to follow.

Reading *The Nature of Blood* alongside Phillips's essay on *Othello*, it does indeed seem, as Warner suggests, that his version is weighted towards the downfall of the protagonist. Phillips explicitly states in his essay that Othello's fate is already sealed by the time of his arrival on Cyprus. If the outcome is certain, the rest of the story becomes redundant. Phillips's Othello betrays all of the traits that render the tragedy inevitable. Lacking a grasp of the language and bewildered by

Venetian custom, he is an isolated and vulnerable figure. Having no one on whom to rely, he turns to marriage as a means of gaining social acceptance, hoping that it might lessen the hostility of the Venetians towards him. He imagines that marriage connects him to the heart of Venetian society. However, he also realises that it irrevocably cuts him adrift from his past. Phillips's Othello, unlike Shakespeare's, already has a wife and child in Africa and he feels uneasy at betraying them in his new marriage. He defensively constructs unconvincing self-justifications: 'I continually reminded myself that my native wife was not a *wife* in the manner that a Venetian might understand the term, yet I wondered if this were not simply a convenience of interpretation on my part' (1997a: 146). The continuing hold on him of the past that he seeks to relinquish is symbolised by the gold bracelet, which represents a link with Venetian society that he can never remove, even as it inescapably recalls the shackles of slavery that continue to bind his consciousness like mind-forged manacles.

On his arrival in Venice, Phillips's Othello walks the streets and alleyways of the city, exploring its every aspect.[1] He is repeatedly described as crossing bridges, which symbolise the potential for cultural crossing in the novel. In his explorations, Othello is confronted with an alternative view of the city which reveals its 'rotting' (109) and 'stagnant' (115) core. Away from the Grand Canal, Venice is a city of 'flimsy structures' (115), a society that is not as stable or secure as it seeks to project. Once he is married, however, Othello ceases his nocturnal wanderings and confines himself indoors. He no longer takes an interest in the view outside: 'I turn from the shuttered windows and [. . .] gaze upon my wife' (107). The shuttered windows mirror the closed windows and windowless walls of the Jewish Ghetto, although Othello remains wilfully blind to this connection. Although he professes to be happy in marriage, there are ominous signs of the impending tragedy. Othello refers to his new wife as 'an object of beauty and danger' (148) and he considers himself to be her 'lord and master' (144). Although she is able to alleviate his misery to some degree, Othello remains doubtful that his wife can 'mollify the more fundamental pain in my heart' (160).

Lest the reader is left in any remaining doubt as to the tragedy to come, Phillips interrupts Othello's story with the voice of a late twentieth-century, African-American black nationalist. The speaker castigates Othello for forgetting his past and seeking to integrate himself into European society, and accuses him of transforming himself into a 'figment of the Venetian imagination' (183). Othello receives clear and unambiguous warning of what is about to happen: 'A wooden ladle lightly dipped will soon scoop you up and dump you down into the gutter. Brother, jump from her bed and fly away home' (183). Although the speaker claims Othello as a brother, his tone is frequently hostile and lambasting. It is also unclear that the solution that he offers provides any answers to Othello's situation. His 'home' is no more in Africa than it is in Venice. The voice, which is not to be confused with Phillips's own, does not take into account the broader import of the novel which demonstrates that in the modern African diaspora, as in the Jewish diaspora, the concept of 'home' is both profoundly unsettled and painfully charged.

In Phillips's rewriting of *Othello* various aspects of intertextuality converge to powerful effect. Interrupting the story on the island of Cyprus, Phillips highlights the role of the reader in interpreting the significance of the text and determining whether Othello can indeed follow a different trajectory. His emphasis on Othello's insecurities and the prejudices of Venetian society suggest that Phillips's protagonist will indeed follow a fatal course, so that the character seems to be caught in a repetition-compulsion. In withholding the ending from us, however, Phillips suggests the possibility of an alternative course and signals the ambiguous status of trauma between departure and return. The twentieth-century voice that interrupts Othello's story is suggestive of a disrupted chronology. A modern speaker with knowledge of Shakespeare's play seeks to intervene in the action and prevent the narrative from reaching its denouement. The story of Othello does not stand alone in Phillips's novel, however. It is placed alongside three other narratives: the Jews of Portobuffole, Eva's story and the narrative of Stern. In what follows, I will consider first the complex and ambiguous relationship that Phillips constructs between Othello and the Jews of Venice.

## In the Ghetto

In *The Nature of Blood*, Phillips draws on the setting of Venice to connect Othello to the Jews of Portobuffole. Bryan Cheyette (2000) observes that Venice has long been represented in literature both as the decaying heart of European civilisation and as a liminal space where Europe and Africa or Europe and the East meet. Through trade, the city attracted a considerable influx of marginal peoples who were barred from official citizenship. In the Renaissance, foreigners lived in Venice as permanent immigrants. Albanians, Turks, Greeks and Germans were segregated from the Venetian population in guarded buildings. Most famously, the Venetians confined the city's immigrant Jews to the segregated space of the Ghetto, which was legally established in 1516. The Jews lived in cramped conditions in the Ghetto, and were obliged to return there at dusk each evening. At nightfall, the gates were locked, the shutters of the houses that faced outwards were closed and police patrolled the exterior. As Richard Sennett comments, the existence of the Ghetto arose out of and was maintained by a conflict of needs in Venice: 'the Ghetto represented a compromise between the economic need of Jews and [. . .] aversions to them, between practical necessity and physical fear' (1994: 216).

Phillips includes an essay on Venice in *The European Tribe*. Here he acknowledges the former imperial might of the city, but also points out that behind its glory lay a pervasive racism and xenophobia: '[s]ixteenth-century Venetian society both enslaved the black and ridiculed the Jew' (1987: 45). Phillips gestures towards *Othello* and *The Merchant of Venice*, and implicitly answers Tony Tanner's query in his study of literary Venice: 'why *did* Shakespeare set his two plays with figures from marginalized groups – a black, a Jew – as protagonists, in Venice?' (1992: 5). Phillips recognises the pragmatism at work in Venice's treatment of the Jews, who were tolerated as usurers. In a passage that resonates with his literary treatment of the Ghetto in *The Nature of Blood*, Phillips observes: 'The Venetian ghetto was the original ghetto, the model for all others in the world – places characterized by deprivation and persecution' (1987: 52). Phillips deploys the Ghetto as a 'model' of racism and segregation in order to construct a history of endless European victimisation and persecution. He places the Venetian Ghetto not only alongside the Jewish ghettos of the Holocaust, but also in connection with those ghettos that have socially and culturally segregated black communities and other minority groups.[2]

In *The Nature of Blood*, Phillips includes an encyclopaedic definition of Venice, which emphasises the city's cultural significance but includes no mention of Othello or the Jews, signalling the omission of foreign or marginalised presences from the official version of history. The ambivalent and hypocritical Venetian attitude to the Jews is revealed in another 'official' document, the Bill of the Grand Council. With superb irony, Phillips reveals the highly compromised attitude of the Venetians to the Jews of the city: 'We intend to tolerate some bullying and maltreatment towards the Jews who reside among us, but we want them to be able to stay and live in our domain without being submitted to excessive damage and insults' (1997a: 99–100). In *The Nature of Blood*, the Jews arrive in Venice as foreigners, and they remain as foreigners within the city. Phillips suggests that this is not exclusively due to Venetian mistrust and suspicion. The Jews contribute to their own segregation through their unwillingness to accommodate to their new surroundings: 'the Jews wished to speak only among themselves. Further, they chose not to eat or drink with the Christians, and they refused to attend to their heavy German accents' (51). The separatism of the Jews forms a stark contrast to Othello's anxious desire to assimilate into Venetian society.

Phillips's description of the Jews' self-segregation refers to Shylock in *The Merchant of Venice* who pursues a similar policy of separatism: 'I will buy with you, sell with you, talk with you, walk with you, and so following, but I will not eat with you, drink with you, nor pray with you' (I, iii, 33–5).[3] In *The European Tribe*, Phillips names Shylock as a figure whom he particularly admires, precisely because of his separatist sentiments: 'Shylock has always been my hero. He makes it uncompromisingly clear that he wants nothing to do with Christians beyond his business' (1987: 55). Linking Shylock's principles to black-identity politics, Phillips argues that 'there is a time when such a debate is necessary' (1987: 55). In *The Nature of Blood*, however, Phillips is more concerned to indicate the dangers of separatism. Although the segregation of the Ghetto is initially imposed on the Jews, it is quickly embraced by them in a defensive mentality, which views the walls of the Ghetto as a 'protection against the many cold hearts that opposed their people' (130). Phillips suggests that separatism renders the Jews particularly vulnerable to attack, for they are 'herded *en masse* and enclosed in one defenceless pen' (130).

The history of the Jews of Portobuffole proves particularly instructive, for they do not assimilate into the surrounding community. The neighbours' ignorance regarding their customs and practices hardens into prejudice, which culminates in accusations that the Jews have murdered a Christian child and drunk his blood. The allegations against the Jews arise out of the wild speculations and rumours regarding their practices which result, in turn, from ignorance. The Portobuffole Jews are tried in Venice, and the ambivalent Venetian attitude towards the Jews is put to the test. Prejudice against the Jews and ignorance of their customs prevail, and the accused are sentenced to die by public burning. If the modern voice that intrudes into Othello's narrative lambasts him for assimilationist attitudes and practices, it is clear that separatism does not provide an alternative solution.

The Venetian Ghetto and the Jews of Portobuffole provide a powerful counterpoint to Othello's narrative. However, Phillips also describes Othello's own entry into the Venetian Ghetto. In *The Nature of Blood*, Othello enters the Ghetto on two separate occasions. His first entry occurs during his nocturnal wanderings through the city and is precipitated by curiosity. Othello finds himself oppressed by the Ghetto and is overcome with relief on finding himself in familiar territory once again. He is puzzled by the nature and strength of his response: 'it appeared somewhat shameful to me that a man who had endured many wars and faced much danger should panic on finding himself in unfamiliar streets in an admittedly civilized environment' (132). Othello's panic results from his realisation that there is a less 'civilized' aspect to Venice, a fact that he has already glimpsed in the shabby and unappealing side canals. Othello recognises as he walks through the Ghetto that 'penalties for offending the morals of the people of Venice were severe' (130). His second entry into the Ghetto occurs as he himself is set on a course which will offend the morals of Venice. He seeks a Jewish scholar to read to him the letter from Desdemona and write down his reply. The insight which Othello gained on his last visit to the Ghetto has been lost and his blindness is mirrored in the effects of the winter fog. Although Othello notes that the Jew responds to his passionate letter by letting 'a smile play around his thin lips' (143), he fails to recognise the danger of his position or to acknowledge the correspondences between his own situation and that of the Venetian Jews. Othello's entries into the Ghetto afford him a clear insight into the xenophobia at the heart of the Venetian empire, but they also chart his increasing blindness with regard to his own situation and predicament.

Phillips's placing of Othello's story in the context of the Venetian Jews and the Jews of Portobuffole (and beyond that, as we shall see, in the context of the Jewish Holocaust and the founding of Israel) is suggestive of a complex interconnection between black and Jewish identity. In *The European Tribe*, Phillips quotes Frantz Fanon, who recalls the advice of one of his teachers: 'Whenever you hear anyone abuse the Jews, pay attention, because he is talking about you' (1987: 54). Discussing this statement, Phillips draws on his own experience to develop an analysis of the interrelationships between blacks and Jews. Growing up in Britain and offered no representations of colonialism or slavery, Phillips found that the Jews were the only minority group discussed in the context of racism. He consequently identified himself with them: 'I vicariously channelled a part of my hurt and frustration through the Jewish experience' (1987: 54). Situating the Holocaust as an internalised component of his own identity configuration, Phillips suggests that his relation to Jewish history is based on a sympathetic approach.[4] *The Nature of Blood* represents his most sustained and ambitious attempt to place the two histories together. However, Phillips is not seeking to combine the two, but rather, in the words of Ledent, to 'set up a dynamic network of overlappings and clashings that preserves the relational fluidity of blacks and Jews' (2002: 153). Phillips's exploration of the complex interrelations between black and Jewish cultures suggests a productive and dynamic cross-culturalism, which works against the tribalisms of both racism and separatist politics.

Phillips's elaboration of the personal significance of the Jewish Holocaust strongly echoes the sentiments of cultural theorist Paul Gilroy. In *Between Camps* (2001), Gilroy notes the pervasive presence of the Holocaust in postwar Britain:

> The world of my childhood included the incomprehensible mystery of the Nazi genocide. I returned to it compulsively like a painful wobbly tooth. It appeared to be the core of the war, and its survivors were all around us. Their tattoos intrigued me. (2001: 4)

Like Phillips, Gilroy identified his own experiences of racism with the Holocaust and he sought to understand the relationship between the two: 'I struggled with the realization that [the Jews'] suffering was somehow connected with the ideas of "race" that bounded my own world with the threat of violence' (2001: 4). Gilroy calls for an intensive and sustained exploration of the interconnectedness of black and Jewish cultures, and he questions: 'why does it remain so difficult for so many people to accept the knotted intersection of histories [. . .]?' (1998: 287). He argues that a dialogue on the community of experience between blacks and Jews could prove invaluable for our understanding of modern racism: 'there might be something useful to be gained from setting these histories closer to each other not so as to compare them, but as precious resources' (1993: 217). *The Nature of Blood* responds to Gilroy, and the latter's writing can be regarded as an important context or intertext for Phillips. Phillips combines Gilroy's call for dialogue between black and Jewish cultures with the setting of Renaissance Venice, which allows him to refer intertextually to Shakespeare's black and Jewish protagonists, Othello and Shylock. In suggesting connections and interrelationships between his characters, and in allowing different instances of trauma to address each other, Phillips departs from the isolation imposed by traumatic experience. Phillips's narrative technique of allowing his characters to speak without the intervention of an authorial voice enables individuals from different cultures and with varied traumatic histories to address each other, and it is the role of the reader to listen to the resonances and dissonances between them. However, in exploring the interrelations between blacks and Jews, Phillips undeniably treads on sensitive ground. In the section that follows, I will explore Phillips's writing of Eva's story as an intervention into contemporary identity politics, and I will suggest that he posits the trauma of racism as a link or connection between blacks and Jews.

## The ghost of Anne Frank

Phillips has recently spent half of each year living and working in the United States and this experience has afforded him insight into the tensions that exist between the Jewish and African-American communities. In *The European Tribe*, he notes: 'One of the aspects of black America that I have never been able to understand fully is the virulent anti-Semitism that seems to permeate much black thought' (1987: 52). Commenting on black–Jewish relations, Bryan Cheyette points to the significance of Louis Farrakhan's increasing influence within the African-American community:

> While anti-Semitism in general is on the decline in the United States, most agree that it is on the increase in the black community which is largely due to the influence of the Nation of Islam on poorer African Americans. Cornell West, Henry Louis Gates and bell hooks have all intervened against the Nation of Islam to rightly temper its worst excesses and its extreme cultural nationalism and politics of separation. (2000: 57)

Cheyette notes that tension between the two communities also arises from the cultural dominance of the Holocaust as the model of racism in the United States.[5] The European Holocaust has at times acted as a welcome and convenient distraction from those instances of historical oppression – the history of slavery, the genocide of the native Americans – which are more immediate and closer to home. In *The Nature of Blood*, Phillips seeks to intervene in this debate by deliberately and provocatively juxtaposing black and Jewish histories. The positive critical reception and success of the novel in the United States may owe something to its European setting, so that although Phillips comments on black–Jewish relations, it does not feel too close to home. As Ledent observes, the novel allows American readers 'to view their identity dilemma from a distance' (2002: 154).

The tensions between Jews and African-Americans extend as far as the literary establishment. Cheyette comments: 'It is clear that the present-day histories of Zionism and black–Jewish relations in the United States [. . .] ha[ve] reinforced the racialised separate spheres between Jews and other ethnicities within the academy' (2000: 59). Against these identity politics, Phillips insists that authorial identity places no restrictions on the fictional or historical imagination. As a black writer, he not only tackles the subject of the Jewish Holocaust, but also assumes the voice of a female Holocaust survivor for one of the novel's primary speakers. This makes a strong political statement, but also complicates and undermines the notion of a fixed identity. His fictional rendering of the Holocaust finds strong endorsement in Salman Rushdie's impassioned observation on literary tribalism:

> Literature is self-validating. That is to say, a book is not justified by its author's worthiness to write it, but by the quality of what has been written. There are terrible books that arise directly out of experience, and extraordinary imaginative feats dealing with themes which the author has been obliged to approach from the outside. Literature is not in the business of copyrighting certain themes for certain groups. Books become good [. . .] when they endanger the artist by reason of what he has, or has not, *artistically* dared. (Rushdie, 1991: 14)

In Eva's story, Phillips makes extensive intertextual reference to Anne Frank's *Diary of a Young Girl.* The ghost of Anne Frank haunts the margins of Eva's narrative in a form which is unsettling precisely because it is oblique and indirect. Eva herself initially seems to represent the figure of Anne Frank. Early in the novel we learn that, like Anne, she has a sister called Margot who is her sole reason for staying alive: 'I simply cling to the image of my sister' (18). Eva starts to keep a diary which she addresses to her absent sister, just as Anne addressed her diary entries to her imaginary friend Kitty. However, Eva does not maintain the journal: 'within a week I gave it up, for I could no longer summon the energy' (67). Once the personalities of the sisters are described, however, it seems that Phillips's Margot assumes the character of Anne Frank as she is popularly conceived. She is 'fanciful' (89) and a 'dreamer' (23). She has a lively interest in fashions, movies and film stars and, like Anne Frank, she has papered the walls of her bedroom with pictures of Hollywood stars. She has a boyfriend named Peter, echoing the name of Peter van Daan. In Eva's imagination, her sister has reached America and fulfilled her ambition of becoming a Hollywood star. Following the posthumous publication of her diaries, 'Anne Frank' was, of course, an over-whelming American success, appearing both in Hollywood and on Broadway.

Ledent argues that one of Phillips's key motivations in invoking the figure of Anne Frank is to challenge the popularised versions of her life and to offer a less anodyne figure: 'Phillips rescues the young diarist from the sanitised interpretations of her writing that cele-brated such sentences as "I still believe people are really good at heart" ' (157). Eva displays all too human faults and prejudices. She dislikes the Jews from Eastern Europe whom she considers to be 'dirty' and 'uncultivated' (170). In despair over her future, she forges a letter from Gerry, the soldier in the camp, inviting her to come to England and marry him. The intertextual references also serve a secondary purpose, however, in constructing a literary version of the Holocaust which is filtered through the text of Anne Frank's *Diary*. In the figure of Rosa, who always has a woollen shawl wrapped around her, Phillips also refers obliquely to Cynthia Ozick's Holocaust novella, *The Shawl* (1990). Through intertextuality, Phillips distances his text from the reality of the Holocaust, providing a space for reflection on the ethics of representation involved in his writing. Phillips's self-consciousness acknowledges his own indirect and highly mediated modes of access to the Holocaust.

Margot and Anne Frank both died of typhus in the concentration camp of Bergen-Belsen in the winter of 1944–45. Phillips signals the horror of their deaths in Eva's dread of typhus in the camps. Eva does not fall victim to typhus, however, for Phillips envisages in the novel an alternative history in which Anne Frank survived, and he imagines what her fate might have been. Ledent argues of Eva's narrative: 'it goes beyond the famous diary and projects the young woman's life into a future she never knew' (2002: 156).[6] Phillips insists that such a future would have been difficult and troubled. Although Eva asserts that the worst is now over, her story reveals that after the war she is broken by loss and grief. Her narrative demonstrates that it is impossible to both 'remember' and 'move on' (157). In a desperate attempt to escape from her past, Eva forges the letter that will enable her to move to London and make a new start. However, her loneliness is reinforced when she realises that Gerry can offer her no support. In hospital, she finds that her past has followed her to Britain in the form of a strange young woman with a 'swathe of red around her mouth' (199). This figure is an uncanny double of Eva herself who, on the eve of her departure for London, sought to distinguish herself from the other women in the camp by wearing lipstick. However, the young woman also represents all of those whom Eva has lost and whose absence she mourns: Margot, Rosa, Bella, her mother. In an attempt to elude this figure, Eva slices her wrists with the knife which is left for her to cut Gerry's cake.

Through Margot's fate, Phillips suggests the vulnerability of those who were in hiding. The Aryan-looking Margot is sheltered in the attic of a family home and she spends eighteen months imprisoned in a tiny room. In her intense loneliness, Margot discovers an imaginary friend named Siggi, who represents a darker version of Kitty. The arrival of Siggi suggests the onset of mental illness in Margot, which worsens when she is raped by the man who is sheltering her. When he comes to her room a second time, Margot screams and is arrested and we learn that she dies 'on a cold grey morning in a country that was not her own' (174). In Eva and Margot, Phillips provides two alternative versions of the Anne Frank story, both aimed at revising and challenging popular myths and misconceptions. In Eva's fate, Phillips insists that survival is not necessarily a happy ending and her suicide echoes the deaths of other famous survivors such as Paul Celan, Jean Amery and Primo Levi.[7] Margot's story demonstrates that not all of those who sheltered Jews were as selfless in their motivations as the helpers of the Secret Annexe.

Phillips's intertextual reference to Anne Frank's *Diary of a Young Girl* serves various narrative functions. He engages in intertextual dialogue with popular misconceptions of Anne Frank's story which highlight a consistently optimistic voice. Phillips suggests that Anne Frank was both more human and more vulnerable than this suggests. His alternative history indicates that death is only one form of suffering and that life itself can sometimes be equally unbearable. Both Eva and Margot choose to die in preference to living in solitude and madness. Intertextuality also affords Phillips a metatextual dimension to his writing, so that his representation of the Holocaust is filtered through previous literary sources and he is able to signal his own position as a writer at a historical and cultural remove from the events that he portrays. The sympathetic and moving rendering of Eva's story becomes all the more powerful because the reader is aware of Phillips's imaginative intervention into the past.

## Imaginary homelands

Eva's solitary contemplation of her future, when she remains in the liberated concentration camp, is interrupted by an interview with an official who asks her if she intends to return home. Eva violently rejects the very notion of 'home': 'How can she use the word "home"? It is cruel to do so in such circumstances [. . .] "Home" is a place where one feels a welcome' (37). In the Displaced Persons camp, Eva encounters the dreams of other survivors that they are soon to find a home in Israel: 'After hundreds of years of trying to be with others, of trying to be others, we are now pouring in the direction of home' (45). Although Eva desperately yearns for a home, she increasingly associates the notion of home less with a geographical place than with her family and the memory of her past, and finally with death. She ominously argues that the place which she must find is the 'place to which Margot now belongs' (46) and, as she is about to commit suicide, she observes: 'I am tired. And I want to come home' (199).

The Zionist sentiments which are expressed by the women in the camp echo the politics of Eva's uncle, Stephan Stern, whom we meet at the opening of the novel at a Displaced Persons camp on Cyprus. It is 1946 and the British, who hold the League of Nations mandate over Palestine, are diverting boatloads of Jewish refugees from Haifa to transit camps in Cyprus. Stern has been active since the 1930s in *Hagganah*, the armed Jewish underground movement, and he has given up his family and homeland to fight for the Zionist cause. He speaks of Israel in idealistic and egalitarian terms as a country which welcomes 'the displaced and the dispossessed' (5). He believes that Israel represents a fresh start both for himself and for the refugees who surround him on Cyprus: 'The new world is just beginning' (9). Like Eva, however, he finds that the past is not so easy to escape. This is suggested in the militaristic impulses of the young refugees who, at the end of the war, 'were acting as though their war had yet to begin' (8). Stern's fantasies of the homeland are also undercut by his own longing for another home, the country which he left behind but which continues to haunt his imagination. For Stern, as for Eva, the notion of home is attached as much to memory as to geography: 'I still carry within me the old world that I once cast aside' (11).

The reality of Stern's projected homeland is glimpsed at the close of the novel, which portrays him in Israel some fifty years later. Phillips portrays a man as isolated in Israel as Eva found herself in

Britain. Elderly and lonely, Stern must go to a club in order to meet 'a companion, someone to talk to, a friend even' (206). Here he encounters Malka, an Ethiopian Jew who is profoundly disenchanted with the Promised Land. During a chaste night spent at a hotel together, Malka tells Stern of her journey to Israel and her experiences there. Like Eva and other Jews who endured the transports, Malka's journey ominously begins with being herded and 'stored like [. . .] cattle' (200). Malka and her family are promised that they are going 'home' (203). However, they arrive in Israel only to find themselves the victims of racial prejudice. Reflecting on Malka's fate, Stern recognises that the Ethiopian Jews 'belonged to another place' (212) although, as in the case of Othello, it is not entirely clear where this might be. This inevitably raises the question of where Stern himself belongs. In his loneliness, he increasingly returns to the past. Inhabiting another place and another time, Stern experiences the mingling of past and present as his nieces, Margot and Eva, play around the bench on which he sits and he finds 'his arms outstretched, reaching across the years' (213). The principles of homecoming and settlement are displaced in Stern's remembering, which represents a movement in time. The exclusion that Malka and Stern experience in Israel is replaced by a gesture of inclusiveness and it seems that, if Stern cannot achieve a new beginning, there is nevertheless a positive ending, which finds value and meaning in the past and views it as a tentative point of departure.

*The Nature of Blood* asserts a diasporic notion of identity, especially in the figure of Malka who, for Coetzee, 'has ended one diasporic exile only to embark on another' (1997: 40). Phillips explores a range of diasporic histories and works in close intertextual dialogue with Gilroy. The concept of diaspora is exemplary for Gilroy because it breaks the dual focus on ethnicity and nationality which has been emphasised in recent Euro-American criticism and theory. He privileges the figure of the diasporic exile or migrant, who does not have secure *roots* tying him to a specific national or ethnic group. Instead, he must continually plot for himself new cultural *routes*, both physical and imaginative, which take him to many places and put him in contact with different peoples. The forging of new cultural routes makes possible the construction of new narrative or literary routes. The notion of diaspora is also important for Gilroy because it connects black and Jewish history and allows him to assert and explore a kinship between the two cultures. The trauma of exile, or the forced separation from one's homeland, finds new meaning as a potential point of connection or dialogue between blacks and Jews.

Phillips has embraced Gilroy's ideas and *The Nature of Blood* represents his most developed exploration of the diasporic theme. We have noted that the hybrid city of Venice allows him to encompass multiple and intertwining histories. Throughout the novel, Phillips evidences sympathy for the Jewish diaspora and suggests complex interconnections between black and Jewish cultures. He also reflects on the intersections between blacks and Jews by carefully paralleling the stories of Othello and Stern. Both characters give up a homeland, a wife and a child to make a new beginning in a different country. Both pass through the island of Cyprus which represents, in Ledent's terms, 'a liminal place, a border zone, halfway between the West and the East' (150). Each finds that a sense of attachment to place, however comforting or reassuring, can prove destructive in the longer term. On Cyprus, Othello looks forward to returning 'home to Venice' (174) and reaching the end of his wandering. He cannot see the protective walls that he is erecting around himself, isolating himself indoors and protecting himself from reality. Stern similarly looks forward to settling in his new homeland, and is likewise blind to the walls of nationalism which will soon be erected in Israel. As Jacqueline Rose points out, even as Israel came into being to bring the migrancy of the Jews to an end, it produced a new people without statehood, 'not just by oversight or brutal self-realizing intention, but as if it had symptomatically to engender within its own boundaries the founding condition from which it had fled' (1996: 13). Ledent likewise observes of Othello and the Jewish refugees respectively: 'Ironically, the new racial and national ghettos that both recreate around themselves after their passage through Cyprus [. . .] are not dramatically different from the ghettos imposed upon them while they were still wanderers, as if the end of exile tended to encourage a form of self-definition relying on the othering of the others' (2002: 141). Once again, it seems that the past is not easy to escape, but returns to haunt both individual and culture.[8]

Influenced by Gilroy's writing, Phillips accords the notion of home considerable significance. Gilroy is sharply critical of the notion of 'home', quoting Nietzsche in *The Black Atlantic*: 'Among Europeans today there is no lack of those who are entitled to call themselves homeless in a distinctive and honourable sense [. . .] We feel disfavour for all ideals that might lead one to feel at home even in this fragile, broken time of transition; as for "realities", we do not believe that they will last' (1993: 1). Phillips does not entirely dismiss the notion of home, but tentatively redefines it as a mnemonic and imaginative site. In *The Nature of Blood*, any attempts to claim a national 'home' seem doomed to failure. Othello does not belong in either Venice or Africa, but he lacks the insight and imagination to forge new cultural routes. Malka belongs in 'another place' (212) which remains unspecified, although it is clearly neither Ethiopia nor Israel. Stern does not belong in modern Israel and looks imaginatively to the old world of Europe, which no longer exists, and the new world of America where his wife and child live but which he himself rejected. Israel itself, in the sense of home, cannot exist in the novel except as a form of yearning or desire. As soon as it is realised in more concrete terms, disenchantment inevitably follows. Phillips reinvests the notion of home, in conjunction with Gilroy's writing, asserting the need for new imaginative and creative forms of interconnection and identification. Along with Rushdie, he believes that it is the task of the modern writer to 'create fictions, not actual cities or villages, but invisible ones, imaginary homelands' (Rushdie, 1991: 10). In his writing, the diasporic and traumatic histories of blacks and Jews form the basis of, and potential for, productive links and dialogue between the two cultures. This dialogue can, in turn, challenge the isolation imposed on both individuals and cultures by traumatic experience. As Jacqueline Rose observes, however, the postmodern celebration of homelessness – of being everywhere and nowhere at the same time – holds its own political dangers. This vision of free-wheeling identity offers the promise that the anxiety of belonging can be redeemed in the present by dispersal. However, for Rose, selfhood and nationhood cannot be so easily willed away. Rose calls into question the validity of a diaspora politics such as Phillips advances, especially when it is associated with Israel: 'But the status of a diaspora intellectual cannot be invoked as a solution when, for the nation in question, the diaspora is the source of the problem, the place where historically it begins' (1996: 14). In seeking to move beyond the bounded politics of nationalism, we risk losing sight of the historic traumas that we unwittingly carry within us, and that transmit and repeat themselves across time.

## Blood ties

In *The Nature of Blood*, Phillips intertwines the histories of Eva and Stern, of Othello and the Jews of Portobuffole, in order to represent the long and bloody history of European racism. Tracing a complex journey through space and time, Phillips confronts his readers with a seemingly unending series of atrocities, in which the violence of the past cannot be laid to rest but inexorably re-emerges in the present. The narratives that Phillips relates are carefully intercut in order to draw out telling analogies. Othello leaves his new wife in order to receive his latest 'orders from the doge and his senators' (149). Phillips cuts to the narrative of the Jews of Portobuffole: by order of the doge and his senators, the trial that will convict the Jews has just begun. In this intersection, Othello's blindness to the racism of the Venetians is both highlighted and confirmed. In a particularly power-ful conjunction, Eva, climbing out of the cattle car at the death camp, is enveloped in the suffocating smell of burning and the air is full of smoke and ash. The smell comes not just from the camp chimneys but from St Mark's Square in Venice, where the Jews of Portobuffole are being burned alive: '[The executioner] threw the ash into the air and it dispersed immediately' (156). The two historical instances of anti-Semitism interconnect and Phillips reinforces the point through repetition. He closes the encyclopaedic definition of the workings of the gas chambers by echoing the concluding words of the account of the burning of the Jews in Venice: 'The ash is white and is easily scattered' (178). In suggesting connections and analogies between different historical instances of trauma, Phillips employs a risky literary strategy. Revathi Krishnaswamy has suggested that one effect of the critical representation of migrancy on which Phillips draws has been a corresponding evacuation of history: 'politically charged words like "diaspora" and "exile" are being emptied of their histories of pain and suffering and are being deployed promiscuously to designate a wide array of cross-cultural phenomena' (1995: 128). There is an element of such promiscuity in Phillips's writing, which deliberately and provocatively spans a wide, cross-cultural range of traumatic experience. Phillips's work is also based in extensive historical research, however, and extends from this basis to explore the cross-cultural implications and potentialities of the material.

The repetition of imagery, in particular the motif of blood, forms a central technique in the novel through which Phillips establishes the interconnectedness of the histories he narrates. Blood provides the novel's title and saturates the narrative. Phillips's constant evocation of the imagery of blood cumulatively represents the violent history of European racism. The continent itself is personified as a cannibal which devours the flesh of the Jews and 'spits the chewed bones' out onto the island of Cyprus (12). Beyond this, Phillips develops the metaphor of blood into a complex and multi-faceted image, so that it becomes a substance which both unites and separates people. Ledent observes of the motif of blood in the novel:

> On the one hand, it is the substance of life that links all human beings together, whatever their race, and hence symbolises the common fund of humanity so forcefully denied by all racist ideologies, not least the Nazis' [. . .]. On the other hand, blood [. . .] symbolises the barrier between the different human groups, whether families or races, thus standing for their irremediable estrangement and the violence this eventually engenders, while simultaneously representing the cement that brings groups of people together, since, as the saying goes, 'blood is thicker than water'. (2002: 139)

Phillips also observes the importance of a newspaper article that he encountered while he was completing the work:

> According to the paper, it appeared that in recent years black Jews in Israel had been donating blood in the hope that it might be used to save lives. However, the Israeli government, fearful of 'diseases' that might be contained in this blood, had instructed the medical teams to dump the 'black' blood. The secret practice had now been exposed, and the black Jews were rioting and demanding that this racist practice now be stopped. I could barely believe what I was reading. (1998: 4)

This story relates most obviously to Malka and the prejudice to which she and her family are subject in Israel. However, it also suggests a broader form of racism which interconnects blacks and Jews and which is 'based solely upon visibility and difference' (1998: 7).

In *The Nature of Blood*, blood defines and demarcates the differences between people: the Venetians marry in order 'to keep the bloodlines pure' (112), but so also do the Jews. Phillips symbolises the Jewish fear of miscegenation through their attitude towards blood itself: 'nothing is more impure than blood – not just from animals, from whom the Jews drain the blood after slaughter, but even from their own women' (149–50). Blood also forms the basis of the Christian allegations against the Jews of Portobuffole. Othello is concerned with his own bloodline and the purity of his descent: 'I [. . .] was born of royal blood, and possessed a lineage of such quality that not even slavery could stain its purity' (159). Blood provides the ingredient which binds societies together, whether Venetian, Jewish or African, but it is also the basis of a damaging and threatening tribalism which Phillips defines as the most pressing issue in Europe today: 'the rise of nationalistic fervour, which leads people to close ranks into groups – or tribes – has become *the* most urgent and seemingly intractable of the many difficulties that now face modern Europe' (1987: xi). Against such separatism, Phillips asserts the value of cultural hybridity and his own 'doggedly "impure" ' blood (2002: 130). The blood flowing through his veins is Caribbean, 'an impure mixture that suggests transcendence and connectivity' (2002: 131).

Blood also represents the violence and brutality that are the endpoints of tribalism and racism. The fire which burns the Jews of Portobuffole 'consume[s] flesh and blood' (155), while the station platform at the death camp comprises an unending 'river of blood' (162). The humiliation of the Jews in the camps is powerfully symbolised in the ripping off of the women's sanitary belts, so that there is '[b]lood everywhere' (164). Eva is haunted by the blood of the camps and she wonders, as she endures the death march: 'How will they cleanse the earth after this?' (186).[9] After the war, she is unable to cleanse her own thoughts of blood and she is haunted by the young woman with a mouth 'red like blood' (197). Longing for the 'bloodless place' (169) of death and oblivion, Eva commits suicide by slitting her wrists, draining her own body of blood as if in a cleansing ritual. Phillips emphasises through repetition that there was a 'lot of blood' (188) when Eva's body was found. The novel offers a vision of European history which comprises an unending and voracious bloodletting. While the Jewish Holocaust forms the central focus, Eva's story is nevertheless firmly situated in the context of a long and ugly history of European racism.

Phillips's extended reflection on the nature of blood also works in intertextual dialogue with *Othello* and *The Merchant of Venice*. In *Othello*, Brabanzio asserts the importance of blood ties and a pure bloodline, as he accuses Desdemona of 'treason of the blood' (I, i 171). Blood is highly susceptible to influence: Othello is accused of persuading Desdemona to marry him 'with some mixtures powerful o'er the blood' (I, iii, 104), while for Iago, love is merely 'a lust of the blood' (I, iii, 333) and his suggestions to Othello work like poison 'upon the blood' (III, iii, 332). Phillips highlights Shakespeare's emphasis on the simultaneous attraction and danger of blood ties and the exclusions in which they can result. He omits Othello's 'most bloody' (IV, i, 90) vengeance on Desdemona, which leaves their bed stained with 'lust's blood' (V, i, 36). This allows him to concentrate on the blood ties which underpin Venetian society and undermine Othello's position and confidence. In *The Merchant of Venice*, it is Shylock who invokes the power of blood relation as he accuses his daughter:

'My own flesh and blood to rebel!' (III, i, 32). He is quickly refuted by Salerio, however, who denies the bond of the bloodline, stating that there is 'more [difference] between your bloods than there is between red wine and Rhenish' (III, i, 36–7). For Shylock, blood is also the sign of a common humanity which transcends ethnic and racial divisions, evident in his plea: 'If you prick us do we not bleed?' (III, i, 60). Phillips's extended, complex and multi-faceted imagery of blood is prefigured in Shakespeare, and Phillips both draws on him and writes in intertextual dialogue with him.

*The European Tribe* forms a companion text to *The Nature of Blood* and the two works can productively be read in intertextual relation. Both books provide powerful testimony to Phillips's conviction that Europe is inherently racist. *The European Tribe* comprises a modern Grand Tour in which Phillips travels through Europe as an outsider, viewing the European sensibility with an anthropological gaze. Phillips criticises European insularity and solipsism: 'Europe's absence of self-awareness seems to me directly related to a lack of a cogent sense of history. [. . .] It is a false history, an unquestioning and totally selfish one, in which whites civilize and discover' (1987: 121). *The Nature of Blood* clearly arises out of Phillips's desire to provide a 'cogent' history of Europe. He contests the selfishness of Europe by giving voice to those who, like himself, are an integral part of European history but are nevertheless regarded as outsiders. His intertextuality does not seek to erase or dismantle the founding narratives of European literature, but rather adds to them by including aspects which those in the West have often preferred to omit or forget.

Phillips presents his readers with the voices of those who are the victims of traumatic violence. He documents the seemingly endless cycle of violence and bloodshed perpetrated under various forms and permutations of European tribalism. The voices bear witness to their own experiences, but it is up to the reader to discern the points of connection and interpenetration between the stories, and to piece together the history of the European tribe which underpins and draws together the various narrative strands. Phillips's polyphonic text is not content to narrate the story of an individual in relation to the events of his or her own past, but gestures beyond this to the way in which individual trauma is always tied up with the trauma of another. Each of the narrators' experiences are profoundly connected to and inextricable from the stories of the other speakers. The question that Phillips leaves unresolved, and that haunts the reader at the close of the narrative, is whether the river of blood which flows from the very heart of Europe can be stopped and there can be an end to the repetition-compulsion of European racism and violence. Phillips suggests that it is precisely that which is not fully known in the first instance which returns to haunt us later on. In articulating the stories of the violent events, but also in dramatising through inter-textuality the ways in which this violence has not yet been fully known or acknowledged as part of European history and culture, Phillips gestures towards a new way of reading and listening which, Caruth suggests, trauma 'profoundly and imperatively demand[s]' (1996a: 9).

# Chapter 5

## *The butterfly man: trauma and repetition in the writing of W. G. Sebald*

In the period leading up to his death in December 2001, W. G. Sebald, Professor of European Literature at the University of East Anglia, established a reputation as one of the key writers of contemporary trauma fiction. A German born in the shadow of the Third Reich, Sebald grew up haunted by an unspoken sense of collective shame. His writing explored both the long aftermath of Nazism and the horrors that resulted from the RAF's devastating bombardment of German cities.[1] Although Bryan Cheyette has termed him a post-Holocaust writer, Sebald was suspicious of the notion of an identifiable genre of Holocaust literature. He was just one year old at the end of the war and consequently did not witness the Holocaust directly. However, he articulated a strong sense of personal implication, observing: 'It's the chronological continuity that makes you feel it's something to do with you' (quoted in Jaggi, 2001: 6). Although the Holocaust pervades his writing, it is evoked rather than represented, a literary strategy which, for Sebald, is connected both with the horrific nature of the events themselves and his own indirect relation to them: 'I don't think you can focus on the Holocaust. It's like the head of the Medusa: you carry it with you in a sack, but if you looked at it you'd be petrified. [. . .] I didn't see it; I only know things indirectly' (quoted in Jaggi, 2001: 7).[2]

In *The Emigrants* (1996), Sebald explores the lives of four twentieth-century émigrés. Two of them are Jewish refugees from Nazi Germany, one is a second-generation Jewish refugee from Lithuania, and one is not Jewish, although his life is inextricably interwoven with those of Jewish emigrants. All four of the émigrés commit suicide. For some this is clearly intentional, like Paul Bereyter who lies down on the railway line to die. For others death is less obviously intended, but nonetheless fervently desired. Max Ferber dies of emphysema, as a result of inhaling the dust generated by his own drawings, while Ambros Adelwarth willingly submits himself to a lethal course of shock treatment. In *Austerlitz* (2001), Jacques Austerlitz slowly and painfully learns over the course of many years that he is a Jewish refugee from Prague who was placed on one of the *Kindertransports* by his mother. Although he does not commit suicide, Austerlitz is a loner with several breakdowns behind him and is unable to form or maintain emotional links with his peers. If the novels explore the themes of time, memory, art and loss, their main subjects are nevertheless the tragedy of the Jews in Europe, and the unending consequences of the Holocaust both for those who escaped death and for the generations after.

Everybody in Sebald's novels is out of their natural place or away from home. His characters are caught in the processes of movement or displacement; they are immigrating, emigrating or in exile. For Sebald, such (e)migrations are a symptom of modernity and arise out of economic as well as political necessity. His own uncles and aunts all emigrated to New York in the late 1920s, because of the Great Depression, and in the aftermath of the Second World War large numbers of Germans moved to the United States. Sebald is primarily concerned with the sense of loss which migration inevitably entails, and which he identifies as a characteristically German preoccupation: 'this whole business of the loss of one's native country, this sentimentality surrounding the notion of *Heimat* is, I think, almost a paradigmatic German concern' (2001b). The displacement that Sebald charts in his novels also affects the natural species. Exotic bird and plant life is repeatedly found in British landscapes, most memorably in the description in *Austerlitz* of the garden at Gerald's family home in Barmouth (114–15). Birds and mammals are likewise transported out of their natural habitat to European museums and zoos. These displacements of Nature are symptomatic of the almost unbearable pressure that humans place on the natural world, which inexorably leads to the unstoppable processes of entropy and decay. Nature is repeatedly portrayed in the novels as 'groaning and collapsing beneath the burden we [have] placed upon it' (1996: 7). As Carole Angier points out, Nature is a 'second victim' (1996: 13) that Sebald commemorates in his work, alongside the Jews.

Sebald's characters are traumatised individuals, living in the shadow of the Holocaust and subject to the contingencies of exile and displacement. They are described in terms which closely replicate Freud's theories of trauma.[3] In *The Emigrants*, Max Ferber is convinced that each detail of his life has been determined by his parents' deportation and more particularly by the delay before he learnt of their deaths.[4] Unable to assimilate the news, he finds himself pursued by the past and discovers in Manchester not the fresh start for which he had hoped but rather a return to the German and Jewish influences which he had sought to escape: 'although I had intended to move in the opposite direction, when I arrived in Manchester I had come home' (1996: 192). Austerlitz is similarly haunted by his unclaimed past and caught in a repetition-compulsion. Echoing Freud's notion of traumatic latency, he notes that it is 'as if an illness that had been latent in me for a long time were now threatening to erupt' (2001a: 173).

In 'Beyond the Pleasure Principle', Freud's understanding of trauma is based on a system of fortification. Freud describes trauma as an extensive breach in the defensive wall surrounding the psyche. The subject's defences are weak if he has not built up a layer of anxiety prior to a shock or an unexpected event. The repetition-compulsion seeks to achieve a retrospective mastery over the stimulus that has breached the defences by developing the anxiety which was previously missing. By continually returning to the traumatic situation, the individual can master the amounts of stimulus which have broken through by binding them together and simultaneously construct a protective shield against trauma after the event. Austerlitz is fascinated by defensive structures, in particular the star-shaped fortress at Breendonk in Belgium. This structure was completed just before the outbreak of the First World War and was subsequently occupied by the Nazis as a prison. During the course of the novel, we learn that Austerlitz's interest in Breendonk itself serves as a defence or screen memory, which conceals behind it the almost identical fortress of Terezín or Theresienstadt, near Prague. This site was used by the Nazis as a ghetto for Czech Jews and was the first destination for Austerlitz's mother when she was deported from Prague. The fortress forms an objective correlative for Austerlitz's trauma, mirroring the internal defensive walls that he has constructed in order to protect himself from anything connected with his own early history. Paradoxically such defences, although constructed as a protective layer, serve to isolate Austerlitz from those around him. After his first memory of arriving in England as a child, Austerlitz dreams of the fortress and recognises that he has developed such complex defences against pain that they will take a lifetime to dismantle: 'I was at the innermost heart of a star-shaped fortress, a dungeon entirely cut off from the outside world, and I had to try finding my way into the open' (2001a: 196).

Sebald's writing closely replicates Freudian notions of trauma at the thematic level, but it is also structured around the notion of repetition in stylistic terms. Images and motifs echo across individual works and across the corpus as whole, so that the novels mimic the effects of trauma in their persistent repetitions and returns. With its obsessive focus on doubling and coincidence, Sebald's work is closely allied to the Freudian notion of the uncanny. Freud completed 'The Uncanny' in March 1919, the same month that he began work on a first draft of 'Beyond the Pleasure Principle', and there is a strong overlap between the two essays. In both works, Freud identifies the repetition-compulsion as a phenomenon exhibited in the behaviour of children and in psychoanalytic practice, and he suggests that this compulsion operates independently of the pleasure principle. In addition to this, however, Freud argues that the feeling of the demonic, arising from the repetition-compulsion, is a particular attribute of the literature of the uncanny or texts of compulsive recurrence. Throughout his novels, Sebald inscribes the repetition-compulsion into his writing, utilising the stylistic conventions which Freud associates with the uncanny. He draws on Freud's classic study of the 'unhomely' in order to explore the phenomenon of exile or the loss of the homeland, and to examine his own inability to identify post-Holocaust Germany as 'home'. Speaking in interview, Sebald observed of his habitual sense of displacement: 'The longer I stay here [in Britain] the less I feel at home. In Germany I feel as distant. My ideal station is probably a Swiss hotel' (quoted in Jaggi, 2001: 7).

'Beyond the Pleasure Principle' has attracted critical interest for its curious literary style in which Freud's writing mirrors or mimics the theories that he is advancing. Jacques Derrida has noted of the work: 'The very procedure of the text itself is diabolical. It mimes walking, does not cease walking without advancing, regularly sketching out one step more without gaining an inch of ground' (1987: 269). In this incessant and paradoxical movement without movement, the endless drive to repeat is clearly inscribed. In *Reading for the Plot* (1984), Peter Brooks has suggestively analysed 'Beyond the Pleasure Principle' as a model for the workings and processes of narrative plot. Brooks extends Derrida's infernal vision of movement without advance, contending that in each narrative plot a tension exists between the drive or impulsion towards the end, and a detour or deferral which delays the arrival at that end. Repetition is crucial to Brooks's understanding of narrative plot, for it serves both to defer the ending, thereby creating a pleasurable tension in the reader, and to bind the various elements of the text together, so that the narrative plot acts as a coherent whole. As I shall demonstrate, Sebald's writing closely corresponds to Brooks's structural analysis. His narratives repeatedly wander into lengthy anecdotes and digressions, the relevance of which is not always immediately apparent. He relates the stories of individuals who are not obviously connected to each other. Threaded through the narrative, however, are repeating devices which bind the incidents together and suggest unanticipated parallels and convergences. Following Brooks, I will argue that Sebald's writing is structured around a diabolical movement which (like trauma) is interminably caught between advance and regress, progression and return.

There is, however, another aspect to the constant repetitions in Sebald's work, which potentially holds a more positive significance. There are occasional hints in Sebald's novels that the inescapable coincidences and correspondences that structure the lives of his protagonists are not exclusively bound to the demonic repetitions and returns of the uncanny. Coincidence may also gesture towards an incomprehensible pattern which is at work in our lives and represents a source of mystery and wonder. While the positive resonances and potential of coincidence in Sebald should not be overstated, I will contend in this chapter that there is nevertheless an element of the sublime in his writing which is frequently overlooked, and which suggests an alternative reading of the significance of trauma in his work.

### Repetition and narrative

In *Reading for the Plot*, Brooks interprets 'Beyond the Pleasure Principle' in intertextual relation to narrative fictions and the processes of plotting. He discerns in the essay Freud's own masterplot, a scheme or model of how life proceeds from beginning to end and how each individual life repeats the masterplot in its own manner. The first problem that Freud confronts in the essay is the evidence of a 'beyond' which does not fit neatly into the pleasure principle. This is exemplified in the dreams of patients suffering from the traumatic neuroses of war: the dreams return to the moment of trauma, to relive its pain in apparent contradiction of the wish-fulfilment theory of dreams. For Brooks this 'beyond', which initiates 'Beyond the Pleasure Principle', also initiates narrative. Narrative is always in a state of repetition; it is, in Brooks's terms, 'a going over again of a ground already covered [. . .], as the detective retraces the tracks of the criminal' (97).

Sebald's novels are concerned with a 'beyond' which the narrator has not himself experienced, but which nevertheless acts for him as a compulsive point of fascination. In *The Emigrants*, the narrator, one 'W. G. Sebald', is a version of Sebald himself who lives in Norfolk, comes from the German village of 'W' and has a companion called 'Clara'. The narrator acts like a detective to uncover the stories of others which he then repeats or passes on to the reader, so that his narrative is necessarily a retracing of ground already covered. The narrator's investigations frame the biographies of the four main protagonists. Each of the four narratives, as J. J. Long points out, also concerns the life of another figure 'whose story either mediates that of the central figure (Aunt Fini, Lucy Landau, Dr Abramsky) or is mediated by it ([Ferber's] mother)' (2003: 122). In *Austerlitz*, the narrator learns of Austerlitz's past during a series of chance encounters in London, Paris and Prague. Over a period of years, Austerlitz gradually unfolds to the narrator the story of his life. The stories are further mediated by the simultaneous passing on of diaries and photograph albums or collections. When the narrator visits Austerlitz's London home for the first time, he is struck by the collection of photographs lying on the table in the front room, which Austerlitz subsequently entrusts to him. In *The Emigrants*, Ferber bequeaths to the narrator a number of photographs and the memoirs of his mother, which were written between 1939 and 1941 and sent to him shortly before her deportation. Lucy Landau hands to the narrator Paul Bereyter's notebooks, in which he copied out stories of suicide prior to taking his own life. When he visits Aunt Fini in America, in his attempts to reconstruct the life of Adelwarth, the narrator is given a photograph album, a postcard album which belonged to Adelwarth and the latter's travel journals. The narrator's stories are illustrated with photographs which are purportedly from their subject's albums, and large sections of the last two stories in *The Emigrants* reproduce extracts from the diaries of Adelwarth and Ferber's mother.

Sebald emphasises his own distance or removal from the events described through the indirectness of his narrative technique. The densely layered structure of the novels allows him to address the subject of the Holocaust and its traumatic legacy, and simultaneously to assert his own highly mediated modes of access to it. However, the narrator also shares much in common with those whose lives he relates; in particular, he is like them a figure in exile. In *The Emigrants*, he leaves Germany to settle first in Manchester and subsequently in Norfolk, while in *Austerlitz* his restless and seemingly unmotivated wanderings parallel and intersect with the travels of Austerlitz himself. This has led Long to assert that the narrator's recuperation of the lives of others is motivated by the desire to find something constant in the face of exile and loss. By suturing himself into the lives of others through identification, the narrator constructs a sense of narrative and biographical continuity:

> [Storytelling] allows the narrator [. . .] to understand his own experience of exile in terms of the narratives of others, and to assert the bonds of kinship and friendship whose durability goes some way towards compensating for the rupture, displacement, and bereavement inflicted on the individual by the vicissitudes of political history. (2003: 131)

Long highlights a redemptive strategy in Sebald's writing which counters the dispersal and dissipation caused by the historical process. However, there is a need for caution when considering the affiliation of the narrator with those whose stories he describes. Sebald has drawn attention to the essential passivity of his narrator and has warned against inserting him into the narrative: 'I try to let people talk for themselves, so the narrator is only the one who brings the tale but doesn't instal himself in it [. . .] I content myself with the role of the messenger' (quoted in Jaggi, 2001: 6). In *The Emigrants*, the narrator likewise reflects on his own attempts to imagine the life and death of Paul Bereyter. He observes that his writing has not brought him 'any closer' to his subject, but rather appears 'presumptuous'; his identification with Bereyter seems to him to represent a form of 'wrongful trespass' (1996: 29).

Brooks's understanding of narrative plot, emerging out of Freud's theorisation of the death instinct, is based on a tension between the urge or impulsion to reach the end and a contrary movement of postponement or delay. Although we tend to think of instincts as a drive towards change, Freud asserts that they may rather be an expression of conservatism. The organism has no desire to change; if the environmental conditions remained stable, it would constantly repeat the same course of life. Modifications in behaviour are the result of external stimuli and they are stored by the organism for further repetition. Freud gives an evolutionary image of the organism in which external influences force living substance 'to diverge ever more widely from its original course of life and to make ever more complicated *détours* before reaching its aim of death' (Freud, 1991, XI: 311). If Freud's notion is superimposed on fictional plots, we can see that what operates in the text through repetition is the death instinct, the drive towards the end. However repetition also delays or postpones the arrival at that end, so that the development of a narrative represents an ever more complicated detour or divergence. For Brooks, the pleasure of reading inheres in precisely such narrative wandering, a pleasure which is located in and derives from delay: 'The desire of the text (the desire of reading) is hence desire for the end, but desire for the end reached only through the at least minimally complicated detour, the intentional deviance, in tension, which is the plot of narrative' (1984: 104).

Sebald's novels exemplify such a vacillation between forward and back, advance and return. As Tim Parks observes, their opening sentences typically offer a 'robust cocktail of date, place and purposeful action' (2002: 83), which suggests a strong narrative thrust or direction. In *Austerlitz*, this is combined with a narrative which has no paragraph or chapter divisions and so rushes onwards, propelling the reader inexorably forwards. The narrative echoes Austerlitz's own internal and unconscious drive to reach the end and uncover his own past. All too soon, however, as in all of Sebald's fiction, the concrete becomes elusive and the narrative disperses into a characteristically rambling and ruminative prose. In *The Rings of Saturn* (1998), the narrator embarks on a walk which follows the Suffolk coastline. The German text is subtitled 'An English Pilgrimage', suggesting a walk which follows a prescribed and well-established route. However, the narrator finds himself repeatedly wandering from the path and losing his way. The walk ends in disaster as the narrator succumbs to paralysis and has to be hospitalised. The pattern of the walk mirrors or replicates the structure of Sebald's narratives, which repeatedly depart from their course to interject some interesting anecdote or piece of factual information.[5] His continual digressions move across time, mediating between the present, the narrator's own past, the more distant pasts of those who are now passing out of living memory and the classic past of historical battles. They also move geographically, like the narrator himself, in a series of routes which criss-cross

Europe. In addition, the narrator ranges across an almost bewildering array of subjects; Gabriele Annan observes that in *Austerlitz* alone

> there are ruminations on subjects as varied as fortresses [. . .], Schumann's madness and death, the creepy museum of the École Vétérinaire near the Gare d'Austerlitz, night moths, the impossibility of thinking about history except in preconceived clichés, concentration camps [. . .], cemeteries and spas. (2001: 27)

Sebald's distinctive prose resonates with Derrida's description of 'Beyond the Pleasure Principle': the narratives are caught in an infernal movement without progression, which threatens to result in paralysis and is suggestive of the endless drive to repeat.

Freud also proposes an alternative function of repetition in his discussion of trauma. The repetition of traumatic experiences in the dreams of neurotics has the function of seeking retrospectively to master the flood of stimuli which has broken through the subject's defences. Repetition performs a mastery or binding of mobile energy through developing that anxiety which was previously lacking – a lack which permitted the breach in the defences to occur and thus caused the traumatic neurosis. Repetition works as a process of binding which seeks to create a constant state of energy and which will permit the emergence of mastery and the restored dominance of the pleasure principle. Repetition in literature may also act as a form of binding, which allows the reader to connect one textual moment to another in terms of similarity or substitution and so make sense of the narrative. Brooks argues that literary binding represents 'a binding of textual energies that allows them to be mastered by putting them into servicable form, usable "bundles", within the energetic economy of the narrative' (1984: 101). It is only once textual energy has been bound or formalised that it can be plotted in a course that leads to significant discharge. 'Binding' in a literary text therefore refers to those formalisations – repetition, repeat, recall, symmetry – which allow us to recognise sameness within difference and to connect up various textual elements or moments.

In Sebald's writing, repetition undoubtedly fulfils the function of textual binding.[6] Carole Angier observes of the four stories in *The Emigrants* that they 'reflect each other like a hall of mirrors' (1996: 10). Correspondences between the lives of the emigrants are established by the repetition, across the stories, of key images and motifs. Certain dates persistently recur, like the summer of 1913. There are beheadings in two of the stories and hermits in three of them. Long argues that the photographs in *The Emigrants* also work to establish patterns of repetition, which can be read within and across the stories. The photographs can be linked in terms of composition or in terms of subject, so that, for example, the cemetery with the yew tree (1996: 3) can be linked to the three photographs that the narrator takes in the Jewish cemetery at Bad Kissingen (1996: 223, 224, 225). These photographs can also be linked to the pictures in Austerlitz's collection of Tower Hamlets cemetery in London (2001a: 320, 321, 324), the Cimetière de Montparnasse (2001a: 361) and the Jewish cemetery behind his home on Alderney Street (2001a: 409). The resulting connections suggest parallels and convergences between Austerlitz's story and the lives of the four emigrants. For Freud, the binding of stray energies works towards a state of constancy and the mastery of the stimulus which has broken through the subject's defences. Likewise, the textual binding in Sebald's writing can be regarded as an attempt, at the level of form, to create patterns of constancy that are repeated within and between the lives of the emigrants. Such constancy allows something stable to be recuperated in the face of the disruptions and dislocations of exile.

The most striking instance of repetition in *The Emigrants* is the butterfly collector, who appears in all four of the stories and is representative of Vladimir Nabokov, a key figure of twentieth-century exile. The figure varies in age, appearing sometimes as a boy and sometimes as a man, but he is always carrying his butterfly net, the key structuring device of evoking in Nabokov's autobiography, *Speak, Memory* (1969). In the first story, Dr Selwyn becomes interchangeable with Nabokov. A slide of Selwyn during his journey to Crete uncannily recalls to the narrator a photograph of Nabokov that he had clipped from a Swiss magazine a few days before. Although the accompanying photograph is indeed of Nabokov (1996: 16), Sebald's characteristic omission of a caption means that the image could also be the slide of Selwyn that trembles on the screen before the narrator. The image represents to Selwyn the return of the past and induces a strong emotional response in him, so that he remains silent as the slide is projected. The figure of Nabokov is evoked in the second story, as Lucy Landau sits reading *Speak, Memory* when Paul Bereyter introduces himself to her. Nabokov appears as the butterfly man to Adelwarth when he is undergoing shock therapy at the sanatorium in Ithaca. His appearance prior to Adelwarth's final treatment session suggests that he represents a harbinger of death. For Ferber, however, the butterfly man acts to prevent death, appearing before him as he contemplates committing suicide. Ferber seeks to portray this mysterious apparition in a painting, but finds himself unable to capture the 'strangeness' of the figure (1996: 174). Nabokov's final appearance is in the diary of Ferber's mother, Luisa Lanzberg. Just before Fritz asks her to marry him, they encounter on their walk near Bad Kissingen two Russian gentlemen, one of whom is Muromzev, the president of the first Russian parliament. Accompanying them is a small boy with a butterfly net, who is reprimanded by Muromzev for spoiling the walk.[7] For Luisa, the boy represents 'a messenger of joy' (1996: 214), and the butterflies released from his specimen box signal her own liberation from her stifling family circumstances.

Nabokov's presence in all of the stories binds the narrative together and suggests correspondences between the lives of the protagonists. However, the figure of the butterfly collector does not act as a stable referent. The photographs of cemeteries which recur throughout *The Emigrants* and *Austerlitz* signify that the lives of the protagonists are constantly shadowed by death and the Holocaust. The butterfly man, on the contrary, represents at various times and to various people a vehicle of memory, a harbinger of death, a deliverer of life and a messenger of joy. Although he is strongly suggestive of a constant pattern threading through the narrative, it is difficult to discern exactly what this pattern of repetition might signify. In Luisa's vision, the butterflies escape from the child's specimen box and flutter away; the figure of the butterfly collector likewise eludes capture and refuses to be pinned down to a single meaning. The loose and undefined connectivity between Nabokov's various appearances has significant implications for Sebald's writing. His repeated presence suggests a pattern of inexplicable but fateful coincidences. This resonates, in the first instance, with Freud's understanding of the uncanny which arises out of involuntary repetition and forces upon us a sense of the inescapable. In interview, Sebald suggests that Nabokov's repeated entrances into the narrative assume a haunting aspect: 'He figures in *The Emigrants* as a kind of spectre that turns up at every corner' (2001b). Sebald also gestures beyond this, however, to a concealed and almost mystical design that lies behind the apparent chaos of history. The remainder of this chapter will be concerned to explore Sebald's treatment of involuntary repetition or coincidence, which is central to his writing in both formal and thematic terms and which, I will argue, holds for him an indeterminate and unresolved significance.

## Repetition and the uncanny

'The Uncanny' is a study of a literary genre and an aesthetic sensation, and Freud's close analysis of E. T. A. Hoffmann's short story *The Sandman* has been widely celebrated in literary criticism. Freud's essay, written contemporaneously with 'Beyond the Pleasure Principle', nevertheless precipitated the uncanny into the more disturbing territory of the death drive. For Freud, the uncanny refers to a particular class of the frightening, which arouses dread and horror in us because it leads back to what is known and long familiar. It is a matter of indifference whether what is uncanny was itself originally frightening; it has become disturbing because it has long been alienated from the conscious mind through a process of repression. Everything that is uncanny (*unheimlich*) fulfils this condition: it is something that is secretly familiar (*heimlich*), which has undergone repression and then returned from it. The uncanny is a source of dread because it acts as a mode of involuntary repetition and forces upon us the idea of something fateful and inescapable. The uncanny reminds us of our own internal and unconscious compulsion to repeat which is represented by the death drive. Arising from the transformation of something homely into something decidedly not so, the uncanny arouses in us the dual responses of spatial fear leading to paralysis of movement, and temporal fear leading to historical amnesia.

Sebald's most explicit evocation of the uncanny occurs in *The Rings of Saturn*, when the narrator visits the home of Michael Hamburger. The house, which he has not visited before, strikes him as perplexingly familiar and therefore evokes a strong sense of the uncanny. On his arrival, the narrator experiences an inexplicable conviction that he himself has once lived there: 'I felt [. . .] as if I or someone akin to me had long gone about his business there' (1998a: 184). The house and its belongings appear strangely familiar to him as if it were he, and not his friend, who had laid aside the piece of writing on the desk in the study. Hamburger represents the narrator's double or doppelgänger, leading him to question: 'How is it that one perceives oneself in another human being?' (1998a: 182). The narrator seeks a rational explanation for his feelings, observing that he has followed the same autobiographical trajectory as Hamburger, another displaced German intellectual living in voluntary exile in East Anglia, and strong feelings of kinship and identification are therefore inevitable. He finds, however, that reason is unable to allay his sense of the unhomely, 'the ghosts of repetition that haunt me' (1998a: 187). The physical symptoms of his unease manifest themselves in a temporary paralysis of movement and of thought, 'as though, without being aware of it, one had suffered a stroke' (1998a: 187). Faced with the uncanny, the narrator, like Freud, links his own sense of dread to the death instinct, the drive towards the end: 'Perhaps there is in this as yet unexplained phenomenon of apparent duplication some kind of anticipation of the end, a venture into the void' (1998a: 187–8).

Freud argues that in literature, the uncanny is evoked through repetitions and doublings. The constant recurrence of the same thing – the repetition of the same features or character traits, of the same names, numbers or dates – arouses in us a strong sense of the fateful or demonic:

> For instance, we naturally attach no importance to the event when we hand in an overcoat and get a cloakroom ticket with the number [. . .] 62; or when we find that our cabin on a ship bears that number. But the impression is altered if two such events, each in itself indifferent, happen close together – if we come across the number 62 several times in a single day, or if we begin to notice that everything which has a number – addresses, hotel rooms, compartments in railway trains – invariably has the same one, or at all events one which contains the same figures. (Freud, 1990, XIV: 360)

In Sebald's fiction, the date of his own birthday, 18 May, obsessively recurs. In *The Emigrants*, the narrator demonstrates Mangold's ability to say on which day of the week any past or future date may fall by citing his birthday, 18 May 1944, which is also the day and the year of Sebald's birth (1996: 40). In the Jewish cemetery at Bad Kissingen, the narrator experiences a shock of recognition at seeing his birthday, 18 May, inscribed as the date of death on the gravestone of Maier Stern (1996: 224). Sebald was inspired to write *Austerlitz* when he watched a Channel Four documentary about Susie Bechhofer, who in mid-life remembered arriving in Wales on one of the *Kindertransports*. The documentary revealed that Bechhofer, the model for Jacques Austerlitz, also shared a birthday with Sebald, a coincidence which struck him as 'very close to home' (quoted in Jaggi, 2001: 6).

The repetition of 18 May establishes close ties between Sebald, the narrator and Austerlitz: sharing the same date of birth, the narrator and Austerlitz form uncanny doubles of Sebald himself. These convergences have led Gabriele Annan to suggest, 'perhaps Sebald sees Austerlitz as his doppelgänger, [. . .] the person he might have been had he been Jewish' (2001: 26). Doubles or doppelgängers, key features of the literary uncanny, haunt Sebald's writing. In *The Emigrants*, Sebald includes the catechist Meier and the beneficiary Meyer (1996: 35) and shop assistants Heinrich Müller and Hermann Müller (1996: 52). Aunt Fini uncannily replicates her own description of Ambros Adelwarth as she waves goodbye to the narrator wearing an overcoat which is too large for her (1996: 104). Austerlitz is haunted by the conviction that he has a double or twin. At the close of the novel, this figure resolves itself into the long repressed memory of his train journey from Prague. His 'twin' may represent a boy who sat beside him on the train and died of consumption during the voyage. Alternatively, it may derive from his own reflection, staring out into the dark, which was subsequently internalised by him as an alternative version of himself, an alter ego whose development and identity were abruptly truncated and denied when he arrived in Wales.

Freud argues that the feeling of the uncanny is experienced with particular intensity in relation to death and dead bodies, and especially to the return of the dead.[8] He observes: 'a particularly favourable condition for awakening uncanny feelings is created when there is intellectual uncertainty whether an object is alive or not, and when an inanimate object becomes too much like an animate one' (Freud, 1990, XIV: 354). In *Camera Lucida* (1993), Roland Barthes famously argued that the essence of every photograph, the terrible thing of which it consists, is the return of the dead. The photograph itself represents a reconstitution: it shows us reality in a past state and at the same time evidences that what we see has indeed existed. By attesting that the object has been real, the photograph surreptitiously induces in us a belief that it is alive; it uncannily suggests a return of the dead. However, the photograph also shifts the reality of the object to the past, evidencing that the thing *has been there*, and so paradoxically suggests that it is already dead. For Barthes, the photograph suggests the 'vertigo of time defeated' (1993: 97) and brings home to us 'the inexorable extinction of the generations' (1993: 84). Barthes's emotional or aesthetic response to the photograph evokes both the uncanny and the temporal disjunctions of trauma, in which the event is missed at the time that it happens: 'I shudder [. . .] *over a catastrophe which has already occurred*. Whether or not the subject is already dead, every photograph is this catastrophe' (1993: 96, original emphasis).

Sebald's inclusion of photographs in his fiction calls into question our notion that photographic evidence is the most incontrovertible by inserting into the narrative photographs which seem to fit exactly into the context. While the vast majority of the images are genuine, some derive from Sebald's extensive collection of 'stray photographs' (Jaggi, 2001: 6).[9] The reader's uncertainty regarding the evidential status of the photograph creates a disorienting effect which, for Sebald, has broad implications in terms of referentiality, for it emphasises the interstices between fact and fiction and so 'acts as a paradigm of the problem which faces all those who write narrative fiction' (2001b). The photographs in Sebald's fictions also occupy an uncertain territory between the living and the dead. Looking through the photographs of Bereyter's life, the narrator cannot avoid feeling that 'the dead were coming back' (1996: 46). In *Austerlitz*, Vera speaks of the mysterious quality of photographs which seem to have 'a memory of their own', and to remember 'the roles that we, the survivors, and those no longer among us had played in our former lives' (2001a: 258). Faced with the photograph of himself as a page boy, Austerlitz feels the boy's 'piercing [. . .] gaze' (reminiscent of Barthes's *punctum*, the photographic detail that can pierce and wound us), which challenges him to avert the misfortune that lies ahead (2001a: 260). As he stares at the photograph, Austerlitz feels that he himself has no place in reality, but is 'unreal in the eyes of the dead' (2001a: 261). In *Austerlitz*, Sebald extends the Freudian un-canny into new territory, inventing a 'disturbing, inverted new take on ghosts, for whom we are the unreal people' (Annan, 2001: 27).

Sebald's uncanny is inextricably linked to the trauma of the Holocaust: the dead who are ever returning to us are those who were exterminated in the concentration camps and who cannot properly be laid to rest. Their photographs in family albums assume a haunting and spectral presence, so that the familiar (familial) is rendered unfamiliar and disturbing. Sebald's evocation of the Ho-locaust depends upon the repetition of key motifs and devices: chimneys, railways and railway stations, and the interconnection of Jerusalem, Manchester and Lodz. In Ferber's narrative, Manchester is reimagined as a post-Holocaust city 'under the chimney' (1996: 192). The narrator's first glimpse of Manchester reinforces this apocalyptic impression, for it appears through the fog 'as if from a fire almost suffocated in ash' (1996: 150). The railway network exerts a powerful fascination for both Bereyter and Austerlitz. Bereyter literally '*end[s] up on the railways*', taking his own life by lying down on the line (1996: 63; italics in original). At the beginning of his studies, Austerlitz visits one of the main stations of Paris daily, and his chance meetings with the narrator almost invariably occur in the waiting rooms of railway stations. For Bereyter and Austerlitz, the railways evoke the deportation of the Jews. In *Austerlitz*, Sebald describes three stations in some detail and each calls forth associations of death: at Antwerp Central Station, the railway passengers resemble the 'last members of a diminutive race which had perished or had been expelled from its homeland' (2001a: 6); Liverpool Street Station recalls to Austerlitz the 'entrance to the underworld' (2001a: 180); while the Gare d'Austerlitz is 'reminiscent of a gallows' (2001a: 406). Sebald powerfully suggests the presence of the Holocaust by the uncanny device of rendering familiar (*heimlich*) urban spaces unfamiliar (*unheimlich*), by revealing them to us through a mental state of projection that elides the boundaries between the real and the unreal in order to provoke a disturbing ambiguity, a slippage between waking and dreaming.

Sebald's fiction habitually occupies spaces that are at once interior and public: railway stations, hotels, municipal buildings, libraries, conservatories and museums. In *The Architectural Uncanny* (1992), Anthony Vidler observes that the uncanny has, not surprisingly, found its metaphorical home in architecture and particularly in the city, where what was once walled and intimate 'has been rendered strange by the spatial incursions of modernity' (1992: 11). Austerlitz is an architectural historian, who is particularly fascinated by the architectural style of the capitalist era. He discerns in 'lawcourts and penal institutions, railway stations and stock exchanges, opera houses and lunatic asylums' (2001a: 44), both a compulsive sense of order and a distinct tendency towards monumentalism. Although Austerlitz does not pursue his research beyond the end of the nineteenth century, he recognises in retrospect that his interest foreshadows the architecture of the Nazi era, that it 'point[s] in the direction of the catastrophic events already casting their shadows before them at the time' (2001a: 197). Hitler's court architect, Albert Speer, produced capitalist architecture and derived his principles from nineteenth-century eclecticism. Sebald observes: 'The architecture of the capitalist era [. . .] prefigures in a quite uncanny sense, if one now looks back on it, the great disasters that were to come' (2001b). He reveals to us that the nineteenth-century capitalist architecture, which is so familiar a feature of our urban spaces, is in an important sense a demonstration of power, enclosure, and imprisonment. He renders unfamiliar the European cities in which we live and move – Paris, London, Manchester and Prague – and suggests that the Holocaust persists as an inescapable and haunting presence throughout Europe.

'The Uncanny' (1919) forms part of a series of essays in which Freud addressed the trauma of war, starting with 'Thoughts for the Times on War and Death' (1915) and 'On Transience' (1916), and continuing into 'Mourning and Melancholia' (1917) and 'Beyond the Pleasure Principle' (1920). Anthony Vidler points out that Freud's study of the unhomely assumes a particular poignancy and relevance when it is considered in relation to its historical context:

> Themes of anxiety and dread, provoked by a real or imagined sense of 'unhomeliness', seemed particularly appropriate to a moment when, as Freud noted in 1915, the entire 'homeland' of Europe, cradle and apparently secure house of western civilization, was in the process of barbaric regression; when the territorial security that had fostered the notion of a unified culture was broken, bringing a powerful disillusionment [. . .] The site of the uncanny was now no longer confined to the house or the city, but more properly extended to the no man's land between the trenches, or the fields of ruins left after bombardment. (1992: 7)

The uncanny emerged as a significant psychoanalytic and aesthetic response to the trauma of war, a trauma that was compounded by its repetition during the Second World War. It offered itself to the Surrealists, in particular, as an instrument of defamiliarisation. Vidler explains that it was 'as if a world estranged and distanced from its own nature could only be recalled to itself by shock, by the effects of things deliberately "made strange"' (1992: 8). Sebald's deployment of the uncanny can also be regarded as part of a surrealist project. In *The Emigrants* and *Austerlitz*, Sebald deliberately and provocatively defamiliarises the urban living spaces of Europe in order to shock us into recalling the Holocaust. He reveals that the catastrophe was uncannily prefigured in late nineteenth- and early twentieth-century domestic and civic architecture and that we must still negotiate its reality on a daily basis, as we continue to inhabit or live among its unhomely remnants. Sebald consistently seeks to make strange the familiar in order to disorient the reader, forcing him to look anew at his everyday surroundings and to readjust his ideas and perceptions, taking into account the troubling and disturbing power of the unacknowledged or repressed.

## Repetition and coincidence

In Sebald's writing, there is a suggestion that the repetitions which haunt the narrator may not be bound exclusively to the demonic returns of the death drive or the uncanny but may correspond to a more creative pattern of coincidence. In an essay on Robert Walser, Sebald notes the similarities between the lives of Walser and his own grandfather. He speculates on the nature of the connections between the two:

> What is the meaning of such similarities, intersections and correspondences? Are they tricks of the memory, self-deceptions, sensory deceptions, or are they the schemata of an order that is programmed into the chaos of human relationships, and extends, while eluding our comprehension, over both the quick and the dead? (1998b: 137–8)

Sebald answers his own query by positing the notion of a sublime and hidden order in which all things are connected and through which the apparent chaos of our lives may potentially be redeemed:

> I have since slowly learned to realise that across time and space, everything is connected with everything else, birth-dates with death-dates, happiness with unhappiness, natural history with the history of industry, the history of homeland and rootedness with that of exile. (1998b: 162–3)

In *The Rings of Saturn*, the narrator similarly seeks to fathom the correspondences which connect the lives of Hamburger and Hölderlin. Again, Sebald gestures towards a concealed order in his mention of 'elective affinities and correspondences' (1998a: 182). He suggests that, although we can gain some understanding of this hidden order in the 'increasing complexity of our mental constructs', we nevertheless know intuitively that we will never fully fathom 'the imponderables that govern our course through life' (1998a: 182). At the heart of his system of correspondences, Sebald seeks to comprehend the relationship between 'the quick and the dead' (1998b: 138). Positing an order or coherence beyond what we can know or understand, he explores the possibility that the dead are linked to us in ways which make possible meaningful connections. If we could penetrate the mysteries of correspondence, he suggests, this may in turn bind us more closely and intimately to the dead.

If a hidden order does indeed exist, Sebald suggests that it can be discerned in the myriad overlooked details of Nature. In *The Rings of Saturn*, he cites Thomas Browne's conviction that a close study of the forms of Nature can reveal the workings of eternity. Browne recorded in his writing the patterns that recurred in Nature and was particularly fascinated by the quincunx, which is formed by using the corners of a rectangular quadrilateral and the point at which its diagonals intersect.

Browne identifies this structure everywhere, in animate and inanimate matter: in certain crystalline forms, in starfish and sea urchins, in the vertebrae of mammals and the backbones of birds and fish, in the skins of various species of snake, in the crosswise prints left by quadrupeds, in the physical shapes of caterpillars, butterflies, silkworms and moths, in the root of the water fern, in the seed husks of the sunflower and the Caledonian pine, within young oak shoots or the stem of the horsetail [. . .]. Examples might be multiplied without end, says Browne, and one might demonstrate *ad infinitum* the elegant geometrical designs of Nature. (1998a: 20–1)

In *The Emigrants*, Sebald's repeated references to Nabokov establish *Speak, Memory* as an important intertext for the novel. In this work, Nabokov explored the pattern of coincidence which structures the individual life and is exemplified in Nature. He was particularly fascinated by the mysteries of mimicry: if a butterfly has to look like a leaf, not only are all the details of the leaf beautifully rendered but markings which mimic the bore-holes of grubs are generously thrown in. For Nabokov, this 'miraculous coincidence' represents 'a form of magic', 'a game of intricate enchantment and deception' (1969: 98). The detail and design, the intricate and often concealed patterns that Nabokov encountered in his study of butterflies became the resources of his writing. In *Speak, Memory*, he demonstrates that tracing patterns or thematic designs through a life and apprehending correspondences have the power to counteract loss. The discovery of pattern is, for Nabokov, a creative act and it is only through such an aesthetic strategy that the traumas of exile and history can be redeemed.

Sebald's exploration of the notion that a thread or pattern may weave through our lives is evident in his interlinking of the moth, the silkworm, the weaver and the writer. We learn in *The Rings of Saturn* that the silkworm moth, *Bombyx mori*, is a member of the *Bombycidae* or spinners (1998a: 274). The caterpillar spins an extensive web on which to support a cocoon and then, reeling out an uninterrupted silken thread which extends to a length of almost a thousand yards, it constructs the egg-shaped casing around itself. Sebald closely links the activity of the silkworm to the process of writing. Theodore Watts-Dunton is reminded of 'the ashy grey silkworm' (1998a: 165) when he looks at Algernon Charles Swinburne, the exemplar or apotheosis of the 'melancholy poet' (1998a: 159). On 1 April 1882, an old master dyer by the name of 'Seybolt' was employed as Keeper of the Silkworms and Superintendent of Carding and Filature in Germany

(1998a: 287). In this historical detail, the date of which may caution the reader against taking its validity too seriously, Sebald connects his own writing with the silkworm and the weaving process. *The Emigrants* closes with the description of a photograph of three young Jewish women working at a loom in the Lodz ghetto, weaving the 'irregular geometrical patterns' of a carpet (1996: 237). The women merge into the three Fates who weave the pattern of our destiny, 'Nona, Decuma and Morta, the daughters of night, with spindle, scissors and thread' (1996: 237). The three women re-emerge in *The Rings of Saturn* as the Ashbury sisters, Catherine, Clarissa and Christina. The bridal gown which they compose out of fragments of silk and embroider with silken thread demonstrates an unattainable 'intricacy and perfection' (1998a: 212) so that the narrator cannot believe his eyes. Like the Jewess weavers, the sisters represent a version of the Fates and sew into their 'cobweb' designs the complex patterns which the writer-narrator seeks to emulate in his prose, but which ever elude him (1998a: 212). Sebald argues that weavers have much in common with writers, for each sits hunched over his work, straining to keep an eye on the complex patterns he has created. In particular, both weavers and writers are afflicted with the condition of melancholy because they are 'engrossed in their intricate designs and [. . .] are pursued, into their dreams, by the feeling that they have got hold of the wrong thread' (1998a: 283). For Freud, melancholy is the opposite of mourning; in mourning we properly let go of the dead, but in melancholy we cling to them and seek to keep them alive within us.[10] Sebald suggests that those who are afflicted with melancholy are those who create complex patterns, those whose work mirrors or mimics the intricate design of Fate (which reveals their underlying preoccupation), but for whom the connecting thread inevitably and necessarily remains elusive.

In his writing, Sebald asserts a pattern of repetition and coincidence which gestures towards a concealed order that structures our lives and experiences. The melancholy of the writer emerges out of his inability to fathom the mysteries of correspondence which, Sebald suggests, would provide a sense of meaningful connection with the dead. However, the very existence of a sublime order, albeit hidden, provides a sense of purpose and acts, as Tim Parks suggests, to counter the disillusionment of Sebald's protagonists, 'to generate that minimum of folly, or we could call it love of life, or even engagement' (2002: 81–2). Parks argues that coincidence, which points towards the underlying mysteriousness of our existence, seems to possess the power of galvanising the melancholic and setting him in motion, so that he sorts through old diaries and photographs or searches through library archives. There is, nevertheless, a need for caution in asserting the positive significance of coincidence for Sebald. As Parks rightly observes, it has a destructive side which is inextricable from Sebald's fundamentally pessimistic vision: 'It has a smell of death about it' (88).

In Sebald's last work, *Austerlitz*, it seems that even the fragile consolation of a hidden order can no longer be sustained. In this novel, Sebald confronts the Holocaust more directly than in his previous works and the repetitions seem inexorably bound to the death drive. Although moths form a key motif in the work, they are no longer linked with an interconnecting thread of Fate. For Sebald, the moth in *Austerlitz* signifies the 'night side' of the butterfly (2001b); if the butterfly, through its connection with Nabokov, represents the workings of memory, the moth forms its dark underside of traumatic forgetting. The moth is also inexorably associated with death and grief: Sebald learnt about moths from a carpenter who worked in his house, a 'passionate moth man' who subsequently took his own life (2001b). The butterfly man who haunts the pages of *The Emigrants* is replaced by Austerlitz, a moth man who collects the mortal remains of the moths that die in his house after flying in from the adjoining Jewish cemetery. The dead moths evidence a surprising durability, showing no signs of decay; likewise, the traumatic memory that haunts Austerlitz does not fade over time. In a particularly resonant and evocative passage, Sebald describes the flight of the moths which Austerlitz and Alphonso attract on the promontory above Andromeda Lodge. In Sebald's description, the nocturnal apparition of the moths merges into a dreamlike and surreal evocation of the ghosts or spectres of the dead. The patterns created by the flight of the moths seem to indicate that something of the dead is left behind them, an aftertrace which arouses our 'deepest feelings' (2001a: 132). However, this impression is quickly dispelled by Alphonso. All that remains to us of the dead, Sebald suggests, is an illusion, a form of deception and enchantment which we are, understandably, reluctant to dispel.

> The trails of light which they seemed to leave behind them in all kinds of curlicues and streamers and spirals [. . .] did not really exist, explained Alphonso, but were merely phantom traces created by the sluggish reaction of the human eye, appearing to see a certain afterglow in the place from which the insect itself, shining for only the fraction of a second in the lamplight, had already gone. (2001a: 131)

Sebald's fiction uses devices of repetition to evoke a melancholic vision of post-Holocaust history, in which the past cannot be properly mourned or let go and threatens to paralyse action and thought. I have demonstrated in this chapter that the style of Sebald's writing powerfully evokes and reinforces the themes of trauma, loss and haunting that are explored in the novels. Sebald gives his readers a sense of the pervasiveness and inescapability of the Holocaust in contemporary European culture, and demonstrates that we are all implicated in its (after-)effects. He locates the Holocaust as a symptom of modernity, which is characterised for him by the traumas of exile and displacement. Even if we are not geographically displaced by the circumstances of history and politics, modernity nevertheless displaces our relation to time and to the spaces we inhabit.

The danger of Sebald's writing is that, like the mazes in which his protagonists are trapped, it offers the reader no escape from the repeated acting out of trauma. The novels respond to trauma by evoking its disorientation and its symptomatic dimensions at a stylistic level, but they do not offer any way of coming to terms with the traumatic experiences which they represent. Sebald's notion of an underlying and mysterious pattern of coincidence relies on the rhetoric of the sublime. Like trauma, the sublime emphasises disruption and discontinuity, for it can never be fully or completely apprehended but necessarily eludes our grasp. Although Sebald's protagonists are given motivation and hope by the prospect of meaning or significance, their melancholy is inevitably increased by their futile attempts to unravel and decipher the design. Sebald's vision of correspondences also risks losing the specificity of the historical event in a generalised pattern. This is powerfully dramatised at the end of *The Emigrants* in Sebald's discussion of the photograph of the Jewish weavers in the Lodz ghetto. The three women are anonymous but the narrator appropriates them for his own narrative purposes, giving them stereotypically East European Jewish names, 'Roza, Luisa and Lea' (1996: 237). This gesture in itself raises questions of historical appropriation and identification. The narrator then replaces the Jewish names with the names of the three Fates, 'Nona, Decuma and Morta' (1996: 237), thereby removing the women from their historical and cultural context. This provides the narrator with a metaphor of destiny or fate which cuts off the narrative, just as the three Fates cut the thread of life. The change of names suggests that Sebald has moved from evoking the history of a trauma or imagining the (Jewish) Holocaust, to implying that history itself is a trauma and as such is both fateful and inescapable. The Jewish women are no longer individuals but represent a trauma or catastrophe that will inevitably return. Although Sebald's writing evokes trauma with remarkable skill and virtuosity, it nevertheless raises problems of identification and generalisation and fails to provide the reader with any means of departure or working through. In the next chapter, I will move on to explore the possibility of working through by reading alongside each other two trauma narratives which are inspired by, and seek to replicate, the improvisational techniques and structures of jazz, namely Toni Morrison's *Jazz* and Jackie Kay's *Trumpet*.

# Chapter 6

## Recomposing the past: trauma and improvisation in Toni Morrison's Jazz and Jackie Kay's Trumpet

Traumatic recollection is characterised by the striking paradox that while its re-enactments are disturbingly literal and precise, they never-theless remain largely unavailable to conscious recall and control. Although the event returns in a vivid and precise form in the traumatic nightmare or flashback, it is simultaneously accompanied by amnesia. Caruth observes that the ability to recover the past is thus closely tied up, in trauma, with 'the inability to have access to it' (1995: 152). The connection in trauma between the elision of memory and the precision of recall – so that there is simultaneously too little and too much memory of the event – is an important element in the work of Pierre Janet. A contemporary of Freud, Janet worked on the effects of traumatic memory on consciousness. For Janet, the traumatic experi-ence was a confrontation with a shocking and unexpected event, which could not be fitted into prior frameworks of understanding. Not fully integrated at the time that it occurred, the event remained unchanged and returned, in its exactness, at a later date. Janet contends that the traumatic cure comprises a transformation of traumatic memory into narrative memory, so that the event is integrated into a chronology of the past and into the individual's life history. Where traumatic memory repeats the past without consciousness, narrative memory recognises the past as past:

> The person must [. . .] know how to associate the happening with the other events of his life, how to put it in its place in that life history which each one of us is perpetually building up and which for each of us is an essential element of his personality. A situation has not been satisfactorily liquidated, has not been fully assimilated, until we have achieved, not

merely through our movements, but also an inward reaction through the words we address to ourselves, through the organization of the recital of the event to others and to ourselves, and through the putting of this recital in its place as one of the chapters in our personal history. (Janet, 1919–25, II: 273)

In his attempts to distinguish between traumatic memory and narrative memory, Janet repeatedly returned in his writing to a particular clinical example: his 23-year-old patient Irène, who was traumatised by the death of her mother from tuberculosis. Irène nursed her mother in the months leading up to her death and, in addition, took in sewing jobs in order to support them both. When her mother died, Irène was in a state of exhaustion and continued to treat and care for the body as if her mother were still alive. Unable to grasp the fact of her mother's death, Irène would not recount any memories of the event, but several times a week she re-enacted in precise detail her actions on that night. After six months of treatment with Janet, Irène gradually began to recount the story of her mother's illness and death and once she succeeded in doing this, her compulsive re-enactments ceased to occur.

Janet observed a number of differences between traumatic memory and narrative memory. Traumatic memory takes too long: it took Irène three or four hours to re-enact the night of her mother's death, whereas it took her only half a minute to narrate the story. The traumatic memory was only evoked under particular conditions, occurring automatically in situations which were reminiscent of the original event. In Irène's case, the re-enactment was triggered if she was positioned near a bed. In traumatic memory, all the elements of the experience followed automatically once one element had been evoked. The traumatic re-enactment, in other words, was not at all adaptive. After retrieving the narrative memory, Irène was able to vary her account from telling to telling, adapting it to present circumstances. Her story could be told anywhere and the memory was triggered by a question. Narrative memory is therefore a social act, taking into account the listener or audience. Traumatic memory, on the contrary, has no social component; it is not addressed to anybody and it does not respond to anyone. In sum, Janet's conversion of traumatic memory into narrative memory aimed to introduce flexibility into the account. Janet sought to enable the patient to improvise around the fixed memory of the event and such improvisations, in turn, removed the unmitigated horror of the original experience.

Trauma theorists have greeted with caution Janet's notion that the goal of therapy is to convert traumatic memory into narrative memory. Ruth Leys points out that contemporary accounts of Janet's work have tended to downplay the extent to which his treatment 'seeks to make the patient *forget*' (2000: 106). Leys maintains that Janet does not sufficiently distinguish the assimilation of trauma from his concept of 'liquidation', and the boundaries between memory and forgetting are accordingly blurred. For Janet, she argues, memory as narration is prioritised over memory as truth-telling: 'If narration cures, it does so not because it infallibly gives the patient access to a primordially personal truth but because it makes possible a form of self-understanding even in the absence of empirical verification' (Leys, 2000: 117). Leys's worries about the extent to which the *content* of trauma is lost in its conversion to narrative are amplified by Caruth's concerns regarding the loss of its *impact*. Narrative memory enables the story to be verbalised and communicated and to be integrated into one's own and others' knowledge of the past, but it simultaneously risks losing 'both the precision and the force that characterizes traumatic recall' (1995: 153). Narrative relies on order and coherence, and it consequently threatens the 'essential incomprehensibility' of trauma, 'the force of its *affront to understanding*' (1995: 154; emphasis in original). For Caruth, the danger of narrative memory 'may lie not in what it cannot understand, but in that it understands too much' (1995: 154).

Jill Matus (1998) correspondingly observes that the orderly and coherent narrative which Janet prioritises closely resembles the 'classic' realist narrative, which emphasises the consistency and continuity of the subject. If recent poststructuralist discourse has acknowledged the unresolved, the discontinuous and the disruptive, a traumatic 'cure' which positions the individual as a transcendent and non-contradictory subject represents for Matus a disappointingly retrograde step: 'one would want to remark the emphasis in accounts of trauma on continuity and coherence, which overlooks the way the category of history and traditional narratives of history have been problematised by recent theorists' (1998: 26). Caruth and Matus both question the *form* of narrative memory. They suggest the need for a narrative form which does not succumb to closure and coherence, but retains within itself the traces of traumatic disruption and discontinuity.

This chapter reads Toni Morrison's *Jazz* (1992) and Jackie Kay's *Trumpet* (1998) in relation to the debates surrounding Janet's work. Both novels open with the traumatic confrontation with a dead body, and in each instance the shock of the death is compounded by a second blow. In *Jazz,* Joe Trace's murder of Dorcas is followed by Violet's attempted desecration of the body at the funeral, while in *Trumpet* Joss Moody's son Colman learns for the first time that his father was a woman. The characters in the novels are grieving and their lives are in a state of disintegration. The novels describe the processes by which the characters remake their lives and reconstruct their identities. At a formal level, the narratives are constructed around the techniques of jazz, which emerges as a process of improvisation, enabling the characters to tell and retell their stories of the dead and transform traumatic memory into narrative memory. The characters perform solo improvisations, so that differing versions of the past counterpoint each other and a flexibility of memory is established. Remembrance becomes a social activity as the characters call and respond to each other. As traumatic memory is resolved into narrative, the characters gradually cease to be haunted by the past. Although it initially seems that the past 'was an abused record with no choice but to repeat itself at the crack' (Morrison, 1992a: 220), the characters learn that it is possible to go round again and get out of the groove in which they have been stuck.

If the novels describe the conversion of traumatic memory into narrative memory, the question arises as to whether the forms of the novels retain the impact of trauma and are marked by its disruptions and discontinuities. I contend that, at several narrative levels, the essential incomprehensibility of trauma is communicated. Each of the novels significantly opens immediately after the death of its central subject. Although the lives of Dorcas and Joss are told and retold, they are present only in the memories of others and their absence is inscribed at the very core of the texts. Morrison has argued that the forms of jazz itself operate against closure and containment. In 'Memory, Creation and Writing', Morrison points out that narrative is, for her, 'the most important way to transmit and receive knowledge' (1996: 216). However, she qualifies this by pointing out that her own narratives, based around the trauma of the 'shattered, splintered life', reflect the fractured perception of the characters in formal terms: 'I fret the pieces and fragments of memory because too often we want the whole thing' (1996: 216). Jazz provides the model for a fragmented mode of writing, because it is an elusive and unsatisfying form:

> Jazz always keeps you on the edge. There is no final chord. There may be a long chord, but no final chord. And it agitates you. [. . .] There is always something else that you want from the music. I want my books to be like that – because I want that feeling of something held in reserve and the

sense that there is more – that you can't have it all right now. (Quoted in McKay, 1994: 155)

Jazz music famously developed from the blues and Morrison's writing, in turn, combines the exuberant rhythms of jazz with the more 'complicated anger' of the blues (1992a: 59). Pain is the essential subject of the blues and Ralph Ellison has influentially described them as a form which resists closure and consolation: 'The blues is an impulse to keep the painful details and episodes of a brutal experience alive in one's aching consciousness, to finger its jagged grain' (1972: 78). In Morrison's fiction, the counter-rhythm of the blues assumes a particular significance. In *Beloved* (1987), Morrison used a blues mode of fiction to explore and pass on the traumatic aftermath of slavery. *Jazz* is concerned with those who were born after Emancipation and who migrated from the rural South to the industrial and urban North to seek a new way of life. The incorporation of the blues demonstrates, however, that the trauma of slavery cannot easily be forgotten, and that its legacy lives on and replays itself long after abolition. Linden Peach observes that there are two undercurrents to the music which sound throughout the novel: 'anger at the violence that blacks in the North experienced at the hands of whites' and the hunger of a people who had been forced under slavery 'to deny their emotional, spiritual and physical needs' (2000: 137–8). If *Jazz* and *Trumpet* explore at a thematic level the modulation from traumatic to narrative memory, this chapter seeks to demonstrate that the novels nevertheless resist at a formal level the closure of trauma that is necessarily risked by such a modulation.

## *Writing jazz*

Both Morrison and Kay are highly innovative writers, reworking the novel form in relation to the structures of jazz. In *The Nature of Blood*, Phillips also experiments with the novel in formal terms, incorporating techniques which reflect the characteristics of black music: antiphony, the repetition of key phrases, improvisations around a central theme. Paul Gilroy has argued that an intense and ambivalent negotiation of the novel form has characterised recent novels by black writers which deal with themes of trauma, memory, history, historiography and slavery. For Gilroy, such formal experimentation is associated with 'a shared anxiety about [the novel's] utility as a resource in the social processes that govern the remaking and conservation of historical memory' (1993: 218–19). However, Gilroy's scepticism regarding the utility of the novel contrasts with Morrison's assertion of its current significance. For Morrison, the novel is crucial to black people at this historical juncture because black music is no longer exclusive to them. The novel has replaced music as the art form which is healing for black people. However, Morrison discerns a need to rework the novel in the style of black music. She is explicit that the novelist should not imitate black music but should rather be informed by its structures and seek to 'reconstruct the texture of it' in her writing (quoted in Gilroy, 1993: 78).

Jazz is a musical form in which the small band or ensemble provides a framework for musical interaction among the players. The players aim to achieve a groove, a feeling which unites the improvisational roles of the piano, bass, drums and soloist into a musical whole. Although the 'front-line' musicians (the wind instruments and horns) are the key soloists, each member of the band is expected to take their turn as solo performer. The musicians respond to and participate in an ongoing flow of music, which can continually change or surprise them. Although the structure of jazz varies endlessly, there is nevertheless a characteristic mode of performance. The musicians initially agree on a 'tune', a melodic or harmonic pattern of a set length. The performance begins and ends with the tune, and one or more of the 'front-line' players will play through the set melody, while the rhythm section iterates its rhythmic or harmonic infrastructure. In between the relatively formal beginning and ending, various players take turns to improvise for one or more choruses each. The structure is sufficiently tight to keep everyone together at the start and finish and to keep the soloist synchronised with the rhythm section. It is simultaneously loose enough, however, to accomodate any number of players and to allow for the spontaneity of performance.

Eusebio L. Rodrigues (1997) contends that Morrison captures the fluidity of music in *Jazz* by leaving her chapters unnumbered and untitled. The novel is divided into ten equal sections, which are divided by blank pages so that the text reads like a musical score. Unlike a symphony, however, in which the sections are clearly demarcated, Morrison's chapters overrun and overlap, resembling the non-stop sequences in a jam session and giving the text a loose, jazz feel. The novel also follows closely the structure of jazz performance. In the opening pages, the narrator relates the story of Joe, Violet and Dorcas, the 'scandalizing threesome on Lenox Avenue' (1992a: 6). The beginning of the novel establishes the narrative pattern which is subsequently retold from the viewpoints of Violet, Joe, Alice, Golden Gray and Felice. The range of narrative voices reflects the multi-instrumentation of the jazz band and the various solo performances which are played by the different band members. The close of the novel concerns the alternative threesome of Joe, Violet and Felice, who contradict the narrator by refusing to replay the pain and trauma of the past. The narrator is surprised by her own creation which asserts itself against a preconceived pattern. As Jill Matus indicates, Morrison thereby demonstrates to the reader that 'improvisation means taking risks, responding spontaneously to what emerges in the process of creation' (1998: 123–24).

*Trumpet* opens with Millie's account of Joss's life, in which her discovery that Joss was a woman seems far less remarkable than the fact that, in death, Joss is no longer there. In the opening chapter, Millie is alone at Torr. The family is fractured and her own identity has been 'swept out to sea' (8). At the close of the novel, the opening is reversed as Colman returns to Torr to be reunited with Millie. In an image which symbolises both the presence of Joss and Millie's new-found ability to let him go, a bird flies into the air 'calling and scatting in the wind' (278). Between these counterpointing melodies, the story of Joss is retold in the novel from the differing viewpoints of the doctor, the registrar, the funeral director, the cleaner, Colman, Sophie Stones, Big Red McCall and Edith Moore. Kay consciously seeks to capture the texture of jazz in the novel:

> The form of the novel in a way equals jazz because you have your solo instruments with the different people who have all been affected by this secret. And then you have the same story being improvised and told over and over again in different ways, with different perspectives. And that's the [. . .] thing that interests me about jazz, how you can take one refrain, one single story, and make it play lots of different ways. (Quoted in Jaggi, 1999: 56)

The different voices or viewpoints are interspersed with a series of chapters entitled 'House and Home', so that the solo improvisations alternate with a melodic pattern that runs through the text. The fluidity of jazz in *Trumpet* reflects Joss's constant reinvention of himself. The multiple narratives resist a fixed position of identification and imply that Joss's identity cannot be contained through standard narrative modes.[1]

The conscious use of repetition is central to the creation of a jazzy prose style. Jazz musicians create forms which repeat themselves in order to structure their improvisatory compositions. The most important of these forms is the riff, a short, melodic phrase which is repeated as a melody or accompanimental background. The riff can act to spur on a soloist or to reassure the audience that the band is still working together. It is repeated without variation in order to stress the melodic development which occurs outside of the short phrase. Morrison uses the repeated phrase to modulate between repetition and variation, and to create stability in an otherwise wandering and circuitous narrative. Dorcas's response to her parents' deaths forms a key riff in the novel: 'But she must have seen the flames, must have, because the whole street was screaming. She *never said. Never said* anything about it. She went to two funerals in five days, and *never said* a word' (57, emphasis mine). Rodrigues suggests that there is variation in Morrison's repetition, a 'rhythm of pause and emphasis and release' (1997: 249). However, the repetition also emphasises the traumatic wound which remains silent and unspoken within the 18-year-old Dorcas, so that its effects tragically play themselves out in her death. Words and phrases which repeat within and between lives in the novel also act as jazz riffs. Alice advises Violet that she should not be a victim of the past, but should actively rework it: 'I'm sayin make it, remake it!' (113). The narrator picks up the riff at the close of the novel, addressing the reader directly and urging her to become involved in the process of creation, to improvise on the themes of the book: 'Say make me, remake me' (229). The riff highlights one of the key themes of the novel: the importance of improvising on trauma and continually making and remaking the narrative of the past.

Jazz performance is structured around antiphony or the pattern of call-and-response. Each musician in a jazz band continually responds to or exhorts the other players. This process reflects the dialogic or conversational character of jazz and emerges out of the calls, cries, whoops and hollas of early African-American culture. Jazz is also characterised by a strong interplay between audience and musicians which reflects the call-and-response interaction between the minister and his congregation in traditional black churches. At jazz perfor-mances, the audience yelps, shouts, claps and dances as immediate ways of provoking or energising the band. Morrison and Kay likewise structure their jazz novels around a call-and-response pattern. Each of the ten sections of *Jazz* ends with a phrase or idea to which the opening lines of the next section respond. When Joe discovers the dwelling of his mother, Wild, he questions: 'But where is *she?*' (184). In the response which opens the next section – 'There she is' (187) – the pronoun no longer refers to Wild but to Dorcas. The substitution reveals that Dorcas is Joe's replacement for his absent mother. The pain of Dorcas's departure is indistinguishable from his mother's abandonment and Joe can no longer discern the difference between searching for Dorcas, tracking Wild and hunting an animal. The last section opens with the narrator's description of her 'sweettooth' for pain (219). This responds to Felice's observation that, rather than hurt Violet's feelings, she drinks water in order to ease the 'pain' of Violet's peppered catfish (216). The narrator's affection for pain leads her to assume that the past cannot change, whereas Felice's compassionate response to Violet demonstrates that it can. In *Trumpet*, the funeral director's narrative closes with his astonishment at Joss's persuasiveness as a man: 'This was a first all right. This was a first' (116). His words are echoed at the start of the next chapter in Colman's description of bringing a girlfriend home: 'The first time, right?' (117). Colman's pained incomprehension of the relationship between Joss and his girlfriend contrasts with the funeral director's amazed acknowledgement of Joss's achievement.

Morrison's involvement of the reader in the construction of the novel also reflects the call-and-response structure. Just as music is enhanced when there is a response from the audience, so Morrison seeks to establish an active sense of connection with the reader. She observes of her attempts to have the reader work with the author: 'I have to provide the places and spaces so that the reader can participate. Because it is the affective and participatory relationship between the artist or the speaker and the audience that is of primary importance' (1985: 341). In *Jazz*, these concerns are most clearly marked in Morrison's use of the second-person address, which invokes the reader directly. The novel closes with a lyrical passage in which the narrator confesses to only having had the kind of secret love affair that Joe and Dorcas shared. She envies Joe and Violet their 'public love' (229) and longs to declare her own feelings openly. In the articulation of her passion, the narrator merges with the book which the reader is holding and the reader in turn becomes the addressee:

> *I love the way you hold me, how close you let me be to you. I like your fingers on and on, lifting, turning. I have watched your face for a long time now, and missed your eyes when you went away from me. Talking to you and hearing you answer – that's the kick.* (229; italics in original)

The narrator exhorts the reader to participate in the process of the novel, to keep its meanings open and continue to improvise on its themes: 'You are free to do it and I am free to let you, because look,

look. Look where your hands are. Now' (229). If Morrison's writing represents a jazz performance, she expects her readers to involve themselves in the manner of a jazz audience. In what Gilroy has termed the 'ethics of antiphony' (1993: 200), Morrison highlights intersubjectivity and seeks to dissolve the boundaries between performer and audience, author and reader. In the manner of all good jazz musicians, she makes it clear that her call demands the audience's response.

## Performing gender

I have argued above that Morrison and Kay structure their novels around the techniques of jazz performance. In their writing, solo improvisation, the jazz riff and call-and-response are creatively adapted to narrative and literary form. Jazz also acts at a metaphorical level in the texts to symbolise women's experimentation with prescribed gender roles and expectations. In *Jazz*, the unpredictability and volatility of the music parallels the contested social space of the City. The context for the novel is the Great Migration, the mass movement of African-Americans from the rural South to the urban North. This move also represented the shift from slavocracy to industrialism. The City acts as a space of negotiation in which men and women explore the new opportunities that are open to them. Like jazz itself, the City shapes and is shaped by people's behaviour and it acts metaphorically as a site for the renegotiation of morality, lifestyles and familial patterns. In *Trumpet*, jazz acts as a metaphor for Joss's reinvention of himself, suggesting the fluidity and elusiveness of gender. For Joss, jazz provides a space outside of the symbolic order which is not inscribed by race or gender. The novel also tells the story of Colman, and Kay explores the ways in which he seeks to improvise his own identity in the wake of his discovery of Joss's secret. Colman seeks to (re)construct the narrative of himself and, as we will see, a crucial aspect of this narrative is his relation to jazz and the forms of identity and identification which it offers to him.

*Jazz* opens with the narrator's confident celebration of the City and the freedoms that it offers. The fast-paced and chaotic nature of jazz mirrors the speed, flux and cosmopolitanism of the City. The music also reflects the optimism and sense of risk which are experienced by those who arrive in the City:

> Here comes the new. Look out. There goes the sad stuff. The bad stuff. The things-nobody-could-help stuff. The way everybody was then and there. Forget that. History is over, you all, and everything's ahead at last. (7)

It quickly becomes apparent, however, that this headlong rush into the future is less a form of optimism than a desperate bid to escape from the trauma of the past, the 'specter' of slavery (33). Underneath the good times, there is 'something evil' and nothing is safe from it, 'not even the dead' (9). Each of the characters in the 'scandalous threesome' which opens the novel seeks to leave behind an unresolved past and for each the trauma centres on the loss of a mother. Violet's mother, Rose Dear, threw herself down a well in desperation when her husband left the family and Violet was brought up by her grandmother, True Belle. Joe was abandoned by Wild and called himself Trace to signify that he was left behind. Dorcas lost her mother and her father within hours of each other and was raised under the stern and watchful eye of Alice. In *Beloved*, Morrison powerfully represented the traumatic impact of slavery through the distortion of the maternal relation which culminated in Sethe's murder of her daughter. The maternal function is significantly not yet restored in *Jazz*, which suggests that the effects of slavery are still very much at work.

Morrison portrays the social and political after-effects of slavery in the novel. Inflation and exploitative conditions led to a series of strikes across the country in 1919. African Americans were especially vulnerable to poor working conditions and racism. The Ku Klux Klan regained popularity and more than seventy African Americans were killed by white mobs during the last nine months of 1919. Black communities responded to the violence against them with increasing assertiveness. This tension erupted in the race riots of the northern cities. In *Jazz*, Dorcas's parents are killed during the East St Louis riots: her father is pulled from a bus and stomped to death, and her mother is burned alive when the house is torched. In this inflammatory context, jazz music assumes a threatening aspect and is criticised by both blacks and whites as a cause of loosening morals and social dislocation. Alice disapproves of the 'lowdown' music (56) when she takes Dorcas to the Silent Protest Parade on Fifth Avenue, organised to protest against the East St Louis riots and other violence. However, jazz is not the cause of what is happening to African-Americans but an expression of their experiences, and Alice dimly perceives this in her reflection that the drums express a 'complicated anger' (59). The music has a powerful political force, providing new sites for social assertion and political negotiation.

Dorcas's reaction to the music counterpoints Alice's, for she embraces as her own the 'life-below-the-sash' (60). Her response is a reaction against her aunt's puritanical upbringing, but it also represents a belated expression of grief for her parents. Dorcas interprets the protest parade as a funeral march for her mother and father. As she watched the house burn with her mother trapped inside, Dorcas swallowed a spark from the fire, which remained within her as an 'inside nothing' (38). The music of the parade causes the spark inside her to sink until it settles 'somewhere below her navel' (61). Dorcas is an incendiary waiting to be set alight and Joe provides the spark, for he shares Dorcas's emptiness as a result of the abandonment of his mother, Wild. With the hoofmarks on her cheeks, Dorcas is marked by Wild and substitutes for her in Joe's imagination. In the story of the spark, Morrison explicitly connects the wildness in Dorcas, which is reflected in the wildness of jazz, with the violence of the race riots.

If jazz music is intertwined with the violence of race relations, the blues articulate a cultural and political struggle over sexual relations and the reclaiming of women's agency. In the 1920s, women blues singers such as Bessie Smith critiqued patriarchal gender relations, male violence and the restrictions of the domestic sphere. In their lyrics, blueswomen sang of leaving violent or unfaithful lovers, they celebrated their own sexuality and they foregrounded lesbian relationships. The blues rhythms which run through the novel articulate the daily abuse of women. The City does not offer a refuge from physical and sexual violence; on the contrary, Alice discovers that the murder of Dorcas occurs against the background of countless similar crimes:

> Every week since Dorcas' death, during the whole of January and February, a paper laid bare the bones of some broken woman. Man kills wife. Eight accused of rape dismissed. Woman and girl victims of. Woman commits suicide. White attackers indicted. Five women caught. Woman says man beat. In jealous rage man. (74)

In response to this litany of violence, the women throughout the City arm themselves with whatever comes to hand. They organise themselves into groups and networks of support, 'leagues, clubs, societies, sisterhoods' (78). Alice both fears and admires these women who are prepared to stand their ground and fight back, and she refers to them as the 'wild women' (81). Confronted with the murderous combination of racial and sexual violence, all of the women in the City are running wild.

The wild woman whom Alice most fears and admires is Violet, the woman who disrupted the funeral of her niece. Alice privately calls her Violent, reflecting Violet's own experience of herself as split or double. There is the woman whom Violet recognises herself to be and then there is '*that* Violet' (90), the woman within her who is wild and seeks to take revenge on a corpse. Like Dorcas, Violet is wild because of her childhood experiences, namely her mother's suicide, which was itself a response to the economic desperation of the Reconstruction period. After Dorcas's death, Violet and Alice meet regularly and enable each other to move forward. Violet helps Alice to confront and recognise her own wildness, her anger against the woman with whom her husband had an affair. She was saved from her own violence by her husband's death and only now does it find expression in her rudeness with Violet. Alice reminds Violet of the value of a sense of humour, the ability to see herself as others see her. She enables Violet to tentatively unite the two halves of herself: 'She buttoned her coat and left the drugstore and noticed, at the same moment as *that* Violet did, that it was spring' (114). Both Alice and Violet reclaim the wild aspects of themselves, reconstructing themselves after Dorcas's death by forming their own sisterhood. Morrison suggests that if women improvise new forms of community this will, in turn, provide them with a means of reclaiming agency in desperate times. However, the figure of Dorcas remains at the core of the narrative as someone who could not leave the trauma of her childhood behind, who could not satisfy the 'inside nothing' which consumed her from within. The healing of Violet and Joe, Alice and Felice, occurs as a result of Dorcas's death, but Dorcas herself remains caught in the traumatic replay of the past and her wildness refuses to be tamed.

*Trumpet* explores the patriarchal aspects of jazz itself. Women were largely excluded from performing jazz because it was believed that they lacked the physical strength to excel on certain instruments, including the trumpet. Success as a jazz performer was closely associated with an ability to survive dangerous performance spaces. This masculinist ethos emerged from early jazz, which was performed in clubs where drug dealing, prostitution, gambling and pimping took place. Eric Porter contends that jazz developed as a 'hypermasculine culture', and that excelling in jazz 'offered access to alternative, expressive capital that challenged American society's denial of the status and rights of manhood to African American men' (2002: 28). For Porter, the improvisational ethos of jazz, in particular, helped to 'validate black male genius' (29) in a society that otherwise denied it. From the outset, then, jazz bands, organisations and unions were established on a patriarchal and fraternal basis.

Joss Moody is based on Billy Tipton, a female jazz pianist who lived as a man so that (s)he could perform as a jazz musician. For Diane Middlebrook, Tipton was a performer or improviser of gender as well as of jazz: 'Billy in a male persona was an artist, improvising with attitude, voice, and gesture. A self-made man, [. . .] in both professional and personal life' (1998: 106). Kay transforms Tipton from a white American pianist into a black Scottish trumpeter, and explores Joss's journey as a 'self-made man'. Joss is named after Josephine Baker, a female performer who sometimes dressed as a man and experimented with the visual creation or invention of herself. In living his life as a man, Joss goes one stage further than this. He succeeds to the degree that, even when those around him discover his secret, they still see him as a man and refer to him using the masculine pronoun. Jazz acts as a metaphor for Joss's improvisation of identity and his playing merges with his self-invention: 'Running changes. Changes running. He is changing all the time' (135). Jazz offers him a site where he can temporarily escape from the cultural inscriptions of race and gender: 'He loses his sex, his race, his memory. He strips himself bare, takes everything off, till he's barely human' (131).

If Joss de- and reconstructs himself through his music, Colman is faced with the problem of how to reconstruct his shattered identity in the wake of Joss's death. The novel charts the process by which he transforms his traumatic confrontation with Joss's naked corpse into a narrative which can make sense of this event in relation to his own life history. Several narrative alternatives offer themselves to Colman. With Sophie Stones, he responds with an aggressive assertion of masculinity and emphasises his own possession of the phallus – '[a] good-sized cock' (181) – which his father lacked. However, this posturing conceals an underlying oedipal anxiety, in which Joss's trumpet acts for Colman as a phallic object which is both prohibited and desired:

*I goes in my father's bedroom. I am six years old. I opens their wardrobe. My daddy keeps his trumpet in here. I opens the big silver box, and there it is, all shiny inside. I touched it. I did touch it. Then I stroke it like I've seen my father do and it purrs. [. . .] Then my mum finded me. [. . .] She says, Colman, what are you doing? Get out of your father's trumpet.* (49; italics in original)

Colman may look like Joss and share his walk and gestures, but he has not inherited his talent as a jazz musician. His identity is further complicated by his adoption, so that he is both Colman Moody and

William Dunsmore. In seeking a narrative for himself, Colman significantly does not trace his birth parents but improvises around Joss's identity and legacy. Crucial to Colman's self-(re)construction is Joss's letter, which offers the story of Joss's own father. In place of a patrilineal identification, Joss bequeaths to his son a history of repeated improvisation and self-invention: 'That's the thing with us: we keep changing names. We've all got that in common' (276). In writing the story of his father, Joss reveals that the familial legacy of improvisation originates in the erasure and denial of black identity. John Moore was the name that Joss's father was given on his arrival in England, but his original name was lost. If Joss's improvisations of identity are positive affirmations of the fluidity and instability of gender, they are nevertheless inextricable from a process of improvisation which was essential to survival in an unfamiliar and bewildering new world. Joss's letter suggests that Colman's narrative of himself must accordingly incorporate an understanding of both his gendered and racial identities.

## Race music

In her autobiography, *The Words to Say It* (1983), Marie Cardinal recorded her feeling of panic when she attended a jazz concert given by Louis Armstrong. Cardinal's mental breakdown dated from this concert and her description of jazz music resonates with the symptoms of her illness: 'The Thing, which on the inside was made of a monstrous crawling of images, sounds and odours, projected in every way by a devastating pulse ma[de] all reasoning incoherent, all explanation absurd, all efforts to order tentative and useless' (15). In *Playing in the Dark* (1992), Morrison argues that Cardinal's experience of jazz as a threatening intrusion from without is symptomatic of a wider pattern in white literature and culture, which is intermittently invaded by a 'language of dread and love that accompanies blackness' (x). Morrison is fascinated by the ways in which black people 'ignite critical moments of discovery or change of emphasis in literature not written by them' (viii). For her, black history and experience comprise one of the forgotten or repressed subtexts of the American narrative of nationhood. In its place, a mythological Africanism was constructed as a psychic defence against the disruptive incursion of the black presence into white American culture. Morrison's fiction, and black literature more broadly, constructs a counter-narrative which asserts what the historical or literary record has 'forgotten'.

Morrison's writing overlaps with psychoanalysis in excavating a buried past and bringing repressed material back to consciousness.

In 'The Belated Postmodern: History, Phantoms, and Toni Morrison', (1996), Peter Nicholls argues that, in her fiction, Morrison reconfigures History – the secure, metaphysical time which is possessed by a contemplative subject – as historicity, a traumatic past which inhabits the subject and exposes him to the shock of a temporality which is always self-divided. For Nicholls, the forgotten history of the black presence assumes the force of a cultural trauma and has 'the power to shake the social and metaphysical forms against which it breaks', giving rise to an idea of history as 'a violent intrusion from somewhere else' (1996: 52). In retrieving this history, Morrison reconfigures narrative itself as historicity, in order to communicate the force or impact of the trauma. Nicholls praises the distinctive rhythms of Morrison's prose, her cross-weaving of temporalities, which produces 'a tension which rends History from within' (1996: 52). In her writing, Morrison commemorates the traumatic impact of black exclusion by inscribing its traces in the creative reconfiguration of narrative form. Jazz provides the form or context in which the black presence asserts itself as an intrusive and disruptive force.

Morrison is centrally concerned with the recovery of forgotten or repressed black experience. She argues that her novels 'centralise and animate information discredited by the West – discredited [. . .] because it is information held by discredited people' (1996: 217). She seeks to write literature which is 'irrevocably, indisputably Black' (1996: 217). In stylistic terms, this depends on an elusive quality which unsurprisingly finds its closest analogy in jazz: 'John Coltrane does not sound like Louis Armstrong, and no one ever confuses one for the other, and no one questions if they are black. That's what I'm trying to get at' (quoted in McKay, 1994: 153). In *The Signifying Monkey* (1988), Henry Louis Gates argues that jazz musicians, such as Armstrong and Coltrane, are connected by a musical tradition which provides the springboard for improvisation. Jazz depends on a history of formal revision and troping in which musicians often make their name by playing 'standards', complexly extending figures that are present in the original version. For Gates, the jazz musician does not seek to surpass or destroy the original; on the contrary, his performance comprises a gesture of admiration and respect. In jazz, Gates observes, 'it is the realignment of the signifier that is the signal trait of expressive genius' (1988: 64).

In articulating a theory of African-American literary criticism which emerges out of jazz, Gates argues that jazz depends on Signifyin(g) – repetition with a signal difference – which emphasises formal revision and intertextual relation and is concerned to address antecedents. Jazz musicians continually quote from and revise one another's work and, as Geoff Dyer observes, 'whether you pick it up or not depends on your knowledge of the music' (1996: x). African-American writers similarly read and revise each other's texts, and continually refigure the canonical tropes of the black tradition. Gates regards the African-American literary tradition as successive attempts to create a new narrative space for articulating black experience. Through the revision of tropes, writers bind themselves to their literary predecessors in 'loving acts of bonding' (1988: xxviii). They also forge a community of interpreters who share their frame of reference, and to whom the textual repetitions and revisions are socially meaningful.

Morrison Signifies not only on the works of other black writers but also, crucially, on her own canon. Each of her novels assimilates and advances the themes and structures of her own former texts. In *Jazz*, Morrison Signifies, in particular, on the text of *Beloved*. Both novels explore the problem of love and the protagonists are confronted with the problem of balancing love for another with self-love and self-preservation. The point of connection between the novels initially seems to be Dorcas. Morrison points out that Beloved re-emerges as Dorcas in *Jazz* and the earlier love story is reconfigured in the Harlem milieu (quoted in Naylor, 1994: 208). The murder of Beloved resurfaces in Dorcas's death, and both victims are paradoxically killed by those who love and need them most. At the end of *Jazz*, Dorcas's blood transforms into a 'bird with a blade of red on the wing' (225), which recalls both the redwings that surround Wild (176) and the hummingbirds which circle Sethe's head and are associated with the murder of Beloved (1987: 262). For Nicholls, however, the figure of Dorcas acts as a false lead and the narrative trail, like Joe's hunt, leads beyond Dorcas to Wild. In interview, Morrison has explicitly connected Beloved and Wild:

> You see a pregnant black woman naked at the end of *Beloved*. It's at the same time [. . .] back in the Golden Gray section of *Jazz*, there is a crazy woman out in the woods. The woman they call Wild (because she's sort of out of it from the hit on the head) could be Sethe's daughter, Beloved. When you see Beloved towards the end [of *Beloved*], you don't know, she's either a ghost who's been exorcised or she's a real person [who is] pregnant by Paul D, who runs away, ending up in Virginia, which is right next to Ohio. (Quoted in Carabi, 1995: 43)

As Nicholls points out, Wild is strongly reminiscent of Beloved in descriptive terms. Wild is a 'naked berry-black woman' (1992a: 144), while Beloved is naked and '[t]hunderblack' (1987: 261) at the close of the previous novel. Like Beloved, Wild is heavily pregnant when she is found by Golden Gray and her stomach is 'big and tight' (1992a: 144; 1987: 261). Golden Gray fears that Wild will 'explode in his arms' (1992a: 153), just as the townsfolk thought that Beloved 'exploded right before their eyes' (1987: 263). If Beloved was indeed pregnant with Paul D's child, then Wild's offspring, Joe, unsurprisingly inherits many of his qualities. The re-emergence of Beloved as Wild and her association with the wildness in Dorcas and the other women powerfully suggests that the trauma of slavery has not been laid to rest. The migration of Joe and Violet from South to North uncannily recalls the desperate flight from slavery of Sethe and Paul D. If the novel's major theme is the impact of their most recent move on the psyche of the African-American people, the presence of Beloved/Wild indicates that this journey reopens wounds which have not yet had sufficient time to heal. The lyrical and optimistic ending of *Jazz* works towards the closure and containment of the trauma. Even here, however, the traumatic memory stubbornly persists. At the end of *Beloved*, the presence of Beloved remained in barely perceptible traces, 'the rustle of a skirt', 'the knuckles brushing a cheek in sleep' (1987: 275). At the close of *Jazz*, it is clear that Beloved has still not been exorcised from the collective imagination or psyche:

> It is out there in the privet hedge that lines the avenue. Gliding through rooms as though it is tidying this, straightening that. It bunches on the curbstone, wrists crossed, and hides its smile under a wide-brim hat. Shade. Protective, available. Or sometimes not; sometimes it seems to lurk rather than to hover kindly, and its stretch is not a yawn but an increase to be beaten back with a stick. Before it clicks, or taps or snaps its fingers. (1992a: 227)

In spite of the consolations of improvisation, of telling and retelling the story, the residue of trauma persists. Morrison extends a political warning that the spectre of the black presence has yet to be fully integrated into the narrative of white American culture.

I have argued that in *Jazz*, Morrison Signifies on *Beloved* in order to highlight the persistence of trauma and its resistance to assimilation. In *Trumpet* Kay, in turn, Signifies on *Jazz*, adopting and adapting Morrison's narrative techniques. As a writer, Kay is very conscious of her predecessors in the black literary tradition – writers such as James Baldwin, Ralph Ellison and Toni Morrison. However, Kay was brought up in Scotland and she regards America as a society which is more driven by race than Britain. Gilroy has argued that black music, and particularly black American music, has played a central role in the configuration of black identity in Britain (1993: 82). For him, music contributes to a sense of the racial self and provides a source for the discourse of blackness within which blacks in Britain can locate their own struggles and experiences. Kay was transracially adopted, and grew up knowing no other black people apart from her brother. She has described her fantasy relationships with various black musicians, including Bessie Smith, Louis Armstrong and Ella Fitzgerald. Bessie Smith was of particular importance to her sense of identity and of an imagined community to which she might belong:[2]

> I will always associate the dawning of my own realization of being black with the blues, and particularly Bessie's blues [. . .] Bessie's blues still fill me with a strange longing. I don't know exactly what for. Blackness? A culture that will wholly embrace me? Who knows? (1997: 138–9)

Kay's experience of adoption is also inextricable for her from the question of her racial identity. In interview, she associates tracing her birth parents with tracing her racial roots, seeking to discover the nature of her relationship to Africa. For her, both represent modes of tracing origins and both can be positive, although they may also prove to be traumatic: 'You can't really merge something that has already been severed [. . .] You can't really repair that split' (quoted in Dyer, 1999: 60).[3]

In *Trumpet*, Joss embraces his split racial heritage. He identifies himself as Scottish, feeling at home once he crosses the border near Carlisle. He also constructs his black identity through identification with various American jazz musicians, 'Louis Armstrong, Fats Waller, Count Basie, Duke Ellington, Miles Davis' (192). Joss's first big hit is significantly entitled 'Fantasy Africa', reflecting his belief that black people across the diaspora have their own imagined identification with Africa, their own imagined communities: 'Every black person has a fantasy Africa, he'd say. Black British people, Black Americans, Black Caribbeans, they all have a fantasy Africa. It is all in the head' (34). In naming Colman, Joss and Millie accordingly seek to pass on to him a dual heritage as both black and Scottish. He is called Colman after the black jazz musician, Coleman Hawkins, but it is spelt in the Celtic form. Colman, however, rejects both affiliations. He feels criminalised and suspected of wrongdoing in Scotland, while he rejects as 'unreal' the notion of an African legacy or history (191).

In the wake of Joss's death, he is left with the painful and seemingly insoluble question: 'What is him?' (190).

Jazz provides Joss with a space in which the musician is free to forge his own relations and identifications. Signifyin(g) becomes the material of self-invention: 'All jazz men are fantasies of themselves, reinventing the Counts and Dukes and Armstrongs, imitating them. Music was the one way of keeping the past alive' (190). Jazz musicians make up their own origins and bloodlines, and Joss urges Colman to do the same: 'Make it up and trace it back. Design your own family tree' (58). Joss improvises his own imaginative 'bloodline' to Colman, regarding his adopted son and the members of his band to be 'related [to him in] the way [that] it mattered' (58). In his last letter to Colman, Joss articulates the ties that bind them together. He reveals that, over three generations, the men of the family have had to improvise or perform their identities, each for different reasons. John Moore's reason was migration, while Colman's reason is adoption. The letter significantly remains silent about Joss's reason, so that we do not know whether he was motivated by his desire to play music or, as Sophie Stones suspects, for other motives. In the letter, Joss hopes that maybe one day Colman will understand his reason for living as a man. Joss recognises, however, that Colman does not *need* to understand him; Joss's story is his own and not Colman's. The letter provides Colman with a jazz 'standard' – the repeated change of name which passes down from father to son to grandson. It is now up to Colman to Signify on it, to perform his own variation, interpretation, improvisation.

## Tracing ancestors

In 'Rootedness: The Ancestor as Foundation', Morrison argues that a valuable approach to black literature is to consider what the writer does with the presence of an ancestor. This figure is a parent or an elder who occupies a benevolent, instructive and protective role in relation to the characters of the novel: 'they provide a certain kind of wisdom' (1985: 343). For Morrison, the presence or absence of an ancestor determines the success or happiness of a character. The absence of an ancestor is invariably threatening or frightening, causing chaos and destruction. Contemporary black fiction has been preoccupied with the importance of keeping in touch with the ancestors, or restoring and creating a 'conscious historical connection' (1985: 344). In *Jazz*, all of the main characters are orphans or were abandoned as children: Joe, Violet, Dorcas and Felice. Even Alice, who raises Dorcas and nurtures Violet, has been profoundly damaged by her own upbringing, so that she fears men and denies her own sexuality. In the course of the novel, the characters come to recognise the wildness in themselves and thereby claim Wild/Beloved as an ancestor figure. I have contended that the 'historical connection' which Morrison seeks to restore in *Jazz* is with slavery, so that the past cannot be escaped or evaded through migration. Although the characters want to start from scratch, they find that trauma cannot be so easily discarded. In *Trumpet*, Colman searches for ancestors and a sense of familial connection. Adoption and the black diaspora represent in the novel a traumatic splitting from origins which may never be healed or restored. I have demonstrated that the novel insists on the importance of improvisation. The characters invent gendered and racial selves and create their own imagined communities. Kay suggests that, through the imagination, new 'bloodlines' can be forged and a sense of historical connection (re-)established. In broader terms, I have argued that black literature is bound up with its own literary ancestors, continually Signifying on its own canon. Thematically, black writers are concerned to recover the forgotten or excluded experiences of black people, and to restore the presence of historical and cultural ancestors. This serves a dual purpose: for black readers, it facilitates the construction of an imagined community, while it confronts white readers with that which has been repressed or 'forgotten' in their own literatures and cultures. Following Nicholls, I have suggested that writers such as Morrison are analogous to psychoanalysts in drawing suppressed material to the surface, in converting traumatic memory into narrative memory. I have also demonstrated that contemporary black fiction radically reconfigures the form of the novel, experimenting with musical and other structures. For Gilroy, this signals a disenchantment with the novel as a vehicle for expression. I have suggested, on the contrary, that such experimentation represents a creative attempt to articulate in formal terms the impact of trauma. Narrative needs to understand enough, so that it can convey a forgotten and excluded history, but it should simultaneously resist understanding too much, so that it can also convey the disruptive and resistant force of a traumatic historicity.

# Conclusion

In this volume, I have sought to introduce and explore the concept of trauma fiction. Many contemporary novels are concerned with traumatic events, whether these emerge out of collective experiences such as war, slavery or the Holocaust, or the more individual experiences of rape or bereavement. The first half of the volume focuses on thematic questions, and I suggest that trauma fiction is influenced and informed by recent developments in trauma theory concerning the nature of traumatic experience itself, the role and function of testimony, and the relation between trauma and place. I have indicated that it is not necessarily that novelists are reading trauma theory, although clearly many of the authors studied in this volume are conversant with the key theorists and ideas, but rather that the rethinking of trauma has been absorbed into the current ideologies of history and memory. In the second half of the volume, I shift attention to stylistic questions and argue that, in representing trauma, many writers have mimicked its symptomatology at a formal level. I have drawn attention, in particular, to the prevalence of repetition, indirection and the dispersal of narrative voice in works of trauma fiction. Fiction is not left unchanged by its encounter with trauma, but has characteristically responded to the challenges of representation that it raises with innovation at the levels of plot, character and narration.

My division of the book into sections on theme and style also, finally, opens up important issues relating to the nature of trauma itself. It reflects one of the major questions that arises in the thinking of trauma, namely whether trauma itself is a content or a form. The

161

knowledge of trauma is composed of two contradictory elements. One is the traumatic event, which is registered rather than experienced. The other is a kind of memory of the event, which takes the form of a perpetual troping of it by the split or dissociated psyche. Trauma, that is, can be defined in terms of specific events or in terms of specific symptomatic reactions to events, and this undecidability recurs throughout the literature on the subject. In the 'Project for a Scientific Psychology' (1895), Freud characteristically divides trauma into two scenes. The earlier scene, occurring in childhood, has sexual content but no meaning; the later scene, occurring after puberty, has no sexual content but is associated with the onset of a symptomatic response. Trauma is suspended between event and symptom, and this model manifests itself throughout Freud's work. It can be discerned in the late essay, 'Moses and Monotheism' (1939), in which trauma represents both a specific event – a railway accident – and the symptomatic responses to that event which emerge a few weeks later. The undecidability of trauma is also evident in the American Psychiatric Association's *Diagnostic and Statistical Manual of Mental Disorders*. When post-traumatic stress disorder was first recognised, the definition of trauma emphasised the specific types of events which caused the condition. In subsequent descriptions, however, the focus has notably shifted to the symptomatic response to trauma.

Geoffrey Hartman suggests that the two aspects of trauma – the event (content) and the symptomatic response to the event (form) – operate in literary terms: 'On the level of poetics, literal and figurative may correspond to these two types of cognition' (1995: 536). His observation resonates with the suspension of trauma fiction between its attempt to convey the literality of a specific event and its figurative evocation of the symptomatic response to trauma through formal and stylistic innovation. As I have suggested above, and as I have sought to reflect in the organisation of the volume into two sections, the double and contradictory nature of trauma also corresponds to the literary distinction between theme and style. In modulating from one to the other across the two halves of the volume, I have sought to allow for both, and to permit the literary undecidability of this distinction within the notion of trauma to inform, to resonate within and to work effectively through and across each of the readings in this volume. In bringing together trauma and fiction, I have aimed to suggest that trauma, like fiction, occupies an uncertain, but nevertheless productive, site or place between content and form.

# Notes

## Introduction to Part I

1. The key Freudian texts in relation to the concept of *Nachträglichkeit* are as follows: 'Analysis of a Phobia in a Five-Year-Old Boy ("Little Hans")' (Freud, 1990, VIII: 165–305) and 'From the History of an Infantile Neurosis (The "Wolf Man")' (Freud, 1991, IX: 227–366). For further discussion of the concept, see Laplanche (1999) and Lacan (1985: 30–113).
2. In accordance with other critics, I will adopt throughout this volume the convention of referring to the author of *Fragments* as Wilkomirski.

## Chapter 1

1. For more detailed discussion of the *Regeneration* trilogy as a narrative of trauma, see Anne Whitehead (1998) and John Brannigan (2003).
2. The original meaning of 'trauma' was a wound inflicted on a body. Unlike the physical wound, the psychological injury resists cure: 'the wound of the mind – the breach in the mind's experience of time, self and the world – is not, like the wound of the body, a simple and healable event, but rather an event that [. . .] is experienced too soon, too unexpectedly, to be fully known' (Caruth, 1995: 4).
3. The image of 'Golgotha' is suggestive of Barker's conflation of the First World War and the Second World War. Pope John Paul II famously referred to Auschwitz as 'the modern Golgotha' and, when Dachau was liberated, the road through the camp was renamed 'The Way of the Cross'. These Catholic appropriations of the Holocaust give rise, in turn, to their own ethical and political problems.

4. Geordie figures himself as a memorial or 'crypt' to the dead of the First World War. Instead of mourning the dead and letting them go, he seeks to incorporate them within himself in a melancholic act of preservation. 'Geordie' is a colloquial term for the people of Tyneside, reinforcing the notion that Geordie embodies his lost comrades.

5. Although Barker's early fiction highlights the role of working-class women in family and community life, her exploration of the First World War in the *Regeneration* trilogy marks a shift in focus to the investigation of masculinity. Fran and Miranda are given secondary roles in *Another World*, and it is Nick who negotiates the stresses of family life and assumes the role of carer for Geordie.

6. Through the Fanshawe narrative, Barker demonstrates that Victorian families were equally fractured and complex. For them, death rather than divorce was the cause of multiple marriages. Muriel and Robert were from their father's first marriage, while James is the child of his second marriage. Barker's emphasis on the faultlines of the Victorian family refutes idealised versions of the past and contests the political rhetoric, prevalent in the 1990s, that sought to inculcate family values through the example of the Victorian family. For further discussion, see Sharon Monteith (2002: 91–3).

7. Miranda's attempted suffocation of Jasper also recalls the Mary Bell murders that took place in Tyneside. In 1968, eleven-year-old Bell was convicted of killing four-year-old Martin and three-year-old Brian by suffocation. The deaths appear in Nick's book on local murders, where he reads that Bell killed one of the boys on 'a stretch of waste land less than a mile from Lob's Hill' (107). The geographical proximity of the killings to the house suggests that the trauma of the Bell murders casts its own shadow over the family. For further discussion of the Bell case, see Gitta Sereny (1995) and Jacqueline Rose (2003: 201–15).

8. In 1993, Robert Thompson and Jon Venables, both aged ten, abducted and murdered the toddler James Bulger in Liverpool. During the Bulger trial, the question of what children 'know' became crucial to determining whether Thompson and Venables could be held accountable for their actions. Although the boys were only ten years old, the law decreed that if they were capable of understanding the difference between right and wrong, then they should stand trial for murder in an adult court. Barker addresses the question of children's accountability more explicitly in *Border Crossing* (2001). Psychiatrist Tom is confronted with the consequences of his decision that the child murderer, Danny, knew the difference between right and wrong, and could therefore be tried and imprisoned for murder. For further discussion of the Bulger case, see Blake Morrison (1997) and Andrew O'Hagan (1995: 89–96).

## Chapter 2

1. Although this chapter focuses on the implications of testimony in the field of Holocaust studies, the issues are relevant across a broad range of contexts. The notion of testimony gives rise to three interrelated questions: the relation between historical or factual referentiality and literary form; the extent to which personal testimony can intervene in cultural memory; and the issue of who is entitled to write testimonial literature in a given area. In the context of the Vietnam War, Tim O'Brien's fiction merges the genres of testimony and the novel; for an interesting discussion of this aspect of his writing, see Mark Heberle (2001). Discussions of Latin-American testimony can be found in Doris Meyer (1992), Linda J. Craft (1997), and Lessie Jo Frazier (1999). Important work on testimony has also been carried out in relation to the literature on AIDS. In this context, see Ross Chambers (2000) and Sarah Brophy (2003). My own emphasis in this chapter reflects the important role played by Holocaust studies in defining and exploring the nature of testimony.
2. The term 'faction' is commonly used by critics to describe the blending of fact and fiction in recent Holocaust novels.
3. For Wiesel, the distortion of the past in his writing is as much an issue of translation as of memory. For further discussion, see Susan Suleiman (2000: 555–6).
4. The text was subsequently republished as *Fragments* (without the subtitle *Memories of a Childhood, 1939–1948*) and prefaced by Stefan Maechler's report on the surrounding controversy. See Maechler (2001).
5. The distinction between *fabula* (story) and *sjuzhet* (plot) emerged out of Russian Formalist criticism and was absorbed into European literary theory, culminating in Gérard Genette's 'Discours du Récit' (1972).
6. Readers wrote to Wilkomirski: 'Your story broke my heart – I could only read a few pages at a time'; 'I barely know how to put into words the sadness I felt' (quoted in Maechler, 2001: 118).
7. Historian Raul Hilberg also recognised that *Fragments* was fiction from the outset because the details of the text did not match the historical record. This argument is problematic, however, because it presumes that all testimonies accord with historical fact, although this is not necessarily the case. For further discussion of this issue, see Shoshana Felman and Dori Laub (1992: 59–63).
8. For a detailed discussion of the relation between *The Painted Bird* and Kosinski's wartime childhood, see James Park Sloan (1996: 7–54).
9. Wilkomirski's psychoanalyst was Israel-based Elitsur Bernstein who encouraged him to write down his memories as they emerged.
10. Villiger's comments were made just a few months before the initial publication of *Fragments*.

11. For an alternative view of the Nazi Gold Affair, which is highly critical of the activities of the World Jewish Congress and regards the claims against Switzerland to be part of a Holocaust industry that has become an extortion racket, see Norman G. Finkelstein (2000: 81–139).

## *Chapter 3*

1. Ben reads to his mother about the effects of a tornado, which gathers up personal possessions, and she, in turn, remembers the piles of belongings in the camp (224). The association of the Holocaust with violent natural phenomena such as tornadoes or lightning gives added significance to Michaels's vision of redemption through nature.
2. As Hillger points out, Jakob's last name, Beer, links to the Hebrew word *be'er*, or 'well'. Scholem observes of the Hebrew term: 'the Torah is likened to a well of fresh water, whence spring ever new levels of hidden meaning' (60). Michaels connects Jakob to a creative and open-ended hermeneutics, which contrasts with the 'poisoned well' of the closed history advanced by the Nazi archaeologists.
3. In *The Prelude*, the guiding influence of nature means that the growth of the child's mind is achieved with the minimum of harm and disruption. Wordsworth registers that, in order for there to be development and progression, there must be trauma or 'shock', but the effect of this is carefully minimised: 'a gentle shock of mild surprise' (1805 *Prelude*, V: 407). Wordsworth emphasises the regenerative action of nature, which almost imperceptibly converts the solipsistic into the sympathetic imagination.
4. Nora observes that archaeological sites are not *lieux de mémoire* because they are overdetermined in significance, exhibiting 'the absolute absence of a will to remember and, by way of compensation, the crushing weight imposed on them by time, science and the dreams of men' (1989: 20). Athos seeks retrospectively to transform Biskupin from the amnesiac site of history's falsification to a site that commemorates both the lives of the prehistoric settlers and the deaths of the Polish archaeologists who worked there.
5. For further discussion of the relation between aesthetics and Holocaust representation, see Michael Rothberg (2000: 25–58).
6. Dominick LaCapra has been critical of the absorption into trauma discourse of Benjaminian messianism, arguing that it does not offer the possibility of working through but suggests an endless repetition of the past and a compulsive implication in trauma. He observes of the response to the Holocaust of those born later: 'Any politics limited to witnessing, memory, mourning dead victims, and honoring survivorship would constitute an excessively limited horizon of action, however desirable and necessary these activities may be' (1998: 198). For him,

Michaels's absorption of Benjaminian messianism into literary fiction would arguably risk legitimising or naturalising this discourse.

7. The word 'golem' appears in *Psalms*, 139: 16.

8. Jakob's collection of poems, *Groundwork*, provides a memorial book for the victims of the Holocaust, while his journals act as a memorial book for Bella.

9. Hartman has suggested that the archive of video testimonies at Yale acts as a memorial space. As Project Director of the Yale Archive, he is concerned that the videos remain on site and are viewed there in full. He argues that the experience of travelling to the library 'reinforces the particular "place" of testimonial memory' (quoted in Ballengee, 2001: 223).

## Chapter 4

1. Othello's nocturnal walks through the city suggest that he is connected with the figure of the prostitute, who is, like him, a tolerated but despised member of Venetian society. Shortly after his arrival in Venice, Othello sees a prostitute, but his practice is condemned by his servant because of his race. Historically, the Jews of Venice were associated with prostitutes. Richard Sennett elaborates: 'the city sought to draw a special connection between prostitutes and Jews, by making them both wear yellow clothing or badges' (1994: 240). The Venetian Jews were required to wear a yellow badge from 1397, while prostitutes and pimps were ordered shortly after to wear yellow scarves. Phillips reverses the association of the prostitute in his suggestion that Venice herself is 'sluttish beneath her regal garb' (1997a: 146), and in Othello's inability to distinguish between the Venetian lady and the courtesan.

2. In *The European Tribe*, Phillips describes his own upbringing in the urban 'ghettos' of white working-class estates in Britain (1987: 3), and he parallels the 'tightly knit ghetto' (1987: 63) of the Parisian-Arab area, *La Goutte d'Or*, with the Venetian ghetto, pointing out that its boundaries are similarly patrolled by the police.

3. Jacqueline Rose observes that Shylock's speech was quoted by Nelson Mandela in May 1990, in an attempt to link black to Jew as members equally, though distinctly, of a persecuted race. Rose observes, however, that the speech has another, darker significance in its emphasis on revenge. Shylock's claim to humanity is based on vengeance, and Rose points out: 'it is through self-perpetuating violence that oppressed and oppressor most often identify' (1996: 95). Rose offers a much more disturbing connection between black and Jew than Phillips suggests.

4. Phillips emphasises his first encounter with Anne Frank's *Diary* at the age of fifteen. It made him realise that he was not 'alone' (2002: 5), although it simultaneously increased his concern over the potential

consequences of racism: 'If white people could do that to white people, then what the hell would they do to me?' (1987: 67).

5. This was particularly the case when the National Holocaust Museum opened in Washington DC in 1993. In spite of intensive lobbying, there is to date no equivalent museum to slavery.

6. Philip Roth's *The Ghost Writer* (1980) also imagines an alternative history in which Anne Frank survived the war. Roth's novel explores the American myth of Anne Frank, created in Hollywood and on Broadway, and its relation to contemporary American-Jewish identity.

7. Although there has been recent debate over whether Primo Levi's death can properly be regarded as suicide, it does seem likely given the evidence of his frequent depressions.

8. Phillips suggests that both Othello and Stern offer the potential for cross-cultural connection. Othello lies in bed marvelling at the white-ness of Desdemona's skin, but his delight is quickly undercut by the modern voice which warns that she will soon be 'lost' (182). Stern lies in bed beside the sleeping Malka and examines her black skin, but he does not bridge the separation between them by reaching out to her. Phillips indicates that we too often remain bounded by the separatism and isolationism of the ghetto.

9. There is an intertextual reference here to Lady Macbeth's lament: 'What, will these hands ne'er be clean?' (*Macbeth*, V, i, 41). By modifying the quote, Phillips emphasises the lasting collective guilt or shame of the Holocaust.

## *Chapter 5*

1. Sebald's fascination with the aerial bombing of German cities is most fully explored in 'Air War and Literature: Zürich Lectures' (2003: 1–107).

2. Sebald's phrasing recalls the fate of Austerlitz, who figuratively carries his Holocaust past with him in the knapsack which is perpetually on his back. *Austerlitz* relates the process by which he is eventually able to confront his past, although it remains unclear whether he can achieve this without being 'petrified' or paralysed by it.

3. Sebald's German deliberately mirrors or replicates Freud's terminology in 'Beyond the Pleasure Principle'. Max Ferber observes of his own childhood memories of Germany: 'The fragmentary scenes that haunt my memories are obsessive in character' (1996: 181). As J. J. Long points out, Sebald uses the German words *Zwangvorstellung* ('a visitation', 'haunting') which is Freud's word for the repetition-compulsion, and *heimsuchen* ('to haunt'), which is used by Freud to refer to the involun-tary invasion of repressed traumatic memories (2003: 125).

4. In the original German version of *The Emigrants*, Max Ferber is called Max Aurach.

5. Sebald implicitly comments on his own 'spiralling prose' in his evocative description of Thomas Browne's writing (1998a: 19).

6. In *The Nature of Blood*, Phillips likewise uses repetition to bind together the stories of Eva, Stern, Othello and the Jews of Portobuffole. Through the binding process, Phillips seeks to establish connections between black and Jewish experiences of racism.

7. Luisa's meeting with Nabokov is closely based on an episode in *Speak, Memory*, which describes a Sunday afternoon excursion in the country with Muromzev (Nabokov, 1969: 103).

8. Sebald has observed that the notion of the return of the dead exerted a strong influence during his childhood: 'Where I grew up, in a remote village at the back of a valley, the old still thought the dead needed attending to [. . .] If you didn't, they might exact revenge upon the living' (quoted in Jaggi, 2001: 6).

9. In interview, Sebald has pointed out that 99 per cent of the photographs in his texts are genuine (quoted in Angier, 1996: 14). Sebald highlights the problematic status of the photograph as evidence in his discussion of the forged photograph of the Nazi book-burning in Würzburg, in 1933 (1996: 183).

10. Freud elaborates on the distinction between the healthy process of mourning and the pathological condition of melancholy in his 1917 essay 'Mourning and Melancholia' (Freud, 1991, XI: 245–68). Sebald also draws on Robert Burton's *The Anatomy of Melancholy*, which first appeared in 1621. Burton devotes an entire section of his compendious study to the 'Miseries of Scholars', and he observes of melancholy: 'Many men [. . .] come to this malady by continual study, and night-waking, and of all other men, scholars are most subject to it' (2001: 301).

## Chapter 6

1. This point is powerfully illustrated when Dr Krishnamurty completes Joss's death certificate. She fills in the 'obvious' details before examining the body, including the sex of the deceased. Linda Anderson observes: 'Signing a death certificate means the registration of the body according to a rigid set of binaries – life/death, male/female – and it is at odds with the doctor's subjective encounter with Joss's body' (2000: 77).

2. For more on 'imagined communities', see Benedict Anderson (1991).

3. Alison Lumsden points out that in Kay's poem 'Pride', the narrator's chance encounter with a Nigerian man, who claims her as part of the Ibo tribe, gives her a momentary sense of cultural ancestry and imagined community (2000: 88). 'Pride' is in the collection *Off Colour* (Kay, 1998b: 62–4).

# Bibliography

Abraham, Nicolas (1987) 'Notes on the Phantom: A Complement to Freud's Metapsychology', *Critical Inquiry*, 13, pp. 287–92.

Abraham, Nicolas and Maria Torok (1994) *The Shell and the Kernel*, Vol. 1, ed. and trans. Nicholas T. Rand. Chicago: University of Chicago Press.

Anderson, Benedict (1991) *Imagined Communities*. London: Verso.

Anderson, Linda (2000) 'Autobiographical Travesties: The Nostalgic Self in Queer Writing', in David Alderson and Linda Anderson (eds), *Territories of Desire in Queer Culture: Refiguring Contemporary Boundaries*. Manchester and New York: Manchester University Press, pp. 68–83.

Anderson, Linda (2001) *Autobiography*. London and New York: Routledge.

Angier, Carole (1996) 'Who Is W. G. Sebald?', *Jewish Quarterly*, 43, 4, pp. 10–14.

Annan, Gabriele (2001) 'Ghost Story', *New York Review of Books*, 1 November, pp. 26–7.

Baer, Ulrich (2000) 'To Give Memory a Place: Holocaust Photography and the Landscape Tradition', *Representations*, 69, pp. 38–63.

Ballengee, Jennifer R. (2001) 'Witnessing Video Testimony: An Interview with Geoffrey Hartman', *Yale Journal of Criticism*, 14, 1, pp. 217–32.

Barker, Pat (1991) *Regeneration*. London: Penguin.

Barker, Pat (1993) *The Eye in the Door*. London and New York: Penguin.

Barker, Pat (1995) *The Ghost Road*. London and New York: Penguin.

Barker, Pat (1998) *Another World*. London and New York: Penguin.

Barker, Pat (2001) *Border Crossing*. London and New York: Viking.

Barthes, Roland (1977) *Image-Music-Text*, trans. Stephen Heath. London: Fontana.

Barthes, Roland (1993) *Camera Lucida: Reflections on Photography*, trans. Richard Howard. London: Vintage.

Benjamin, Walter (1973) *Illuminations*, ed. Hannah Arendt, trans. Harry Zohn. London: Fontana.

Benjamin, Walter (1978) *One-Way Street and Other Writings*, trans. Edmund Jephcott and Kingsley Shorter. London: Harcourt Brace Jovanovich.

Bettelheim, Bruno (1976) *The Uses of Enchantment: The Meaning and Importance of Fairy Tales*. London: Thames & Hudson.

Brannigan, John (2003) 'Pat Barker's *Regeneration* Trilogy', in Richard Lane, Rod Mengham and Philip Tew (eds), *Contemporary British Fiction*. Cambridge: Polity, pp. 13–26.

Brooks, Peter (1984) *Reading for the Plot: Design and Intention in Narrative*. London and Cambridge, MA: Harvard University Press.

Brophy, Sarah (2003) *Witnessing AIDS: Writing, Testimony and the Work of Cultural Mourning*. Toronto: University of Toronto Press.

Buchanan, Brad (2003) 'Caryl Phillips', in Richard Lane, Rod Mengham and Philip Tew (eds), *Contemporary British Fiction*. Cambridge: Polity, pp. 174–90.

Buck-Morss, Susan (1991) *The Dialectics of Seeing: Walter Benjamin and the Arcades Project*. Cambridge, MA and London: MIT Press.

Burton, Robert [1621] (2001) *The Anatomy of Melancholy*, ed. Holbrook Jackson. New York: New York Review of Books.

Carabi, Angels (1995) 'Interview with Toni Morrison', *Belles Lettres*, 10, 2, pp. 40–3.

Cardinal, Marie (1983) *The Words To Say It*, trans. Pat Goodheart. London: Pan Books.

Caruth, Cathy (ed.) (1995) *Trauma: Explorations in Memory*. Baltimore, MD and London: Johns Hopkins University Press.

Caruth, Cathy (1996a) *Unclaimed Experience: Trauma, Narrative and History*. Baltimore, MD: Johns Hopkins University Press.

Caruth, Cathy (1996b) 'An Interview with Geoffrey Hartman', *Studies in Romanticism*, 35, 4, pp. 631–53.

Caruth, Cathy and Deborah Esch (eds) (1996) *Critical Encounters: Reference and Responsibility in Deconstructive Writing*. New Brunswick, NJ: Rutgers University Press.

Chambers, Ross (2000) *Facing It: AIDS Diaries and the Death of the Author*. Ann Arbor, MI: University of Michigan Press.

Cheyette, Bryan (2000) 'Venetian Spaces: Old-New Literatures and the Ambivalent Uses of Jewish History', in Susheila Nasta (ed.), *Reading the 'New' Literatures in a Postcolonial Era*. Cambridge: D. S. Brewer, pp. 53–72.

Coetzee, J. M. (1997) 'What We Like to Forget', *New York Review of Books*, 6 November, pp. 38–41.

Craft, Linda J. (1997) *Novels of Testimony and Resistance from Central America*. Gainesville, FL: University Press of Florida.

Darling, Marsha (1994) 'In the Realm of Responsibility: A Conversation with Toni Morrison', in Danille Taylor-Guthrie (ed.), *Conversations with Toni Morrison*. Jackson, MS: University of Mississippi Press, pp. 246–54.

Derrida, Jacques (1987) *The Post Card: From Socrates to Freud and Beyond*, trans. Alan Bass. Chicago and London: University of Chicago Press.

Dwork, Debórah (1991) *Children With a Star: Jewish Youth in Nazi Europe*. New Haven, CT and London: Yale University Press.

Dyer, Geoff (1994) *The Missing of the Somme*. London: Hamish Hamilton.

Dyer, Geoff (1996) *But Beautiful*. London: Abacus.

Dyer, Richard (1999) 'Jackie Kay in Conversation', *Wasafiri*, 29, pp. 57–61.

Ellison, Ralph (1972) *Shadow and Act*. New York: Vintage.

Eskin, Blake (2002) *A Life in Pieces*. London: Aurum.

Faulks, Sebastian (1994) *Birdsong*. London: Vintage.

Felman, Shoshana and Dori Laub (1992) *Testimony: Crises of Witnessing in Literature, Psychoanalysis and History*. New York and London: Routledge.

Fine, Ellen S. (2001) 'Intergenerational Memories: Hidden Children and the Second Generation', in Margot Levy (ed.), *Remembering the Future: The Holocaust in an Age of Genocide*, Vol. 3. Basingstoke: Palgrave, pp. 78–92.

Finkelstein, Norman G. (2000) *The Holocaust Industry: Reflections on the Exploitation of Jewish Suffering*. London and New York: Verso.

Frank, Anne (1997) *The Diary of a Young Girl*, eds Otto Frank and Mirjam Pressler, trans. Euan Cameron. London and New York: Penguin.

Frazier, Lessie Jo (1999). '"Subverted Memories": Countermourning as Political Action in Chile', in Mieke Bal, Jonathan Crewe and Leo Spitzer (eds), *Acts of Memory: Cultural Recall in the Present*. Hanover, NH and London: Dartmouth College, pp. 105–19.

Freud, Sigmund (1973–82) *The Penguin Freud Library*, 24 vols, eds Angela Richards and Albert Dickson, trans. James Strachey. London and New York: Penguin.

Freud, Sigmund [1895] (1966) 'The Project for a Scientific Psychology', trans. and ed. James Strachey, *The Standard Edition of the Complete Psychological Works of Sigmund Freud*, Vol. 1. London: Hogarth Press, pp. 283–398.

Freud, Sigmund [1909] (1990) 'Analysis of a Phobia in a Five-Year-Old Boy ("Little Hans")', in Angela Richards (ed.), *Case Histories I*, Penguin Freud Library VIII, trans. Alix and James Strachey. London and New York: Penguin, pp. 165–305.

Freud, Sigmund [1915] (1991) 'Thoughts for the Times on War and Death', in Albert Dickson (ed.), *Civilization, Society and Religion*, Penguin Freud Library XII, trans. James Strachey. London and New York: Penguin, pp. 57–90.

Freud, Sigmund [1916] (1990) 'On Transience', in Albert Dickson (ed.), *Art and Literature*, Penguin Freud Library XIV, trans. James Strachey. London and New York: Penguin, pp. 283–90.

Freud, Sigmund [1917] (1991) 'Mourning and Melancholia', in Angela Richards (ed.), *On Metapsychology*, Penguin Freud Library XI, trans. James Strachey. London and New York: Penguin, pp. 245–68.

Freud, Sigmund [1918] (1991) 'From the History of an Infantile Neurosis (The "Wolf Man")', in Angela Richards (ed.), *Case Histories II*, Penguin Freud Library IX, trans. James Strachey. London and New York: Penguin, pp. 227–366.

Freud, Sigmund [1919] (1990) 'The Uncanny', in Albert Dickson (ed.), *Art and Literature*, Penguin Freud Library XIV, trans. James Strachey. London and New York: Penguin, pp. 335–76.

Freud, Sigmund [1920] (1991) 'Beyond the Pleasure Principle', in Angela Richards (ed.), *On Metapsychology*, Penguin Freud Library XI, trans. James Strachey. London and New York: Penguin, pp. 269–338.

Freud, Sigmund [1939] (1990) 'Moses and Monotheism', in Angela Richards (ed.), *The Origins of Religion*, Penguin Freud Library XIII, trans. James Strachey. London and New York: Penguin, pp. 237–386.

Freud, Sigmund and Joseph Breuer [1895] (1991) *Studies on Hysteria, 1893–5*, ed. Angela Richards, trans. James and Alix Strachey, Penguin Freud Library III, London and New York: Penguin.

Gates, Henry Louis (1988) *The Signifying Monkey: A Theory of African-American Literary Criticism.* Oxford and New York: Oxford University Press.

Gathercole, Peter and David Lowenthal (eds) (1994) *The Politics of the Past.* London and New York: Routledge.

Genette, Gérard (1972) 'Discours du récit', *Figures III.* Paris: Seuil.

Gilbert, Martin (1997) *Holocaust Journey: Travelling in Search of the Past.* London: Wiedenfield & Nicolson.

Gilloch, Graeme (2002) *Walter Benjamin: Critical Constellations.* Cambridge: Polity.

Gilroy, Paul (1993) *The Black Atlantic: Modernity and Double Consciousness.* London and New York: Verso.

Gilroy, Paul (1998) 'Afterword: Not Being Inhuman', in Bryan Cheyette and Laura Marcus (eds), *Modernity, Culture and 'the Jew'.* Cambridge: Polity, pp. 282–97.

Gilroy, Paul (2001) *Between Camps: Nations, Cultures and the Allure of Race.* London and New York: Penguin.

Glob, P. V. (1969) *The Bog People.* London: Faber.

Grourevitch, Philip (1999) 'The Memory Thief', *New Yorker*, 14 June, pp. 48–68.

Halbwachs, Maurice (1992) *On Collective Memory*, ed. and trans. Lewis A. Coser. Chicago and London: University of Chicago Press.

Hanks, Robert (1996) 'Where Naughty Children Get Murdered', *The Independent*, 8 December, p. 31.

Hartman, Geoffrey (1995) 'On Traumatic Knowledge and Literary Studies', *New Literary History*, 26, 3, pp. 537–63.

Hartman, Geoffrey (1996) *The Longest Shadow: In the Aftermath of the Holocaust.* Bloomington and Indianapolis, IN: Indiana University Press.

Hartman, Geoffrey (1997) *The Fateful Question of Culture.* New York: Columbia University Press.

Heaney, Seamus (1975) *North.* London: Faber.

Heberle, Mark A. (2001) *A Trauma Artist: Tim O'Brien and the Fiction of Vietnam.* Iowa City: University of Iowa Press.

Henderson, Mae G. (1991) 'Toni Morrison's *Beloved*: Re-membering the Body as Historical Text', in Hortense Spillers (ed.), *Comparative American Identities.* London: Routledge, pp. 62–86.

Hillger, Annick (1999) '"Afterbirth of Earth": Messianic Materialism in Anne Michaels' *Fugitive Pieces*', *Canadian Literature: A Quarterly of Criticism and Review*, 160, pp. 28–45.

Hungerford, Amy (2001) 'Memorizing Memory', *Yale Journal of Criticism*, 14, 1, pp. 67–92.

Huyssen, Andreas (1995) *Twilight Memories: Marking Time in a Culture of Amnesia.* London and New York: Routledge.

Iser, Wolfgang (1978) *The Act of Reading: A Theory of Aesthetic Response.* Baltimore, MD and London: Johns Hopkins University Press.

Jaggi, Maya (1999) 'Jackie Kay in Conversation', *Wasafiri*, 29, pp. 53–6.

Jaggi, Maya (2001) 'Recovered Memories', *The Guardian*, 22 September, pp. 6–7.

James, Henry [1898] (1999) *The Turn of the Screw*, eds Deborah Esch and Jonathan Warren. New York and London: Norton.

Janet, Pierre (1919–25) *Les medications psychologiques*, 3 vols. Paris: Société Pierre Janet.

Kay, Jackie (1997) *Bessie Smith.* Bath: Absolute Press.

Kay, Jackie (1998a) *Trumpet.* London: Picador.

Kay, Jackie (1998b) *Off Colour.* Newcastle upon Tyne: Bloodaxe Books.

Keneally, Thomas (1982) *Schindler's List.* New York: Simon & Schuster.

King, Nicola (1999) '"We Come After": Remembering the Holocaust', in Roger Luckhurst and Peter Marks (eds), *Literature and the Contemporary: Fictions and Theories of the Present.* Harlow: Longman, pp. 94–108.

King, Nicola (2000) *Memory, Narrative, Identity: Remembering the Self.* Edinburgh: Edinburgh University Press.

Kosinski, Jerzy (1965) *The Painted Bird.* New York: Bantam.

Krielkamp, Ivan (1997) 'Caryl Phillips: The Trauma of "Broken History"', *Publishers Weekly*, 24, 17, pp. 44–5.

Krishnaswamy, Revathi (1995) 'Mythologies of Migrancy: Postcolonialism, Postmodernism and the Politics of (Dis)location', *Ariel*, 26, 1, pp. 125–46.

Kurlansky, Mark (2002) *Salt: A World History.* London: Jonathan Cape.

Lacan, Jacques (1985) *Écrits: A Selection*, trans. Alan Sheridan. London and New York: Routledge.

LaCapra, Dominick (1998) *History and Memory After Auschwitz.* Ithaca, NY and London: Cornell University Press.

LaCapra, Dominick (2001) *Writing History, Writing Trauma.* Baltimore, MD and London: Johns Hopkins University Press.

Langer, Lawrence (1991) *Holocaust Testimonies: The Ruins of Memory.* New Haven, CT and London: Yale University Press.

Laplanche, Jean (1999) 'Note on Afterwardsness', in John Fletcher (ed.), *Essays on Otherness.* London: Routledge, pp. 260–5.

Lappin, Elena (1999) 'The Man With Two Heads', *Granta*, 66, pp. 7–66.

Ledent, Bénédicte (2002) *Caryl Phillips.* Manchester and New York: Manchester University Press.

Lejeune, Philippe (1975) *Le pacte autobiographique.* Paris: Seuil.

Levi, Primo (1988) *The Drowned and the Saved*, trans. Raymond Rosenthal. London: Abacus.

Leys, Ruth (2000) *Trauma: A Genealogy.* Chicago and London: Chicago University Press.

Long, J. J. (2003) 'History, Narrative and Photography in W. G. Sebald's *Die Ausgewanderten*', *Modern Language Review*, 98, 1, pp. 117–37.

Luckhurst, Roger (1999) 'Memory recovered/recovered memory', in Roger Luckhurst and Peter Marks (eds), *Literature and the Contemporary: Fictions and Theories of the Present.* Harlow: Longman, pp. 80–93.

Lumsden, Alison (2000) 'Jackie Kay's Poetry and Prose: Constructing Identity', in Aileen Christianson and Alison Lumsden (eds), *Contemporary Scottish Women Writers.* Edinburgh: Edinburgh University Press, pp. 79–94.

Lyotard, Jean-François (1990) *Heidegger and 'the Jews'*, trans. Andreas Michel and Mark S. Roberts. Minneapolis, MN: University of Minnesota Press.

McKay, Nellie (1994) 'An Interview with Toni Morrison', in Danille Taylor-Guthrie (ed.), *Conversations with Toni Morrison.* Jackson, MS: University Press of Mississippi, pp. 138–55.

McLeod, John (2000) *Beginning Postcolonialism.* Manchester and New York: Manchester University Press.

Maechler, Stefan (2001) *The Wilkomirski Affair: A Study in Biographical Truth*, trans. John E. Woods. London: Picador.

Matus, Jill (1998) *Toni Morrison.* Manchester: Manchester University Press.

Mbalia, Dorothea Drummond (1993) 'Women Who Run With Wild: The Need For Sisterhoods in *Jazz*', *Modern Fiction Studies*, 39, 3–4, pp. 623–46.

Meyer, Doris (ed.) (1992) *Lives on the Line: The Testimony of Contemporary Latin-American Authors.* Berkeley, CA: University of California Press.

Michaels, Anne (1997) *Fugitive Pieces.* London: Bloomsbury.

Middlebrook, Diane Wood (1998) *Suits Me: The Double Life of Billy Tipton.* London: Virago.

Middleton, Peter and Tim Woods (2000) *Literatures of Memory: History, Time and Space in Postwar Writing.* Manchester and New York: Manchester University Press.

Monson, Ingrid (1996) *Saying Something: Jazz Improvisation and Interaction.* Chicago and London: University of Chicago Press.

Monteith, Sharon (2002) *Pat Barker.* Tavistock: Northcote House.

Morrison, Blake (1997) *As If.* London: Granta.

Morrison, Toni (1985) 'Rootedness: The Ancestor as Foundation', in Mari Evans (ed.), *Black Women Writers*. London: Pluto Press, pp. 339–45.

Morrison, Toni (1987) *Beloved*. London: Vintage.

Morrison, Toni (1992a) *Jazz*. London: Vintage.

Morrison, Toni (1992b) *Playing in the Dark: Whiteness and the Literary Imagination*. New York: Vintage.

Morrison, Toni (1996) 'Memory, Creation and Writing', in James McConkey (ed.), *The Anatomy of Memory: An Anthology*. New York and Oxford: Oxford University Press, pp. 212–18.

Nabokov, Vladimir (1969) *Speak, Memory: An Autobiography Revisited*. London: Penguin.

Naylor, Gloria (1994) 'A Conversation: Gloria Naylor and Toni Morrison', in Danille Taylor-Guthrie (ed.), *Conversations with Toni Morrison*. Jackson, MS: University Press of Mississippi, pp. 188–217.

Newman, Judie (1995) *The Ballistic Bard: Postcolonial Fictions*. London and New York: Arnold.

Nicholls, Peter (1996) 'The Belated Postmodern: History, Phantoms and Toni Morrison', in Sue Vice (ed.), *Psychoanalytic Criticism: A Reader*. Cambridge: Polity, pp. 50–74.

Nora, Pierre (1989) 'Between Memory and History: *Les Lieux de Mémoire*', trans. Mark Rondebush. *Representations*, 26, pp. 7–25.

Nora, Pierre (1998) *Realms of Memory: Rethinking the French Past*, trans. Lawrence D. Kritzman. New York: Columbia University Press.

O'Brien, Tim (1995) *If I Die in a Combat Zone*. London: Flamingo.

O'Hagan, Andrew (1995) *The Missing*. London: Picador.

Owen, Wilfred (1994) *The War Poems*, ed. Jon Silkin. London: Sinclair-Stevenson.

Ozick, Cynthia (1990) *The Shawl*. New York: Vintage.

Parker, Michael (1993) *Seamus Heaney: The Making of a Poet*. London: Macmillan.

Parks, Tim (2002) *Hell and Back: Selected Essays*. London: Vintage.

Peach, Linden (2000) *Toni Morrison*, 2nd edn. London: Macmillan.

Phillips, Caryl (1987) *The European Tribe*. London: Faber.

Phillips, Caryl (1997a) *The Nature of Blood*. London: Faber.

Phillips, Caryl (1997b) *Extravagant Strangers: A Literature of Belonging*. London: Faber.

Phillips, Caryl (1998) 'On "The Nature of Blood" and the Ghost of Anne Frank', *CommonQuest: The Magazine of Black–Jewish Relations*, 3, 2, pp. 4–7.

Phillips, Caryl (2002) *A New World Order: Selected Essays*. London: Vintage.

Porter, Eric (2002) *What Is This Thing Called Jazz? African American Musicians as Artists, Critics, Activists*. Berkeley, Los Angeles and London: University of California Press.

Rashkin, E. (1988) 'Tools for a New Psychoanalytic Literary Criticism: The Work of Abraham and Torok', *Diacritics*, 18, pp. 31–52.

Reiter, Andrea (2000) *Narrating the Holocaust*. London and New York: Continuum.

Rice, Alan (1994) 'Jazzing It Up a Storm: The Execution and Meaning of Toni Morrison's Jazzy Prose Style', *Journal of American Studies*, 28, 3, pp. 423–32.

Roberts, Michèle (1993) *Daughters of the House*. London: Virago.

Rodrigues, Eusebio L. (1997) 'Experiencing *Jazz*', in Nancy J. Peterson (ed.), *Toni Morrison: Critical and Theoretical Approaches*. Baltimore, MD and London: Johns Hopkins University Press, pp. 245–66.

Rose, Jacqueline (1996) *States of Fantasy*. Oxford: Clarendon Press.

Rose, Jacqueline (2003) *On Not Being Able To Sleep: Psychoanalysis and the Modern World*. London: Chatto & Windus.

Roth, Philip (1980) *The Ghost Writer*. London and New York: Penguin.

Rothberg, Michael (2000) *Traumatic Realism: The Demands of Holocaust Representation*. Minneapolis, MN and London: University of Minnesota Press.

Rubenstein, Roberta (1998) 'Singing the Blues/Reclaiming Jazz: Toni Morrison and Cultural Mourning', *Mosaic: A Journal for the Comparative Study of Literature*, 31, 2, pp. 147–63.

Rushdie, Salman (1991) *Imaginary Homelands: Essays and Criticism 1981–1991*. London: Granta.

Sassoon, Siegfried (1983) *The War Poems*, ed. Rupert Hart-Davis. London: Faber.

Scarry, Elaine (1985) *The Body in Pain: The Making and Unmaking of the World*. New York and Oxford: Oxford University Press.

Schama, Simon (1996) *Landscape and Memory*. London: Fontana.

Scholem, Gershom (1965) *On the Kabbalah and its Symbolism*, trans. Ralph Manheim. New York: Schocken Books.

Schwarz, Daniel (1999) *Imagining the Holocaust*. Basingstoke: Palgrave.

Scott, Ann (1996) *Real Events Revisited: Fantasy, Memory and Psychoanalysis*. London: Virago.

Sebald, W. G. (1996) *The Emigrants*, trans. Michael Hulse. London: Harvill; first published as *Die Ausgewanderten* in 1993.

Sebald, W. G. (1998a) *The Rings of Saturn*, trans. Michael Hulse. London: Harvill; first published as *Die Ringe des Saturn* in 1995.

Sebald, W. G. (1998b) *Logis in einem Landhaus: Über Gottfried Keller, Johann Peter Hebel, Robert Walser und andere*. Munich: Hanser.

Sebald, W. G. (1999) *Vertigo*, trans. Michael Hulse. London: Harvill; first published as *Schwindel. Gefühle* in 1990.

Sebald, W. G. (2001a) *Austerlitz*, trans. Anthea Bell. London: Hamish Hamilton.

Sebald, W. G. (2001b) 'Interview', *Nightwaves*, Radio 4, 5 October.

Sebald, W. G. (2003) *On the Natural History of Destruction*, trans. Anthea Bell. London: Hamish Hamilton; first published as *Luftkrieg und Literatur* in 1999.

Sennett, Richard (1994) *Flesh and Stone: The Body and the City in Western Civilization*. London and New York: W. W. Norton.

Sereny, Gitta (1995) *The Case of Mary Bell: A Portrait of a Child Who Murdered*. London: Pimlico.

Shakespeare, William (1998) *The Complete Works*, eds Stanley Wells and Gary Taylor. Oxford: Oxford University Press.

Sloan, James Park (1996) *Jerzy Kosinski: A Biography*. London and New York: Dutton.

Spiegelman, Art (1986) *Maus: A Survivor's Tale: My Father Bleeds History*. New York: Pantheon.

Spiegelman, Art (1991) *Maus II: A Survivor's Tale: And Here My Troubles Began*. New York: Pantheon.

Suleiman, Susan (2000) 'Problems of Memory and Factuality in Recent Holocaust Memoirs: Wilkomirski/Wiesel', *Poetics Today*, 21, 3, pp. 543–99.

Tal, Kali (1996) *Worlds of Hurt: Reading the Literatures of Trauma*. Cambridge: Cambridge University Press.

Tanner, Tony (1992) *Venice Desired*. Oxford and Cambridge, MA: Blackwell.

Todorov, Tzvetan (1975) *The Fantastic: A Structural Approach to a Literary Genre*, trans. Richard Howard. New York: Cornell University Press.

Vice, Sue (2000) *Holocaust Fiction*. London and New York: Routledge.

Vidler, Anthony (1992) *The Architectural Uncanny: Essays in the Modern Unhomely*. Cambridge, MA and London: MIT Press.

Wardi, Dina (1992) *Memorial Candles: Children of the Holocaust*. London and New York: Routledge.

Warner, Marina (1997) 'Its Own Dark Styx', *London Review of Books*, 20 March, pp. 23–4.

Whitehead, Anne (1998) 'Open to Suggestion: Hypnosis and History in Pat Barker's *Regeneration*', *Modern Fiction Studies*, 44, 3, pp. 674–94.

Wiedmer, Caroline (2001) 'Bordering on the Visible: Spatial Imagery in Swiss Memory Discourse', in Margot Levy (ed.), *Remembering for the Future: The Holocaust in an Age of Genocide*, Vol. 3. Basingstoke: Palgrave, pp. 466–77.

Wiesel, Elie (1960) *Night*, trans. Stella Rodway. New York: Bantam.

Wiesel, Elie (1995) *All Rivers Run to the Sea: Memoirs Vol. 1*. New York: Alfred A. Knopf.

Wilkomirski, Binjamin (1996) *Fragments: Memories of a Childhood, 1939–1948*, trans. Carol Brown Janeway. London: Picador.

Wood, Nancy (2000) *Vectors of Memory: Legacies of Trauma in Postwar Europe*. London: Berg.

Wordsworth, William (1979) *The Prelude, 1799, 1805, 1850*, eds Jonathan Wordsworth, M. H. Abrams and Stephen Gill. New York and London: W. W. Norton.

Young, James E. (1993) *The Texture of Memory: Holocaust Memorials and their Meaning*. New Haven, CT and London: Yale University Press.

# Index

179